CHILDREN OF ATHENA

PROCEEDINGS OF THE 1998 UNDERGRADUATE PHILOSOPHY CONFERENCE

EDITED
BY

DOUGLAS W. SHRADER

ONEONTA PHILOSOPHY STUDIES
HISTORICAL AND CULTURAL PERSPECTIVES

Published by Oneonta Philosophy Studies

Library of Congress Cataloging-in-publication Data:

Title: *Children of Athena*
Editor: Douglas W. Shrader
Subject: Philosophy

ISBN 1-883058-67-8

Distributed by:

Global Publications, IGCS, Binghamton University,
State University of New York at Binghamton
Binghamton, New York, USA 13902-6000
Phone: (607) 777-4495 or 6104; Fax: (607) 777-6132
e-mail: pmorewed@binghamton.edu
http://ssips.binghamton.edu

Dedicated to

BARBARA

my best friend,
my wife

ONEONTA PHILOSOPHY STUDIES
HISTORICAL AND CULTURAL PERSPECTIVES

Department of Philosophy

SUNY ONEONTA

Oneonta, NY 13820-4015

http://www.oneonta.edu/~shradedw/ops.html

CONTENTS

Contents

PREFACE

In October of 1995, I invited a select group of students to attend a conference on Greek and Islamic Philosophy. The weekend proved exceptional in many ways. Several students began talking about holding a conference of their own, for undergraduate students. With a bit of encouragement and a lot of work, we hosted our first conference during March of 1996. Three years later I continue to be amazed by the response and support we have received, the quality of the papers that have been submitted, and the dedication of our own students. Even as I write this preface, one of my students is busy in another office, creating the program for our fourth annual conference. That he is doing so on his spring break only serves to reinforce my conviction that somewhere, somehow, we must have done something right.

Part of what we have done right, I believe, is to treat students with respect and professionalism. By encouraging excellence, we have been rewarded in kind. The current volume represents the best of our third conference (April 3-4, 1998). Seven of the twelve student papers published here received special awards, described below. The others, as will be obvious to anyone who reads the essays, made decisions concerning those awards especially difficult.

The conference itself was a dynamic interplay of personal commitment, intellectual energy, and youthful exuberance. Thirty remarkable papers were presented by students from twenty prestigious institutions: Adelphi University, Alfred University, American University, Clark University, Fordham University, George Washington University, Hunter College, Marymount University, Nazareth College, SUNY Buffalo, SUNY Oneonta, Syracuse University, Taylor University, United States Military Academy, University of New Hampshire, Vassar College, Wheaton College, College of William and Mary, Xavier University, and Yale. As evidenced by the program (pp. 297-323), their papers covered a wide range of exciting topics, including: Moral Philosophy, Racial Prejudice, Physician-Assisted Suicide, Justice, Love, Tibetan Buddhism, Hermeneutics, the Ontological Argument Concerning the Existence of God, and the Philosophical Views of Derrida, Foucault, Heidegger, Kant, Nietzsche, Ricouer, Rousseau, Plato, Putnam, and Wittgenstein.

Each paper represented an exceptional student's best work. In most cases, it was the first time the student had presented a paper beyond the confines of a classroom. The inherent intimidation of presenting one's work in public, combined with the knowledge that it would be subject to critical blind review, resulted in a significant measure of self-selection. I know many capable students who elected not to submit. But for those who summoned the courage, the experience was remarkable. Presentations were clear, insightful, and informed. Discussion was spirited and robust. Selecting conference awards was not easy. Nor was it easy to decide which papers to include in the present volume.

President's Awards

President's Awards honor student presentations that most clearly exemplify the standards and ideals of the conference. For 1998, these awards were presented to (alphabetic order):

Daniel Bristol (*SUNY Oneonta*)
Kevin Goetz (*SUNY Oneonta*)
John Hartmann (*Alfred University*)
Litia Perta (*Vassar College*)
Amanda Joy Schwarz (*SUNY Oneonta*)
Clinton Tolley (*Wheaton College*)

Ninash Foundation East-West Awards

East-West Awards honor student presentations that exhibit special expertise and insight in Asian and Comparative Philosophy. For 1998, these awards were presented to (alphabetic order):

Daniel Bristol (*SUNY Oneonta*)
Meghan Tadel (*George Washington University*)

Spirit of Conference Awards

Spirit of Conference Awards honor students who contribute to the conference in diverse, sometimes unexpected ways. Special consideration is given to contributions that enhance the academic, intellectual, and positive social atmosphere of the conference. For 1998, these awards were presented to (alphabetic order):

Daniel Bristol (*SUNY Oneonta*)
Kevin Goetz (*SUNY Oneonta*)
Amanda Joy Schwarz (*SUNY Oneonta*)

Kerri Lynn Nicholas Heart and Soul Awards

Named in honor of an alumna who helped found the conference, Kerri Lynn Nicholas Heart and Soul Awards provide special recognition to those who have made truly exceptional, lasting contributions to the conference. In 1998, the inaugural award was presented to:

Kerri Lynn Nicholas

to honor her foundational role in the creation of the SUNY Oneonta Undergraduate Philosophy Conference, and to recognize her tireless commitment to the planning and conduct of the 1996, 1997, and 1998 conferences.

A second Heart and Soul Award was presented to:

Amanda Joy Schwarz

to honor her pioneering role as the first student chair of the conference planning committee.

Other Awards

The English Club presented awards to papers with literary themes. Specifically, the award for *The Best Philosophy Paper with Historical Literary Themes* went to:

Amy Katrin Ferrara (*SUNY Oneonta*)

The award for *The Best Philosophy Paper with Overall Literary Excellence* was presented to:

Gary Jay Schwenk (*Nazareth College*)

Editing the conference proceedings continues to be a labor of love. On the one hand, the project demands far more time and attention to detail than I had originally intended. On the other hand, the students with whom I have worked—from other institutions as well as from SUNY-Oneonta—have been sources of joy, inspiration, and delight.

A formal list of acknowledgments follows the student preface. Still, I would be remiss if I did not take this opportunity to thank my family (Barbara, Callie, and Sterling) for their patience, encouragement, and support. I also owe a special note of appreciation to Gary Hardcastle and Jere Surber, our keynote speakers, for gracing our conference with their presence, their insights, and their infectious enthusiasm. I am especially grateful to them for allowing us the honor of including their presentations in the proceedings.

Without the assistance of faculty, staff, and administrators here at Oneonta, neither the conference nor this volume would be possible: thank you. Perhaps less obviously, without the editorial assistance of the 1998/1999 Undergraduate Conference Committee I would still be poring over manuscripts, searching for errant commas or misplaced computer codes: special thanks to Morgan Brenner, Daniel Bristol, Meghan Callahan, Kevin Curran, Howard Fitzpatrick, Gotti Jicha, Denise Nicoletti, Keith Reischmann, George Savvas, and—especially—Cindy Budka.

Douglas W. Shrader
Oneonta, New York

STUDENT PREFACE

With Ludwig Wittgenstein's arguments against private language, and Roland Barthes' proclamation of the death of the author, the notion of a signature or name which can guarantee the meaning of a text—even a name like Wittgenstein or Barthes—has imploded, collapsed upon itself. Authorship has been swallowed up, twisting deep within the belly of that most wretched beast, postmodernism.

And yet, we still sign our names on contracts. We still cherish the names of certain authors, and bandy them about like the lost prayers of the American academic. Perhaps most importantly, we still attach our name, our seal of approval, to the texts we write, and the presentations we give.

Is this simply habit? Yearning for days of yore, when the stamp of the King produced the same effect as his very word? For a time when a name (especially our own name) felt tight, unique, and not as just another character string within an exponentially expanding bandwidth of useless information?

What's in a name, anyway?

A name is *as a trace*—evidence of various forces (in a decidedly Nietzschean sense) which come together, at a certain time, to hybridize and create the fictional locus we recognize as the self. Our names, the graphemes as well as the phonemes, contain within their trace the trajectories of innumerable influences, acquaintances, and ignorances. Our names carry our neighborhoods, our politics, our loves and our losses. In short, our names are our 'shorthand' for the nebulous complexities that are each and every human subject, in this and in all times and places.

In this volume, the reader will find the names and texts, and the words and thoughts, of a handful of (then) ambitious undergraduate philosophers. It is not possible to elucidate what is at stake within the names of each of these men and women, much less any one of them specifically. In place of vain attempts at such an impossible task, I would like to, instead, pull out and examine one common thread immanent within all of these names—that of the experience of philosophical inquiry, and especially as it relates to the Oneonta Undergraduate Philosophy Conference.

I do not mean to hyperbolize, nor to deify, but to say that the Conference at Oneonta is as an oasis within a vast desert is not too great a comparison to make. For those of us for whom philosophy is more than simply hobby or vocation—for those of us for whom philosophy is a *calling*—the Conference at Oneonta is perhaps the first entrypoint into a world where such a calling is not only accepted, but understood. Over a span of two days, young thinkers from distinctly different backgrounds push one another towards better and deeper thought. Viewpoints previously unencountered are digested and integrated towards the end of a more comprehensive picture of one's inquiries.

The aims of philosophical thought and a thoughtful life, being quite unvalued by society—I cannot count the number of times I've been asked, "Philosophy? Whaddaya gonna do with that?!"—find at the Undergraduate Conference at Oneonta sustenance, nourishment, and a medium in which to flourish and grow. In terms of my own development, it was a crucial step taken in Oneonta, with my first public presentations of my work (and reception of the first public criticisms!), as well as in terms of the friends I've made through my experience there. The beauty of the Conference lies in the idea that philosophical discourse need not simply appear within the confines of the Conference room, but in the hallways, the diner, and the local "watering hole." For two days, Conference participants exist in a world in which the utility of inquiry is not questioned but fostered, not shunned but valorized. It is, to say the least, a very pleasant world in which to, even if temporarily, reside.

For my own part, I would like to take this opportunity to acknowledge a number of people and institutions for the parts they have played in my own situation, and the immanence they hold within my own name-trace. First, to SUNY-Oneonta and the President's Office, innumerable thanks are due for financial and moral support of the Conference. To Dr. Douglas Shrader and the rest of the Philosophy Department at Oneonta, not only for the invitation to pen this student preface, but for the opportunities afforded me at two Undergraduate Conferences, as well as the encouragement. To my own undergraduate teachers—John Gilmour, Emrys Westacott, Beth Ann Dobie, Bill Cassidy, and Bill Dibrell—for their erudition, their friendship, and their undying patience. Finally, to LB, for the fact that her signature, her name, still etches itself within my own, even to this very day.

Having said this, I can in good conscience sign my own name...

John R. Hartmann
Stony Brook, New York

ACKNOWLEDGEMENTS

The conference and this volume depend on the contributions and good will of many. The following organizations and local merchants provided generous financial and/or professional assistance:

SUNY Oneonta Student Association
The Ninash Foundation
The Philosophy Club
The English Club
The Religious Studies Program
The Philosophy Department
Oneonta Philosophy Studies
Organization of Ancillary Services
Campus Grocery
Center Street Deli
Drury Lane Bakery and Cafe
Elena's Sweet Indulgence
Hannaford Foods
J & B Subs
Oneonta Bagel Company
P & C Food Market
Subway
Wal-Mart
Woody's Market
Gary's Flowers and Gifts
Stoeger Florist
Wyckoff's Florist

Acknowledgements

Special appreciation is extended to:

Gary Hardcastle and Jere Surber for donating nearly a week of their precious time to our conference

Amanda Joy Schwarz for tireless commitment as the first student chair of the conference planning committee

The rest of the1997/1998 conference planning committee: Daniel Bristol, Kevin Goetz, Alissa Kokkins, Kerri Nicholas, David Schaaf, and Lilly Stolzberg

Marjorie Holling for secretarial support

Morgan Brenner, Daniel Bristol, Cynthia Budka, Meghan Callahan, Kevin Curran, Howard Fitzpatrick, Gottlieb Jicha, Denise Nicoletti, Keith Reischmann, and George Savvas for editorial assistance

SUNY Oneonta faculty for patiently reviewing and evaluating a multitude of manuscripts—especially Michael Green, Michael Koch, Achim Köddermann, Ashok Malhotra, and Anthony Roda

SUNY Oneonta administration for support and encouragement—especially Dean Michael Merilan, Provost Anne C. Federlein, and President Alan B. Donovan

Parviz Morewedge, IGCS, SAGP, SSIPS, and Global Publications for financial and in-house support of this series

Finally, a heartfelt Thank You is extended to all the Presenters, Chairs, and Discussants—for without them there would have been no Conference.

Classic Philosophical Issues

TEMPORAL INCONGRUITY IN ZENO OF ELEA AND ITS PHILOSOPHICAL CONSEQUENCES[1]

Jeffery M.J. Murphy
Xavier University

When the antinomies and paradoxes of Zeno of Elea are analysed, one can observe a dual description of temporality. In the antinomies against plurality, Zeno treats time conceptually as if it were continuous, non-discrete, infinitely divisible, and not composed of individual "nows," whereas in the paradoxes against motion, time is treated as discontinuous and finitely divisible into indivisible units of no temporal magnitude, beyond which no further division is possible. What is drawn from Zeno's treatment of time are that: (1) time is treated conceptually in two different ways—as infinitely divisible in proofs against plurality and finitely divisible in proofs against motion, and (2) in order to disprove motion, Zeno was forced to concede to a lesser species of theoretical plurality and in order to disprove plurality, he was forced to concede to a lesser species of theoretical motion.

As finite and temporal creatures, there exists to human beings perhaps no more obvious and absolute notion than the passing of time. We are beings who live in time and, as such, have matured personally and culturally with a strong acclimation to the presence, past, and futurity of time, both real and potential. This recognition is in and of itself no more philosophical than the recognition of length, width, or breadth in the world about us. Even before the dawn of the philosophical age in Greece, the importance of time in the Universe was recognised in theogonical mythology, as seen in Hesiod:

Temporal Incongruity in Zeno of Elea

> *But great Cronos the wily took courage and answered his dear mother: "Mother, I will undertake to do this deed, for I reverence not our father of evil name, for he first thought of doing shameful things."*[2]
>
> — *Theogony, 168-172.*

According to Hesiod, time is a distributor of justice—the final justice allotted to temporal beings. Due to the elusive nature of its subject, however, the assessment and contemplation of the recognition of time presents problems much more significant than the simple measurement of spatial dimension. While spatial extension would seem to "hold still" long enough to be significantly observed and understood, the essence of time seems always to have passed us by before we have had the opportunity philosophically to consider its presence and/or meaning. The mysterious nature of time was noted still after the rise of philosophical speculation in Greece, considered in the earliest philosophers in what remained a largely mythological sense, as in the Anaximander fragment:

> ... κατὰ τὸ χρεών: διδόναι γὰρ αὐτὰ δίκην καὶ τίσιν ἀλλήλοις τῆς ἀδικίας κατὰ τὴν τοῦ χρόνου τάξιν— *KRS #110 (DK 12A9)*
>
> *... According to what is necessary, for they pay the penalty and retribution to each other for their injustice according to the assessment of time.*[3]

While he did indeed consider the observable world in a quite abstract light, Anaximander continued to endow time with poetic overtones.[4] And the tone in pre-Socratic philosophy regarding time remained much the same until the advent of the Eleatic school of thought.[5] Parmenides' elucidation of Eleatic philosophical beliefs in his extensive poem the *Truth* describes a "One" reality which "Justice has never...allow[ed] to come to be or perish," which is unchanging, continuous, and "*never was, nor will be, since it is now*, all together, one..."[6] Thus do we receive the first outright philosophical contemplation of time, what it is, how it extends, and how (when) it exists. Immediately following upon the *Truth* of Parmenides were composed Zeno's (in)famous antinomies against plurality and paradoxes against motion, six surviving contrived logical conundra in which the 'One' of "father Parmenides" is made painfully obvious through illustration of the absurdity of the opposite notion (that the universe is multiple, rather than unitary). The proofs of Zeno depend heavily upon his conception of the nature of time for their force,[7] a force which seems to have been intended to bolster the teachings of Parmenides.[8] However, when Zeno's paradoxes are analyzed specifically with respect to their temporal content, they can in certain situations be shown to argue contrarily to the philosophy of Parmenides. In fact, the analysis of time in Zeno's antinomies and paradoxes can even be turned back upon him; one Zenonian assertion can at times be used to cast doubt upon another. A particular discrepancy can be noted between the prevalent notions of time in the antinomies and the paradoxes.

According to Plato's *Parmenides* (128c), Zeno's purpose in composing his paradoxes was as an "argument against those who would try to make fun of it [Parmenides' philosophy] ... it pays them back in their own coin" (KRS # 327, DK 29A12); in short, as a physical buttress to his mentor's pre-existing metaphysical system. Thus, when considering Zeno's philosophy, one ought to have recourse to Parmenides, whose conception of time has been quoted above (*et* n. 6). Parmenides' time, as far as can be extrapolated, consisted of an "infinite present" in which what *is* exist—temporal duration limited only in its immediacy, but not in its extension. In addition, this present is described as "ὁμοῦ πᾶν" (all together as one) and "ξυνεχές" (continuous). "Συνεχής" is the same word used by Aristotle to express the concept of "continuous" in the *Physics*,[9] in which time is defined as *continuous* in that it is not "composed of individual nows (συγκεῖσθαι ἐκ τῶν νῦν)" — (*Phys*. 239b30). Thus, we can assume from the predominant philosophical use of the Greek term that Parmenides' conception of time was as a continuous flow rather than a set of instants (the latter being a view argued against quite intensely by Aristotle, who actually assumed it to be Zenonian in origin, *Phys*. 239b). With a firm grasp of Parmenides' temporal order in hand, we can now examine the temporal philosophy of Zeno.

Unfortunately, the temporal pattern illustrated by Zeno is not nearly as easy to understand as that of Parmenides. In addition, upon close scrutiny of the antinomies and the paradoxes, one can actually arrive at opposed descriptions of Zenonian time. Such a scrutiny will be attempted herein, after which the relation of Zeno's time scheme to that of Parmenides, and its consequences upon Zeno's own philosophical system, will also be examined.

By and large, Zeno's arguments offer little information in disagreement with Parmenides; this stands to reason, considering Zeno's assumed purpose in the composition of his work, as quoted above. This is not to say that no differences are to be found, however; in regard to all four paradoxes, Zeno's time diverges markedly from that proposed by Parmenides, and even from Zeno's own time as understood in the antinomies. Let us then examine the content of the antinomies and the paradoxes with respect to the temporal patterns exhibited in each, beginning with the antinomies against plurality and afterward considering the paradoxes against motion:

Antinomy 1 (*a.k.a.* 'Argument A')

In Antinomy 1 (henceforth referred to as 'Argument A'), Zeno, having assumed the postulate that there are many things, proceeds to illustrate that, were this the case, that they would have to be both limited (in the sense that they are just as many as they are) and unlimited (in the sense that there exists within any magnitude an infinite number of potential divisions or "semi-magnitudes").[10] In rationally proving each half of this argument to be true, while at the same time diametrically opposed, Zeno's has, in effect, negated the original postulate whence the incongruity arose. In order for 'Argument A' to maintain its force, both of its halves must be effective, for without a second half against which the first half might be foiled, the first half must be left to stand alone, leaving no incongruity, no antinomy, and therefore no proof. It ought be noted, therefore, that in order for this antinomy to prove anything, both halves must be able to stand up.

The first half of 'Argument A,' although applicable to spatial and material extensions, says little in regard to temporal composition; it will therefore be kept in mind, but not further considered.

The second half of 'Argument A,' ("if there are many things, then they are unlimited, for there are always others between those that are, and still others between those...") however, is much more illuminating. There is no specification given in the text as to what exactly Zeno' subject was—he simply describes πολλά, "many *things*;" we may, therefore, assume that Zeno was referring to the properties of "things" in general, *qua* things (or plurality *qua* plurality), for if he were referring to the divisibility of certain things or aspects of reality but not others, we may assume that he would have made this clear.[11] With this in mind, it can then be considered from the text of the second half of 'Argument A' that Zeno considered time to be *infinitely* divisible, just as the rest of the πολλά. This conclusion is obvious, since, for the second half to hold force, "things" must exhibit divisibility *ad infinitum*—therefore making them infinite and unlimited.

What then are the temporal consequences of infinite divisibility of time? If the duration between one second and another were divided again and again, *ad infinitum*, the result, according to Zeno's logic, would seem to be an infinite amount of time in one second. What then would be the amount of time in two seconds? Mathematically, it would be twice infinity; consideration of the concept of infinity, however, reveals the fact that twice infinity is equal to once infinity is equal to *n*-infinity.[12] Therefore, one second could be considered equal to two seconds, equal to ten seconds, or equal to ten thousand seconds. The natural result of this consideration, then, is that infinitely divisible time *must be thought of as continuous*, not made up of discrete units (if time were made up of discrete units, then these units would have *no meaning*, and as such, nor would time itself, as shown above).[13]

Thus, it can be stated that the concept of time in 'Argument A' is one of a *continuous and non-discrete process*, as a result of the infinite divisibility needed to legitimise the antinomy's second half.

Antinomy 2

Antinomy 2 deals exclusively with spatial magnitude (μέγεθος), solidity (πάχος), and bulk (ὄγκος).[14] It says little outside of what is strictly spatial, and is not very illuminating regarding Zeno's ideas of time. It will therefore not be further considered.

Having thus examined the antinomies, we may then turn our attention to the four paradoxes of motion. Since time is a necessary component of motion (or even lack thereof), it is to be expected that the paradoxes ought address the concept more specifically than the antinomies. In examining the temporal content of the paradoxes, we must assume that Zeno's actual conception of time is the one which would allow the paradox to be *paradoxical*; thus in each case, we must be aware of why each paradox is a paradox.

Achilles and the Tortoise

The 'Achilles' states that, were a tortoise given a head start in a race with Achilles, Achilles could never overtake the tortoise because, in order to reach the tortoise's position, he would first have to reach the position whence the tortoise had departed, and by the time he had reached this position, the tortoise will have moved further away, thus always holding a lead.[15] How then does time figure into this scenario? Either time must be taken as composed of discrete, indivisible 'nows' of no magnitude, or as continuous and non-discrete;[16] the question which must be asked, then, is which conception of time allows the paradox to remain paradoxical and which conception negates it? Unfortunately, a clear-cut answer cannot be truly reached in this particular case.

If time is considered to be discontinuous, composed of discrete 'nows' (a presumption attributed to Zeno by Aristotle),[17] then the 'Achilles' is indeed quite paradoxical. Recalling the second half of 'Argument A,' the space, which Achilles would be required to traverse, would be infinite, due to the infinite divisibility of spatial extension.[18] Were time assumed to be composed of *finitely* divisible instants beyond which no further division were possible, then Achilles would be presented with the task of traversing an infinite space in a finite time, or, more clearly, of performing an infinite number of discrete physical acts (touching various "takeoff points") in a finite amount of time.[19] This task is indeed logically unattainable, and thus the paradoxical force is retained by the conception of *finitely divisible, discrete time*. Unfortunately, infinitely divisible time allows also for a paradoxical conclusion.

If time were considered to be infinitely divisible, and therefore *continuous*, as it is in 'Argument A,' then the logical impossibility of Achilles' task would seem to be averted. Since a space which is infinitely divisible can in Zeno's system be thought of as an infinite space ('Argument A'), then a time which is infinitely divisible could similarly be thought of as an infinite time. It would then seem that the task facing Achilles would be the performance of an infinite number of discrete, physical tasks in an infinite interval of time—which, despite its practical absurdity, would seem to be logically possible, since the time allotted would be sufficient for the completion of the assigned tasks. The scenario would then appear possible, and therefore non-paradoxical. We are, however, also presented with the fact that Achilles' goal, the tortoise, is constantly moving *away* from him; considered in this light, even given the fact that Achilles is allotted an infinite time in which to complete his tasks, his tasks are constantly increasing,[20] since by his own motion the tortoise is continuously placing *new* "halfways" between himself and his pursuer. Thus, even with infinitely divisible time, it would seem that Achilles would still never be able to overtake the tortoise.[21] The paradoxical force is then retained also in the scenario of infinitely divisible, continuous time.

Thus it would seem that the 'Achilles' presents a paradox no matter which concept of time is postulated; both concepts are *equally effective* in the 'Achilles.' Since we cannot say conclusively which concept of time Zeno intended to incorporate into the 'Achilles' (since, in either case, a paradox still results), it will not be further discussed. Fortunately, Zenonian time is much more visible in the three remaining paradoxes.

The Dichotomy

The 'Dichotomy,' which asserts that a runner can never traverse a stadium (nor even leave his present location) because of the infinite divisibility of spatial extension, is much like the 'Achilles' in many ways; indeed, Aristotle remarked in the *Physics* (239b24-5) that the Achilles is merely "a theatrical version of the 'Dichotomy'."[22] In this scenario, the runner is again presented with the accomplishment of an infinite number of discrete, physical acts in the task of touching each intervening "halfway" between his starting point and his goal,[23] just as was Achilles. The 'Dichotomy' and the 'Achilles' are not exactly similar, however, as Aristotle believed them to be; the difference between the two lies in the fact that, in the 'Achilles,' the goal (the tortoise) is constantly *receding*, whereas in the 'Dichotomy,' it is *stationary*. The problem encountered in the analysis of the 'Achilles' is then averted. It would then seem that, in the case of the 'Dichotomy,' one conception of time will produce a paradox, while the other nullifies the paradoxy of the situation.

If time is considered to be discontinuous in the 'Dichotomy' (finitely divisible into discrete, indivisible instants), then the task facing the runner is indeed impossible. For in this case, the runner would be required to touch an infinity of "halfways" in a finite amount of time, which is logically and physically impossible. Thus, the conception of time as finitely divisible and discrete retains the paradoxical force of the 'Dichotomy;' the task facing the runner is, in this case, impossible.

If time is thought of as continuous and infinitely divisible, however, Zeno's argument would seem to fall apart. Just as was the case in the 'Achilles,' if an infinite divisibility of space can be thought of as producing an infinite spatial extension ('Argument A,' pt. 2), then an infinite divisibility of time could also be thought of as producing an infinite temporal duration. In contrast to the Achilles, however, the runner's goal does not move away from him in the 'Dichotomy;' so, in this sense, the runner is presented with the task of completing an infinite number of discrete, physical acts, but is given an infinite amount of time in which to do so. When Achilles was given an infinite amount of time to perform his infinity of tasks, he still could not complete them, because more and more tasks were always being added by the tortoise's motion;[24] in the case of the 'Dichotomy,' however, the amount of tasks presented to the runner does not change. It would seem, then (theoretically, at least), that the runner could indeed perform an infinity of tasks (touch an infinity of halfway points) if given an infinite amount of time to accomplish them; the tasks would equal the time allotted, since $\infty = \infty$. In addition, the problem, which faced Achilles of the regression of the goal, is no longer present in the 'Dichotomy,' and thus the task of traversing the stadium *is* possible with the postulate of *continuous, non-discrete, infinitely-divisible* time. Continuous time, therefore, can effectively remove the paradoxical force from the argument, since it removes its impossibility.

Taking into consideration the guideline stated above, that Zeno's conception of time must be the one which allows his paradoxes to be paradoxical, we can then assume that, in the case of the 'Dichotomy,' Zeno's idea of time *must* be the one which allows for a paradox; *in the 'Dichotomy,' therefore, Zeno's time is finitely divisible, consisting of discrete indivisible "nows"* (otherwise there is no paradox).

The Arrow

The 'Arrow' paradox attempts to illustrate the impossibility of motion by stating that a flying arrow is throughout its path at rest because at each instant of its flight, it occupies a space just its own size. Zeno then assumes that, if an arrow is at rest at each instant of its flight, it must be at rest throughout the entire flight.[25] It would seem upon first glance that this is a paradox concerning the logical impossibility of motion and that it has little to do with Zeno's concept of time (or lack thereof).[26] Time must figure into the contemplation of the arrow's motion, however; there must be a stretch of time over which the arrow is at rest, for instantaneous rest proves nothing and does not give a paradox, just an interesting thought. In order to arrive at the correct conclusion regarding Zeno's conception of time in the 'Arrow,' the idea of time which preserves the paradox must be located—i.e. the one which allows the arrow to be at rest.

If time is considered as infinitely divisible, and not composed of indivisible nows in the 'Arrow,' then it is obviously impossible that the arrow would be able to stay still at any period of its flight. For in such a continuous time scenario, every possible time interval can be subdivided into sub-intervals *ad infinitum*, and can as such be considered to be always composed of smaller sub-units, no matter how many times it has been previously divided (note 'Argument A,' pt. 2). So, through any given time interval, the arrow could conceivably possess motion, since each interval will always be composed of sub-intervals, *giving it always some amount of magnitude* (duration). In a continuous (infinitely divisible) time scheme, then, there always would exist to the arrow a temporal beginning point and a temporal stopping point of the duration over which it is being observed; since this duration has extension and magnitude, the arrow would then be free to move through it from the beginning to the end.

It can therefore be concluded that in a continuous, infinitely divisible time scheme, the arrow could always move, no matter how small the instant over which it is observed. This conclusion obviously is non-paradoxical, so it can be assumed that this was *not* Zeno's intended temporal usage in the 'Arrow.'

The assumption of finitely divisible time composed of indivisible instants, however, allows the paradoxical force of the 'Arrow' to be preserved; in fact, for the 'Arrow' to be paradoxical at all, we *must* assume this sort of time scheme.[27] An instant must be indivisible in order for the arrow to be at rest within it, otherwise it would necessarily be composed of sub-instants, giving the interval a beginning and an end over which the arrow could travel. For the arrow to be stationary, time must be composed of indivisible "nows" which could themselves possess no magnitude (if they did possess magnitude, then once again the arrow would have a beginning and an end to the time interval through which it could travel). Thus it can be concluded that, in order for the 'Arrow' to remain paradoxical, its time scheme must be one of fragmentary, *finitely divisible, time made up of indivisible "nows."*

The Moving Rows (a.k.a 'The Stadium')

The 'Moving Rows' is the most abstract and most difficult to visualise of Zeno's paradoxes. It presents a scenario in which a row of "alphas" sits stationary and is passed from the left by an equally long row of moving "betas" of the same size and from the right by an equally long row of "gammas" of the same size moving at the same speed as the "betas." It was illustrated by Simplicius (*In Phys.* 1016, 14)[28] in such a way that by the time that the leading beta and the leading gamma have reached the outermost alphas, the leading beta will have passed two alphas, but four gammas, and the leading gamma will have passed two alphas, but four betas, all in the same amount of time. If all characters are taken to be of the same size, then it would appear that the amount of time taken to traverse a given distance (i.e. one letter-size) is equal to the time taken to traverse twice that distance or, that twice t is equal to t is equal to $\frac{1}{2}t$, ($2t = t = \frac{1}{2}t$).[29] This conclusion is obviously paradoxical—it makes no temporal sense. In looking for the proper concept of time in the 'Moving Rows,' then, we must find the one which allows the scenario to make no temporal sense, the one which allows $t = 2t = \frac{1}{2}t$ to be irrational and absurd.

If time is considered to be continuous and infinitely divisible, then it would be perfectly logical for $2t$ to equal t and $\frac{1}{2}t$, since in any time interval t, there would exist an *infinite* number of potential sub-divisions. Thus, we could say that in one interval t, there is an infinite amount of time. How much time would then exist in twice t? Mathematically speaking, it would equal twice the amount that is present in t, which is ∞; and it can be stated mathematically and logically that $2\infty = \infty$.[30] Therefore, if a continuous, infinitely divisible time scheme is assumed in the 'Moving Rows,' it is perfectly logical that t could equal $2t$ or $\frac{1}{2}t$—the force of the paradox is lost. Thus, continuous time cannot be assumed to be Zeno's intention in the 'Moving Rows.'

The 'Moving Rows' only retains its paradoxical force if the time in it is assumed to be discontinuous and *finitely* divisible into *indivisible* units. The assumption that t is equal to twice t is nonsensical only if t is *defined* and *limited.* If we assume that time is composed of indivisible "nows" in the 'Moving Rows,' then the paradox is retained due to the fact that an instant, which ought be indivisible, appears to be divisible[31] (this fact does not matter if time is thought of as infinitely divisible). In the scenario, the time required for a beta to pass four alphas is equal to twice the time required for a beta to pass four gammas—if this situation is extrapolated downward to the point that it would take one instant or "now" for a beta to pass an alpha, it would then require ½ of a "now" for a beta to pass a gamma. In this time scheme, however, a "now" must be thought of as indivisible. Thus, in the case of finitely divisible time, the paradoxical force is preserved. In the 'Moving Rows,' therefore, we can conclude that Zeno assumed a *discrete, finitely divisible time* composed of indivisible nows, since this is the only situation in which the paradox is a paradox.

In total, then, we can see that Zeno's time scheme is different in some places than it is in others. In 'Argument A,' Zeno assumes a continuous and infinitely divisible time, which agrees more with the philosophy of his mentor Parmenides, whereas in the 'Arrow,' the 'Dichotomy,' and the 'Moving Rows,' he seems to require a discrete, fragmentary, instantaneous time which is divisible only up to a given point, beyond which instants ("nows") are indivisible. In the 'Achilles,' he plausibly exhibits elements of both. What then are the consequences of this dualistic nature of Zenonian time?

Let us first consider the relation of Zenonian time to the Eleatic "One" championed by Parmenides. 'Argument A' produces a concept of time, which coincides with the Eleatic "One" in many respects.[32] Continuous (συνεχής) time which is infinitely divisible cannot be quantified into discrete units,[33] as demonstrated above (since if this attempt is made, one second can logically be made equal to ten-thousand seconds). Since temporal quantity and its expiration are the essence of motion and change, in this respect continuous time is quite Parmenidean: "Nor is it divided, since it all exists alike; nor is it more here and less there, which would prevent it from holding together, but it is all full of being. So it is all continuous" (Parmenides, *Truth* ll. 22-25, *via* Simplicius, *In Phys.*, 144, 29).[34] But in the 'Dichotomy,' the 'Arrow,' and the 'Moving Rows,' Zeno also required a scheme of finitely divisible, fragmentary time made up of instants—an obviously non-Parmenidean scenario in its seeming plurality and implicit endorsement of change and motion. In a way, the Zenonian time of the final three paradoxes is almost atomistic in that they rest on the assumption that time, rather than being "One," is an aggregate of indivisible "nows." And indeed, the time scheme employed in the final three paradoxes can effectively counterbalance 'Argument A' in addition to the Parmenidean leanings of Zeno.

When observed *en masse*, the extant works of Zeno leave us with two conflicting, but still apparently true temporal alternatives. It would seem, then, that Zeno implies both poles of a diametrically opposed system to be equally correct. Such a dual use of time leaves us an ideal criterion for another of Zeno's favorite philosophical usages, the *reductio ad absurdum*. If Zeno's assertions are applied (with an eye toward their temporal ramifications) to the structure of the *reductio ad absurdum*:

$$p \supset q$$
$$p \supset \sim q$$
$$p \supset (q \;\&\; \sim q)$$
$$p \supset \sim (q \;\&\; \sim q)$$
$$\therefore \sim p$$

the following relationship results:

> Zeno's assertions [*'Argument A' and Eleatic 'One'*] ⊃
> continuous, infinitely divisible time
>
> Zeno's assertions [*Dichotomy, Arrow, Rows*] ⊃
> discontinuous, limited time
>
> Zeno's assertions ⊃
> (continuous time and discontinuous time)
>
> Thus ~ (continuous and discontinuous time)
>
> ∴ Zeno's Assertions ⊃ ~ (Zeno's Assertions)

In this way, Zeno's assertions can be seen to imply their opposites. As noted above, however, Zeno's antinomies and paradoxes were composed for the purpose of denying plurality and motion, and were not explicitly concerned with the structure and passage of time. Application of the *reductio ad absurdum* to his arguments is then perhaps a bit harsh in this case. Despite Zeno's intentions and apparent lack of temporal concern, however, the relation still exists and must be considered philosophically. The philosophical conclusions to be drawn from Zeno's differential treatment of time in the antinomies and the paradoxes are twofold: 1) in order to disprove motion, Zeno was forced to concede to a lesser species of theoretical plurality, and 2) in order to disprove plurality, Zeno was similarly forced to concede to a lesser species of theoretical motion.

Whatever Zeno's attitude toward time really was (if indeed he even formulated such an attitude), in order to keep the force of all his arguments, it must have been able to address and incorporate equally well the concepts and consequences of both fragmentary, discrete time which is finitely divisible into indivisible "nows" (quasi-"time-atomism") and continuous, flowing time which is infinitely divisible (quasi-Parmenidean time). This "half-and-half" temporal dichotomy is perhaps fitting for Zeno, however, falling as he does directly between the *floruit* of Eleatic monism and the rise of Democritean atomism.

NOTES

1 The author wishes to thank Professor Robert Rethy, under whose instruction and suggestion the original version of this paper was composed, and all others who have read or listened to preliminary versions and offered comments or suggestions. Whatever infelicities remain are those of the author.

2 Translation as taken from Loeb Classical Library, *Hesiod: Homeric Hymns, Epic Cycle, Homerica*, translated by Hugh Evelyn-White (Cambridge, 1914). Although the identification of Κρόνος with Χρόνος is not undisputed, the allegory is generally accepted and will be treated as such here for the sake of conciseness.

3 Translation as taken from G. S. Kirk, J. E. Raven, and M. Schofield, *The Presocratic Philosophers*, henceforth KRS, (Cambridge, 1957), #110, 117-18.

4 As Simplicius, in whose treatise on Aristotle's *Physics* Anaximander's fragment survives, notes of Anaximander's account: "ποιητικωτέροις οὕτως ὀνόμασιν αὐτὰ λέγων." — *He thus describes these things in rather poetical terms* (KRS 110, H. Diels & W. Kranz, *Die Fragmente der Vorsokratiker* (Berlin, 1951-52) — henceforth DK, 12A9).

5 Time was treated lightly by the Pythagoreans, who stated merely that it occurred in cycles. They did not, however, speculate philosophically on its nature or composition. A somewhat obscure reference to the cosmic significance of time can perhaps also be noted in Heraclitus' statement: — αἰὼν παῖς ἐστι παίζων, πεσσεύων. παιδὸς ἡ βασιληΐη (DK frg. 52).

6 KRS, #296, 249-50. "The statement...seems to claim not merely that what is will not *come to exist*, but that it will not exist *at all* in the future. Probably what Parmenides means to ascribe to what *is* is existence in an eternal present not subject to temporal distinctions of any sort" (italics included in the original).

7 Since motion is dependent upon time, and time itself depends upon change, which implies multiplicity (the very premise which Zeno supposedly had attempted to disprove), the cardinal relevance of time to Zeno's system can be noted.

8 This conclusion has, however, been questioned, e.g., by N. B. Booth, "Were Zeno's Arguments a Reply to Attacks upon Parmenides?" *Phronesis* 1 (1957) 1-9; and "Were Zeno's Arguments Directed against the Pythagoreans?" *Phronesis* 1 (1957) 90-103. See also N. B. Booth, "Zeno's Paradoxes," *Journal of Hellenic Studies* 78 (1957) 189-201.

9 *Physics*, 227a10-7, 232b24-5, 268a6-7; also *Metaphysics* 1069a5-9.

10 KRS, #315, 265-66.

11 The *argumentum ex silentio* contained herein is acknowledged. Since the subject of Eleatic philosophy was not specificity, but the nature of reality and the universe as a whole, however, I believe that the inclusion of "everything" under Zeno's statement is justified in this case.

12 This is not to imply the existence of multiple infinities, the idea of which is absurd, but simply to compare the quantity of infinity with itself theoretically.

13 Aristotle reaches a similar conclusion in regard to συνεχής, but from the opposite direction, in the *Physics*. He derives infinite divisibility from continuousness, rather than continuousness from infinite divisibility. "A property of continuity is infinite divisibility."

14 KRS, #316, 260.

15 KRS #322, 272.

16 Adolf Grünbaum, *Philosophical Problems of Space and Time* (New York, 1963), 160.

17 *Physics* VI, 239b, 5-9, KRS # 323 (DK 29A27) : "for time is not composed from indivisible nows, just as neither is any other magnitude." — as cited by Jonathan Lear, "A Note on Zeno's Arrow," *Phronesis* 26 (1981) 91-103.

18 In my opinion, the infinite divisibility of spatial extension may be safely inferred from 'Argument A' without the need for further examination, as time is examined above. Infinite spatial divisibility is required for the retention of force in all the paradoxes and antinomies. It would seem that Zeno's statements were composed with an eye toward the three physical dimensions especially, and that, in this respect, Zeno's actual words are clear enough.

[19] D. J. Furley, "Zeno and Indivisible Magnitudes," in Alexander P. D. Mourelatos (ed.), *The Pre-Socratics* (Princeton, New Jersey, 1974), 316; and John McKie, "The Persuasiveness of Zeno's Paradoxes," *Philosophy and Phenomenological Research* 47 (1986-87) 631-9.

[20] S.M. Corbett, "Zeno's 'Achilles'," *Philosophy and Phenomenological Research* 49 (1988-89), *passim*.

[21] *Ibid.* It is acknowledged that this assertion can be seen to imply an unusual notion of infinity. This is a conceptual problem that has been dealt with by many; it can be summarised by the question "if a quantity is added to infinity, does this make infinity larger?" Such a question, however, leads into consideration of the question of whether or not there could be anything outside of infinity which one could add to infinity—if not, then the possibility of addition to infinity is absurd, but if so, then would infinity really be infinity? It is my opinion that this problem rests on one's interpretation of the term itself, much like one's interpretation of Anaximander's ἄπειρον—should one consider it as "a quantity which extends and increases without limit" or as "that which possesses no internal delineations?" I base the assertions made in *this* paper upon the authority of the majority of writers on this subject. This topic, however, cannot in and of itself be treated fully here.

[22] KRS, 272.

[23] KRS #318-320 (DK 29A25), 269-271.

[24] Corbett, *op. cit.* (n. 20).

[25] Cf. KRS, 273; Lear, *op. cit.* (n.17) 91; Furley, *op. cit.* (n. 19), 361.

[26] The hypothesis that Zeno's 'Arrow' has nothing at all to do with his concept of time is argued by KRS, 273: "His argument requires no determinate assumption about the structure of space and time; all he requires for the validity of his inference is that what is true of something *at every moment* of a period of time (whether or not moments are indivisible instants) is true of it *throughout* the period" (italics in the original). I disagree, along with Furley, *op. cit.* (n. 19), 361-2, and Lear, *op. cit.* (n. 17), *passim*.

[27] Lear, *op. cit.* (n. 17), *passim*.

[28] For an illustration, see KRS, #326, 274; Mourelatos, *op. cit.* (n. 19), 362.

[29] John Immerwahr, "An Interpretation of Zeno's Stadium [Moving Rows] Paradox," *Phronesis* 23 (1978) 22-6.

[30] Or, since the division in this case is into ever-decreasing and infinitesimally small units, the process could be described by the function:

$\lim_{t \to 0}$, in which case the relation $\lim_{t \to 0} = 2 \lim_{t \to 0}$

would hold true and would further indicate the inadequacies of infinitely divisible time in the 'Moving Rows.' Thus, this situation can be evaluated with an eye toward both the infinite and the infinitesimal.

[31] *Ibid.*

[32] Stephen Makin, "Zeno on Plurality," *Phronesis* 27 (1982) 223-34: "Zeno is concerned precisely with something συνεχής, which is also ἀδιαίρετον, and ἓν ... τὸ ὄν is συνεχής."

[33] Adolf Grünbaum, "Modern Science and Zeno's Paradoxes of Motion," 423-24 in Richard Gale (ed.) *The Philosophy of Time* (New Jersey, 1968).

[34] KRS #297, 250-51.

REFERENCES

Apostle, Hippocrates G. (ed.). *Aristotle: Selected Works*. Grinnell, Iowa: The Perpatetic Press, 1983.

Corbett, S. M. "Zeno's Achilles: A Reply to John McKie." *Philosophy and Phenomenological Research* 49 (1988): 325-331.

Dillon, V. J. "More Evidence on Zeno of Elea?" *Archiv für Geschichte Der Philosophie* 19 (1981): 221-222.

Engman, Joyce. "Cosmic Justice in Anaximander." *Phronesis* 36 (1991): 1-25.

Evelyn-White, Hugh G. (ed.). *Hesiod: Homeric Hymns, Epic Cycle, Homerica* (Loeb Classical Series). Cambridge: Harvard University Press, 1914.

Freeman, Eugene and Wilfrid Sellars (ed.). *The Philosophy of Time*. LaSalle, Illinois: Open Court Publishing, 1971.

Gale, Richard M. (ed.). *The Philosophy of Time*. New Jersey: Humanities Press, 1968.

Grünbaum, Adolf. *Philosophical Problems of Time and Space*. New York: Alfred A. Knopf Inc., 1963.

__________. *Modern Science and Zeno's Paradoxes*. Middletown, Connecticut: Wesleyan University Press, 1967.

Immerwahr, John. "An Interpretation of Zeno's Stadium Paradox." *Phronesis* 23 (1978): 22-26.

Jaques, Elliott. *The Form of Time*. New York: Crane Russak, 1982.

Kirk, G. S., J. E. Raven, and M. Schofield. *The Presocratic Philosophers*. Cambridge: Cambridge University Press, 1957.

Lazerowitz, Morris. "The Paradoxes of Motion." *Proceedings of the Aristotelian Society* 52 (1952): 261-280.

Lear, Jonathan. "A Note on Zeno's Arrow." *Phronesis* 26 (1981): 91-103.

Makin, Stephen. "Zeno on Plurality." *Phronesis* 27 (1982): 223-238.

McKie, John R. "The Persuasiveness of Zeno's Paradoxes." *Philosophy and Phenomenological Research* 47 (1986): 631-640.

Mourelatos, Alexander P. D. (ed.). *The Pre-Socratics*. Princeton, New Jersey: Princeton University Press, 1974.

Shamsi, J. A. "Toward a Definitive Solution of Zeno's Paradoxes." *Revue Philosophique de la France et de l'etranger* 166 (1976): 231-232.

VanFraasen, Bas C. *An Introduction to the Philosophy of Time and Space*. New York: Random House, 1970.

Vlastos, Gregory. "A Note on Zeno's Arrow." *Phronesis* 11 (1966): 3-18.

__________. "Zeno's Race Course." *History of Philosophy* 4 (1966): 95-108.

__________. "Plato's Testimony Concerning Zeno of Elea." *Journal of Hellenic Studies* 95 (1975): 136-162.

Waterlow, Sarah. "Instants of Motion in Aristotle's Physics VI." *Archiv für Geschichte der Philosophie* 65 (1983): 128-146.

White, Michael J. "Zeno's Arrow, Divisible Infinitesimals, and Chrysippus." *Phronesis* 27 (1982): 239-254.

DOES THE ONTOLOGICAL ARGUMENT NEED SALVAGING? AN ANALYSIS OF ST. ANSELM'S AND PLANTINGA'S THEISTIC PROOFS

Erin Kathleen Carter
Taylor University

Since St. Anselm formulated the first ontological argument in the eleventh century, philosophers and theologians have debated whether such an argument is sound and thus succeeds in proving the existence of God. In the course of this paper, I examine whether St. Anselm's original formulation of the ontological argument succeeds as a theistic proof, and if not, whether Alvin Plantinga's modal version circumvents the problems in the Anselmian argument.

Since St. Anselm of Canterbury formulated the first ontological argument in the eleventh century, philosophers and theologians have debated whether such an argument is sound and thus succeeds in proving the existence of God. It seems that more people reject than accept the ontological argument in any of its numerous forms but, as P.J. McGrath notes, "while it is widely believed that the argument is unsound, there is little agreement as to what precisely is wrong with it."[1] Schopenhauer referred to it as a "charming joke,"[2] and McGrath calls it a "hydra-headed monster,"[3] but most recent critics of the ontological argument are simply content to claim that it begs the question, that is, it presupposes that which it is attempting to prove. Though the ontological argument can take many forms, so many that it seems misleading to refer to "*the* ontological argument," today it appears to be widely accepted that there are six standard versions, three of which are modal, or having to do with possible worlds. In the course of this paper, I wish to examine whether St. Anselm's original formulation of the ontological argument succeeds as a theistic proof, and if not, whether Alvin Plantinga's version circumvents the problems found in the Anselmian argument.

It has been said that St. Anselm never intended to prove the existence of God, per se. Indeed, some argue that Anselm did not succeed in proving that God exists, if one defines *to prove* as "to achieve absolute cogency and clarity by means of a single brief course of reasoning."[4] Since Anselm's motives were not to conclusively demonstrate God's existence by way of one *a priori* argument, this "failure" can hardly be understood as a strong criticism against him. In addition, it is important to note that Anselm's ontological argument does not necessarily prove the existence of God as defined by Christian theism, with a triune nature and the ability to participate in the Incarnation. The ontological argument is, however, strong enough to support the idea that a greatest conceivable being exists. This being may not be first apprehended as the God of Christianity, but it could still be possible to arrive at the Christian God using the being posited in this argument as a foundation of sorts.

Anselm formulated the first ontological argument while in a state of "prayerful meditation," during which he requests, "Let me discern Your light whether it be from afar or from the depths. Teach me to seek You, and reveal Yourself to me as I seek, because I can neither seek You if You do not teach me how, nor find You unless You reveal Yourself."[5] Further in the *Proslogium*, Anselm writes that God is "something than which nothing greater can be thought."[6]

From this definition, Anselm proceeds to formulate his ontological argument, the conclusion of which is as follows:

> Therefore, if that, than which nothing greater can be conceived, exists in the understanding alone, the very being, than which nothing greater can be conceived, is one, than which a greater can be conceived. But obviously this is impossible.
>
> Hence, there is no doubt that there exists a being, than which nothing greater can be conceived, and it exists both in the understanding and in reality. And it assuredly exists so truly, that it cannot be conceived not to exist. For, it is possible to conceive of a being, which cannot be conceived not to exist; and this is greater than one, which cannot be conceived not to exist. Hence, if that, than which nothing greater can be conceived, can be conceived not to exist, it is not that, than which nothing greater can be conceived. But this is an irreconcilable contradiction. There is, then, so truly a being than which nothing greater can be conceived to exist, that it cannot even be conceived not to exist; and this being thou art, O Lord, our God.[7]

If one were to make a formal representation of Anselm's argument, it would take one of two forms, the first of which is as follows:

(1) I have an idea of that than which nothing greater can be conceived (G).

(2) That which exists in reality (and not only in my mind) is greater than that which exists only in my mind.

(3) If G existed only in my mind, G would not be that than which nothing greater can be con-

ceived (because I can conceive of it existing in reality, not only in my mind).

(4) *Therefore, G exists in reality.*[8]

The second version of the ontological argument contained in Anselm's *Proslogium* is:

(1) It is possible to conceive of a being which cannot be conceived not to exist (G).

(2) If G is conceived of as not existing, then G is not G (which is a contradiction).

(3) Therefore, G cannot be conceived of as not existing.

(4) Therefore, G exists necessarily (or G's existence is logically necessary).[9]

The first argument concludes that *G* exists in reality, while the second maintains that *G* exists necessarily; combining the two versions provides a clear definition of the being for which Anselm is arguing—one than which nothing greater can be thought (version 1) and who must necessarily exist in reality (version 2). In both of these versions, Anselm is attempting to reason from the idea of God to His existence in the actual world. This is an *a priori* theistic proof for it does not reason from a person's experience to the existence of God. Rather, it calls first for one to imagine a greatest conceivable being, and then leads the "conceiver," through reason alone, to the conclusion that this mighty being actually exists.

As would be expected, there are many criticisms, some famous and others obscure, to Anselm's ontological argument. Although Hartshorne cites as many as twenty objections,[10] only four will be discussed here, the first of which is presented by Gaunilo, a contemporary of Anselm. Gaunilo claims that one can conceive of many objects than which nothing greater can be thought; just because one can formulate the idea of such a thing in one's mind does not necessarily imply that it exists. The example given by Gaunilo is that of the most perfect island. One can imagine the most perfect island, with palm trees and white sand and beautiful waves crashing upon the shore, but just because one can conceive of this landmass as existing does not necessarily mean that it exists in some ocean somewhere. Similarly, he argues, just because one can conceive of a most perfect being as existing does not mean that the being does indeed exist.

St. Anselm's response to this objection is that Gaunilo fails to understand that the ontological argument is not positing a being "that is *in fact* greater than any other, but one such that a greater *cannot be conceived*; a being than which it's *not possible* that there be a greater."[11] Since this is the case, as Plantinga notes, Gaunilo's

> famous lost island argument isn't strictly parallel to Anselm's argument; his conclusion should be only that there is an island such that no other island is greater than it—which, if there are any islands at all, is a fairly innocuous conclusion.[12]

One could counter Plantinga by restating Gaunilo's objection, so that the island is one than which it is not possible that there be a greater, but even this seems to fail as a criticism of Anselm's argument. As Plantinga notes, the idea of a greatest possible island is incoherent, because there is no "intrinsic maximum" available for land masses and other objects. Beings, on the other hand, have characteristics for which there are intrinsic maximums, i.e., knowledge, power, goodness, etc. Assume that possession of palm trees is considered a "great-making" property and that there is an island, which has thousands of palm trees. While this may be a great vacation spot, it is still not the greatest conceivable island, since one can always imagine an island with hundreds of thousands of palm trees, which would in turn make it greater than the previous island. A being, however, can be all-knowing, all-powerful, and all-good, thus making it the greatest conceivable being. One cannot conceive of a being with more knowledge and more power than an omniscient and omnipotent being; to attempt to do so creates a contradiction.[13]

Thomas Aquinas rejected Anselm's argument on the grounds that it makes an illicit transition from the ideal to the real. He writes in his *Summa Theologica* that to

> know that God exists in a general and confused way is implanted in us by nature. This, however, is not to know absolutely that God exists; just as to know that someone is approaching is not the same as to know that Peter is approaching, even though it is Peter who is approaching.[14]

Aquinas claims that all that is proven by Anselm's argument is that "if we think of God at all, we must *think* of Him as existing; it does not prove that He actually exists."[15] By way of reply, one could argue that Aquinas' objection

> neglects the peculiar character of God, of the Being than which no greater can be thought. Such a Being is its own existence and if it is possible for such a Being to exist, it must exist. The Being than which no greater can be thought is the Being which exists necessarily, it is the necessary Being, and it would be absurd to speak of a merely possible necessary Being.[16]

Aquinas seems to be ignoring premises (2) and (3) of the first version of Anselm's argument, the former being, *"That which exists in reality (and not only in my mind) is greater than that which exists only in my mind,"* and the latter, *"If G existed only in my mind, G would not be that than which nothing greater can be conceived (because I can conceive of it existing in reality, not only in my mind)."* Both of these premises lead to the conclusion that *G*, that than which nothing greater can be thought, has to exist in reality—it is a *requirement*, not an option—and thus cannot just be a result of one's mental processes. In light of this response, it appears that Aquinas' claims against Anselm's argument do not form much of an objection at all. This may account for why it is not cited as often as those postulated by Gaunilo, Kant, and more recent philosophers such as McGrath and Sennett.

Though theologian Karl Barth referred to Immanuel Kant's criticism of the ontological argument as "so much nonsense on which no more words ought to be wasted,"[17] it is still the most well-known objection to the Anselmian argument cited to date. In addition to accusing Anselm of begging the question, Kant maintained that there is a "contradiction in introducing the concept of existence...into the concept of a thing which we profess to be thinking solely in reference to its possibility."[18] He argued that "existential propositions are always synthetic, always true or false as a matter of fact rather than as a matter of definition,"[19] hence existence is not a real predicate. That is, it is "not a concept of something which could be added to the concept of a thing."[20] In Kant's understanding, existence is presupposed whenever we discuss an object or being; if he is correct, then God's existence is already presupposed when we speak of Him.

One can counter this objection by arguing that we do not always presuppose existence when discussing a being or object. For example, when my younger sister and I watch "Sesame Street" and see Big Bird, neither one of us assumes that somewhere there really is a very yellow, six-foot English-speaking bird who answers to the quite descriptive name "Big Bird." We can, and do, talk about Big Bird without presupposing his existence. It seems that people refer to fictitious beings quite often (i.e., The Cat in the Hat, Cookie Monster, etc.) without assuming that such beings exist somewhere.

There are those who maintain that Kant is objecting to what he perceives to be an attempt by Anselm to define God into existence, by listing existence as a property which God, the greatest possible being, must have as a matter of necessity. If this is the case, Plantinga's response that this Kantian objection is irrelevant seems appropriate: "Where did he [Anselm] try to define God into being by adding existence to a list of properties that defined some concept?"[21] In neither of his versions of the ontological argument does Anselm mention existence as an added property. Rather he arrives at the conclusion that God must exist necessarily instead of assuming His existence from the outset.

Many recent philosophers who reject Anselm's ontological argument do so solely on the basis that it begs the question. P.J. McGrath maintains that the Anselmian argument, when viewed as a *reductio ad absurdum*, "implies that the existence of the greatest conceivable being is logically impossible and this contradicts something that is assumed to be true, namely, that it is logically possible that the greatest conceivable being exists."[22] McGrath formulates Anselm's argument in the following manner:

(1) *If it is logically possible that the greatest conceivable being exists, then it actually exists.*

(2) *But it is logically possible that it exists.*

(3) *Therefore, it actually exists.*[23]

McGrath maintains that the "second premise of this argument cannot be true, granted the truth of the first premise, unless the conclusion is true,"[24] hence his claim that this ontological argument begs the question. McGrath further solidifies his objection by arguing that the greatest conceivable being is

> such that it exists in either all possible worlds or in none. To show that [this being] is logically possible, it is not enough to show that the concept of [it] involves no contradiction, one must show in addition that the concept is exemplified in all worlds, and therefore in the actual world.[25]

The above argument justifies McGrath's claim that if "it is correct to say that the existence of the greatest conceivable being is logically possible only if it actually exists, then one would need to know that it actually exists in order to know that its existence is logically possible."[26]

William Vallicella has attempted to refute McGrath's criticism by arguing that one need not know God exists in order to know that His existence is logically possible. Vallicella argues that what McGrath is basing his argument upon is

> a distinction between two senses of 'logically possible', one that applies to contingent, the other to necessary, beings. In the first sense, to say of the GCB [greatest conceivable being] that it is logically possible is just to say that the concept thereof is internally coherent. But in the second sense it is to say that the

> concept is both internally coherent *and* actually exemplified.[27]

Vallicella's claim is that this separation "does not show up on the conceptual level. Conceptual coherence is the same for both contingent and necessary beings."[28] Since McGrath's criticism hinges upon this distinction, when Vallicella dissolves the differentiation at the conceptual level, it appears that he causes McGrath's objection to disintegrate as well.

One might be able to formulate another response to McGrath's criticism based upon his wording of Anselm's argument, by claiming that he rewords the argument to make it fit with his objection. Consider the second version of Anselm's argument once again:

> (1) *It is possible to conceive of a being which cannot be conceived not to exist (G).*
>
> (2) *If G is conceived of as not existing, then G is not G (which is a contradiction).*
>
> (3) *Therefore, G cannot be conceived of as not existing.*
>
> (4) *Therefore, G exists necessarily (or G's existence is logically necessary).*

This argument does not begin with the premise that *G* actually exists. Rather, Anselm proposes only that a person has the ability to conceive of a being, which cannot be conceived not to exist. The first premise is not asserting *G's* existence per se, as McGrath's formulation appears to do. While it is possible that McGrath's wording of the ontological argument begs the question, it seems doubtful that conclusion could be supported using one of the two Anselmian versions outlined at the beginning of this paper.

Although the ontological argument as formulated by St. Anselm appears to withstand the aforementioned criticisms, there are still those who believe it to be insufficient for proving the existence of a being than which nothing greater can be conceived. This is due, at least in part, to the underlying assumption that an argument such as this, which appears to be so simple to comprehend, must be seriously flawed. Charles Hartshorne writes that one scholar advised him in this way regarding the traditional Anselmian argument: "People's minds are closed, on this subject...you should not openly defend the Old Proof. Label it differently, appear to be talking about something new."[29] Another philosopher, D. Elton Trueblood, claims that the main reason the ontological argument "does not carry conviction today [is] largely because it represents a prescientific mentality ... [and it] seems irrelevant."[30] Because of the tendency to shy away from Anselm's argument, and move toward more "scientific" proofs for the existence of God, several philosophers have recently tried to formulate their own ontological arguments, many of which deal with possible worlds.

Although Alvin Plantinga notes that it is "doubtful...that any person was ever brought to a belief in God by this argument [Anselm's ontological argument], and unlikely that it has played the sort of role in strengthening and confirming religious belief that, for example, the teleological argument has played,"[31] he nonetheless has formulated his own argument, designed to circumvent the problems he finds in Anselm's original version. Plantinga's ontological argument is one of the three standard modal versions, the other two being postulated by Charles Hartshorne and

Norman Malcolm. Plantinga presents Anselm's argument as follows:

> *(1) God [the Greatest Conceivable Being] exists in the understanding but not in reality.*
>
> *(2) Existence in reality is greater than existence in the understanding alone. (premise)*
>
> *(3) God's existence in reality is conceivable. (premise)*
>
> *(4) If God did exist in reality, then He would be greater than He is. (from 1 & 2)*
>
> *(5) It is conceivable that there is a being greater than God is. (3 & 4)*
>
> *(6) It is conceivable that there is a being greater than the being than which nothing greater can be conceived. (5, by definition of "God")*
>
> *(7) It is false that God exists in the understanding but not in reality. (because 6 is absurd and self-contradictory)*[32]

After phrasing Anselm's argument in this way, Plantinga introduces the discussion of possible worlds by making three claims: (1) an object may exist in some possible worlds, but not others, (2) an object can have different properties in different worlds, and (3) if a person can have different properties in different worlds, then he can have different degrees of greatness in different worlds.[33] With these presuppositions in mind, Plantinga rephrases Anselm's ontological argument in modal terms:

> *(1) God does not exist in the actual world.*

(2) *For any being x and worlds W and W′, if x exists in W but not in W′, then x's greatness in W exceeds x's greatness in W′.*

(3) *There is a possible world in which God exists. (restatement of original premise (3))*

(4) *If God does not exist in the actual world, then there is a world W′ such that the greatness of God in W′ exceeds the greatness of God in the actual world.*

(5) *So there is a world W′ such that the greatness of God in W′ exceeds the greatness of God in the actual world.*

(6) *So there is a possible being x and a world W′ such that the greatness of x in W′ exceeds the greatness of God in actuality.*

(7) *Hence it is possible that there is a being greater than God is.*

(8) *So it's possible that there is a being greater than the being than which it's not possible that there be a greater.*

(9) *But it's not possible that there be a being greater than the being than which it's not possible that there be a greater.*

(10) *Therefore, (1) is false—so the actual world contains a being than which it's not possible that there be a greater, that is, God exists.*[34]

The problem, as Plantinga sees it, is that the above modal argument begs the question, in that one can accept the inference from premise (2) to premise (4) only if one already knows the conclusion that God exists is true. Because of this perceived difficulty with Anselm's argument, Plantinga proposes the following argument as a successful modal ontological argument for the existence of God:

(1) There is a possible world in which maximal greatness is instantiated [represented by a concrete example].

(2) Necessarily, a being is maximally great only if it has maximal excellence in every possible world.

(3) Necessarily, a being has maximal excellence in every possible world only if it has omniscience, omnipotence, and moral perfection in every possible world.

(4) The actual world is a possible world.

(5) Therefore, an omniscient, omnipotent, and morally perfect being exists in the actual world.[35]

While this argument seems to be valid, it is not without its critics. James Sennett has opposed Plantinga's modal ontological argument based on what he refers to as "universe indexed properties." A universe indexed property is a property which, if a being is going to possess it, that being must possess it in every possible world, including the actual world;[36] Sennett then identifies unsurpassable greatness as one such property. Sennett's basic claim is that these properties, when applied to "non-abstract objects like God,"[37] are not exemplifiable. If this is the case, then Anselm's greatest conceivable being has just become a "metaphysically contingent omnipotent being,"[38] and is unable to exhibit characteristics such as unsurpassable greatness and maximal excellence in every possible world. Rather than fully elucidate this point, Sennett calls for the philosopher to rely upon his or her "modal intuitions" to come to the conclusion that "Plantinga's version of the OA [ontological argument] is...more rationally rejected as unsound than accepted as sound."[39] Aside from noting the dangers inherent in appealing to one's intuitions, especially considering that the concept of a "metaphysically contingent omnipotent being [seems to be] wildly counter-intuitive,"[40] the response given by Vallicella is that, regardless of the discussion of universe indexed properties, Sennett has still not provided good evidence for his claim that it is more rational to reject rather than to accept the ontological argument.[41]

P.J. McGrath, who maintains that this revision of the ontological argument fares no better than any other standard version, offers another criticism of Plantinga. His claim is that "[i]mplicit in Plantinga's argument is the assumption that if the notion of a maximally great being is internally coherent, then there is a possible world in which a maximally great being exists."[42] What McGrath seems to be arguing is that it could be the case that a being could be maximally great and yet not exist in any possible world, and for Plantinga to assume otherwise is to beg the question.

According to Plantinga's argument, however, a being which did not exist in any possible world would not be maximally great, given premise (2),*"A being is maximally great only if it has maximal excellence in every possible world,"* and premise (3),*"A being has maximal excellence in every possible world only if it has omniscience, omnipotence, and moral perfection in every possible world."* It is interesting to note that McGrath bases his criticism on the first restatement of the ontological argument offered in Plantinga's book, *God, Freedom, and Evil*, but does not address the final version given a few pages later, in the section titled, "The Argument Triumphant."[43] Although McGrath's criticism might carry some weight with the first of Plantinga's arguments, it fails to address the final version at all, especially in light of the fact that Plantinga prefaces his "triumphant" argument by saying that it has been restated "in such a way that it no longer matters whether there are any merely possible beings that do not exist."[44]

Given that St. Anselm's version of the ontological argument appears to be both valid and sound, it seems as though Plantinga's reformulation of it is unnecessary. Indeed, Plantinga's modal ontological argument appears to be more susceptible to potentially insurmountable criticisms than does Anselm's traditional and simpler argument. In addition, it is possible that introducing into this discussion the question of possible worlds confuses, rather than clarifies, the issues at hand. If, however, one prefers to argue for the existence of God in terms of possible worlds, and is also able to comprehend the modal logic utilized within the discussion, Plantinga's argument is strong and worth focusing one's attention upon.

NOTES

1 McGrath, P.J., "The Refutation of the Ontological Argument," *The Philosophical Quarterly*, April 1990: 195.

2 Arthur Schopenhauer, as quoted in P.J. McGrath, 195.

3 McGrath, 212.

4 Hartshorne, Charles, *The Logic of Perfection* (La Salle, Illinois: Open Court Publishing, 1962) 31.

5 St. Anselm, as quoted in Patrick Sherry, ed., *Philosophers on Religion* (London: Geoffrey Chapman, 1987) 43.

6 St. Anselm, as quoted in Patrick Sherry, ed., 43.

7 St. Anselm, *Proslogium; Monologium; An Appendix in Behalf of the Fool by Gaunilon; and Cur Deus Homo*, Trans. Sidney Norton Deane (La Salle, Illinois: Open Court Publishing, 1944) 8-9.

8 Spiegel, Dr. James, "Theistic Proofs" handout, Philosophy of Religion, Spring 1997.

9 Spiegel, "Theistic Proofs" handout.

10 Hartshorne, 44-47.

11 Plantinga, Alvin, *God Freedom, and Evil* (Grand Rapids, Michigan: William B. Eerdmans, 1974) 90.

12 Plantinga, 90.

13 Plantinga, 91.

14 St. Thomas Aquinas, as quoted in W.T. Jones, *A History of Western Philosophy* (New York: Harcourt Brace Jovanovich College Publishers, 1969), II, 218.

15 Jones, 219.

16 Copleston, Frederick, *A History of Philosophy* (New York: Doubleday, 1950), II, 338.

17 Barth, Karl, *Anselm: Fides Quaerens Intellectum*, Trans. Ian W. Robertson (New York: Meridian Books, 1962) 171.

18 Immanuel Kant, as quoted in Patrick Sherry, ed., 131.

19 Hick, John, "Ontological Argument for the Existence of God," *Encyclopedia of Philosophy* (New York: Macmillan, 1972), V, 539.

20 Immanuel Kant, as quoted in Alvin Plantinga, 94.

---

21 Plantinga, 97.

22 McGrath, 198.

23 McGrath, 199.

24 McGrath, 199.

25 McGrath, 199.

26 McGrath, 201.

27 Vallicella, 99.

28 Vallicella, 99.

29 Hartshorne, 32.

30 Trueblood, D. Elton, *Philosophy of Religion* (Grand Rapids, Michigan: Baker Book House, 1957) 92.

31 Plantinga, Alvin, *God and Other Minds* (Ithaca, New York: Cornell UP, 1967) 26.

32 Plantinga, *God, Freedom, and Evil*, 87.

33 Plantinga, *God, Freedom, and Evil*, 99.

34 Plantinga, *God, Freedom, and Evil*, 99-101.

35 Spiegel, "Theistic Proofs" handout.

36 Sennett, James F., "Universe Indexed Properties and the Fate of the Ontological Argument," *Religious Studies*, March 1991, 73.

37 Vallicella, 106.

38 Vallicella, 107.

39 Vallicella, 106.

40 Vallicella, 107.

41 Vallicella, 109.

42 McGrath, 211.

43 Plantinga, *God, Freedom, and Evil*, 111.

44 Plantinga, *God, Freedom, and Evil*, 111.

References

Barth, Karl. *Anselm: Fides Quaerens Intellectum*. Translated by Ian W. Robertson. New York: Meridian Books, 1962.

Copleston, Frederick. *A History of Philosophy*. New York: Doubleday, 1950.

Jones, W.T. *A History of Western Philosophy*. New York: Harcourt Brace Jovanovich College Publishers, 1969.

Hartshorne, Charles. *The Logic of Perfection*. La Salle, Illinois: Open Court Publishing, 1962.

Hick, John. "Ontological Argument for the Existence of God." *Encyclopedia of Philosophy*. New York: Macmillan, 1972.

McGrath, P.J. "The Refutation of the Ontological Argument." *The Philosophical Quarterly*, April 1990.

Plantinga, Alvin. *God and Other Minds*. Ithaca, New York: Cornell University Press, 1967.

_______. *God Freedom, and Evil*. Grand Rapids, Michigan: William B. Eerdmans, 1974.

Sennett, James F. "Universe Indexed Properties and the Fate of the Ontological Argument." *Religious Studies*. March 1991.

Sherry, Patrick (ed.). *Philosophers on Religion*. London: Geoffrey Chapman, 1987.

Spiegel, James. "Theistic Proofs" handout. Philosophy of Religion class, Spring 1997.

St. Anselm. *Proslogium; Monologium; An Appendix in Behalf of the Fool by Gaunilon; and Cur Deus Homo.* Translated by Sidney Norton Deane. La Salle, Illinois: Open Court Publishing, 1944.

Trueblood, D. Elton. *Philosophy of Religion.* Grand Rapids, Michigan: Baker Book House, 1957.

PUTNAM, REALISM, AND PERCEPTION

Clinton Tolley
Wheaton College

Hilary Putnam has spent much time trying to navigate a *via media* between the Scylla of Relativism and the Charybdis of a Metaphysical Realism with a capital 'R.' *En route*, Putnam has come to espouse an epistemology of 'direct realism' to aid in his defense against charges of relativism: the mind perceives the real world directly, not through some intermediary such as the modern 'way of ideas' or the positivist's 'sense-data.' *The mind just perceives the world.*

The Realists (such as John Haldane) appear delighted at such a move, for if the mind is to apprehend the real world directly, and one gives any kind of weight to the notion of intentionality, it would seem that the world must already be divided into 'objects' *in itself* (Aristotelian *hylomorphs*, Tractarian *Sachverhalte*, etc.) prior to perception for the mind to then have something to intend. Can Putnam maintain this insistence on a *direct* encounter with a world, which endures independently of the mind, and still escape the Realist's other (unwanted) metaphysical baggage?

My intention is to tease out the relevant subtleties of Putnam's own position, while giving ear to the Realist's counterclaims, as well as offering a quasi-Kuhnian interpretation of the general notion of *Gestalt* switches as lending a helping hand to non-Realist perceptual theory.

I. "On Coming Home"

Professor John Haldane suggests in one of his recent publications that Hilary Putnam has finally "come home" to a position that is commensurable with, if still not identical to, his own brand of orthodox metaphysical realism. For Haldane, the motivation for exploring the possible return of the Prodigal Putnam to his earlier Realist convictions is found in Putnam's growing trend of incorporating elements of Metaphysical Realism into his own "realism with a lower case 'r.'" Haldane writes, "Given the direction of his subsequent investigations, and the repeated qualifications of their conclusions, the question that arises is whether he has now returned, perhaps unwittingly, to metaphysical realism."[1] Perhaps the most decidedly Realist direction of Putnam's present course is his return to what he has called "a second naiveté"—an acceptance of the direct realist's account of perception: direct perceptual contact with the real world without the use of any sort of intermediary interface. But, having assured us that, at least in this review, he "is not aiming to assess the overall cogency of Putnam's arguments or the merits of his conclusions,"[2] Professor Haldane cannot resist the temptation to offer at least one critique of Putnam's position:

> I want to suggest that *without* the idea of objective natures of the sorts in question Putnam's newly acquired account of perception and thought may not be intelligible.... Without the Aristotelian idea of formal structures characterizing world and mind it remains obscure how Putnam's version of perceptual realism is possible.[3]

It is my hope to take up just this challenge. I wish to bring out of 'obscurity' how the direct realist's account of perception might be commensurable with Putnam's own realism, including his constant dismissal of the intelligibility of the Metaphysical Realist's additional convictions about "objective natures and "formal structures" and the like.

II. Direct Realism

Is what we encounter the *Real* world, or only a representation of it? The recourse by modernist epistemology to the "way of ideas" persuaded us of an account of our interaction with the world as a *rendezvous* with images (and images *alone*) of the substantive world rather than an apprehension of the world itself. The substantive world always conceals its "that-which-we-know-not-what." This disconnection between subjects and the Real world as object led Bishop Berkeley to suggest that the "that-which-we-know-not-what" (and will-never-know-what) might as well not even exist. If we encounter only the ideas of the Real world, then why could not *they* just be the Real world itself? If both secondary *and* primary properties exist merely in the realm of the mental, and there has never been cognitive contact with Substance-as-such, what work is this Unknowable actually doing for us? Why posit our contact as being with the less-than-Real ideas if it is precisely these ideas which are all that are ever to be Really known?

The idealist's insistence that we *are* in direct contact with the Real world (even if it is a Berkeleyan world shorn of any external independent nonmental stuff-ness) has its realist counterpart. Putnam's own Brains in Vats experiment points implicitly to this same conclusion: if all we encountered as Brains in Vats were computer-induced images (similar to Berkeleyan God-induced imagery), then our thoughts and conceptions could never refer to some extra-vat Real world of substantive existence because we would have had no contact with that existence. The ability to refer to a world has the prerequisite of having had immediate contact with that world. If we can only have contact with one world, then we can only refer to that world (Brains in

Vats can only refer to their vat-image world).[4] Where Putnam and the metaphysical idealists differ is that Putnam *affirms* the mind-independent existence of the world: "if language-users had not evolved, there would still have been a world."[5] Putnam retains the intuition that the existence of the world is not dependent upon the mind and will continue to endure even in the event that the minds of the human race (or any other minds, for that matter) do not; in other words, the world's *esse* is not in its *percepi*.

In Putnam's direct realism *cum* mind-independent reality, the mind does not encounter the idea of the thing, nor is the thing merely a projection of the mind, but rather it encounters a mind-independent *thing itself*; or, perhaps put more critically, the mind does not encounter the idea of the world, but rather a mind-independent *world itself*. There is no screen of representation before which the mind's eye lazily reclines, nor is there a world behind a screen projecting forth images (or sense-data), all the while evading the mind's attempt to connect to the world's true existence-in-itself. Simply put, *the mind just knows the world directly*. To speak of an additional "in-itself" which has the mysterious ability to project accidental properties while remaining essentially hidden from the mind is to speak useless nonsense. There is no need for a "world-in-itself," for either Berkeley or Putnam. There is only the world, a world that is "external" to the mind and is known directly. The content of our knowing is the world itself.

III. An Ontological Commitment?

But what does this content look like? Even after recovering the plausibility of direct realism in terms of the direct encounter between the mind and the Real world, what are we to say about the status of our various conceptions of this world to which we are immediately related? In particular, it appears that our relation is never to an undistinguished world-as-such, but rather to the world of things, of objects, of events. Are these thing-perceptions perceptions of that which has been thing-distinguished prior to the mind's apprehension? Or, in directly relating to the world, have our minds imposed this thing-conceptuality upon a world, which would have been otherwise without distinction?

The issue turns on the question of whether or not the necessarily thing-orientedness of our perception reflects a *thing*ed-ness essential to the world itself or whether our perception is merely mobilized by our own conventions placed upon the world by our own mind. In other words, the question is whether the world is already essentially cut at joints into discrete *things* to which the mind must connect in order to truly perceive, or whether the mind cuts the world of its own accord, cuts unprecedented by a more primordial thing-ness of the world itself.[6]

But it is not only thingness-as-such that raises the dilemma of what it means to have true connection to the Real world. Things are never merely *things*. Things are always a some *kind* of thing—a cat, a bike, a college professor, etc. Again, are these particular thing-classifications *in* the world? Is the world sorted out into kinds of things *by* the world itself, into what Putnam calls "Self-Identifying Objects?"[7] Or are kinds merely stamped *upon* the world by our minds? What is the nature of that which populates the world?

By way of summary before moving on, I offer three brief statements recounting what seems to be of central issue to our discussion:

1. We do not perceive the world as a completely undifferentiated milieu of nonmental external "stuff."
2. We cannot just perceive whatever, but are *constrained* (in some sense).
3. In encountering the world, our perception is always perception-of-some*thing*; there is never *pure* perception of no thing in particular.[8]

IV. "No Epistemology without Ontology": The Aristotelian Idea of Formal Structure

Haldane sees the turn to direct realism as a "welcome development from the point of view of Thomist-*cum*-Aristotelian realism."[9] The "inescapable question" to which any candidate for the title of direct realist must provide an answer, is "how it is possible that a mental act of the subject should have some state of the world as its object."[10] For the Realist the answer is simple—the Realist's world is precut, and offers itself to us in terms of particular objects. And not only are the world and its objects really 'out there,' but so are the relations within the world. For example, the relation to which 'north of' refers would remain even if there were no humans to point it out or put it into language or refer to it. With the early Russell, the Realist would say "we merely apprehend a fact that was there before we knew it."[11] Our direct encounter with the world is an encounter of a world that has relations and things already packaged and ready for the mind's passive apprehension.

Haldane's Aristotelianism with a Thomist face provides us with sufficient example of how such a response unfolds, one of a considerable degree of sophistication. The world is made of two modes of being: actuality and potentiality. Anything existing (except God himself) exists as an actualized potentiality. There are particulars because there are particular Forming principles (the Forms) and there is an individualizing That-which-is-formed (Matter). The mind knows the things by way of their Form. This is not knowing *via* 'a way of ideas,' nor a representational theory of knowledge. For anything to be known, it must be *actually present* in the knower, in all its actuality.[12] St. Thomas takes the liberty of expanding this "direct realist" interpretation of an Aristotelian account of epistemology:[13]

> As Aristotle says, it is not the stone that is in our mind but its likeness. Yet it is the stone that we know, not its likeness (unless we are reflecting on our own knowing), for otherwise we would not know things but ideas.[14]

The ability of the mind to take on the Forms of the world constitutes the connection between the two. The world is made of Forms actualizing Matter; the world is known by virtue of the mind's capability to receive the Form of an object, and thus be "identical in character with its object without being the object."[15] The Form ("abstracted species") is then the means by which we know the world. There have been some (including Putnam) who have given an interpretation of Aristotle's theory as being a precursor to the modern projects as it identifies the object-as-such and the object-as-known as being in some ways different. The thrust of this interpretation is diminished, if only slightly, when one takes into account the different Aristotelian senses of "object." In the formal sense (the sense, which defines the "thing" metaphysically), the object-as-such and the object-as-known are identical as they share the Form. It is in the material sense that the object-as-such and the object-as-known are different as one is physical and one is mental.[16] The relation of mere similarity is not in their respective thing-ness; both *are* the object Formally. They are discernible (and thus only similar) in this aspect: one is physical and one is not; one is actualized matter, one is actualized mind.

"Any form material things assume can be common to many such things."[17] Things in the world are similar if they have a same Form. It is through experience of things that we learn to abstract the common Forms from various particular things. We come to identify "the one beside the many which is a single identity within them all."[18] Thus, for the Realist, not only things, but *kinds* of things have a metaphysical reality completely independent of the mind.

V. The non-Realist Rejoinder

The allure of Aristotelian hylomorphism is that it appears to provide sufficient answer to Haldane's "inescapable question." It does justice to this common intuition, that, as Putnam puts it, "mind and language could not hook onto the world if that which is to be hooked onto did not have intrinsic or 'built-in' form."[19] The mind's inherent intentionality would appear to necessitate an anteperceptive *thing*ed-ness inherent in the world, and thus a truly external differentiation of the world *by* the world itself into objects.

"But," as Putnam would reply, "what counts as an 'object,' in your sense of 'Formed objects in the world'? Is there some single meaning of 'object' which is *in* the world itself?" The situation becomes obviously problematic:

> 'Object' itself has many uses, and as we creatively invent new uses of words, we find that we can speak of 'objects' that were not 'values of any variable' in any language we previously spoke. (The invention of 'set theory' by Cantor is a good example of this.)[20]

In discussing the evolution and extension of the domain of reference of the concept of an 'object' within the context of quantum mechanics, Putnam notes that the term's movement within this field alone "is a wonderful example of how with the development of knowledge... our idea of what counts as even a *possible* object, and our idea of what counts as even a *possible* property are all subject to change."[21] Which, we might ask, conception of 'object' is *the* one that populates the world?

To further illuminate the difficulties, Putnam gives the simple example[22] of a world W that is populated by three individuals, *x, y,* and *z*. How many 'objects' are there in W? One answer would be to take 'object' as meaning 'individual,' and thus give the answer three—*x*, *y*, and *z*. Yet, according to some Polish mathematicians interested in mereological studies, there is another 'object' which is 'the sum of every two particulars,' so that there are then seven 'objects' in W—*x*, *y*, *z*, *x*+*y*, *x*+*z*, *y*+*z*, and *x*+*y*+*z*. Still others hold the null set (0) to be an additional 'object,' raising the number of 'objects' to eight. So, which is the correct number of 'objects' in W? To make his point completely clear, Putnam submits another paradox, this time from Euclidean geometry. Are points *concrete* parts of which a plane is the sum, or are points just *abstract* limits of converging spheres? In both cases, the 'existence' of 'objects' is *essentially* different (concrete vs. abstract), according to the relative perspective. The root problem in both examples is the equivocation of meaning of 'object' (how many *objects*?) as well as of 'are' (*are* there? What *are* points?).

But the hope of finding *the* fixed meaning of either 'object' or 'are' (or any other word) which has a one-to-one correspondence to that which populates W is precisely the Realist's hope of finding an absolute meaning of 'object' and 'are' essential to W itself, unaffected by our ever-changing perspectives toward the world. 'Object' has come to be used in so many different ways that "there is no one property common to all the things to which the word correctly applies."[23] It can never hope to betray anything like the Aristotelian "one beside the many which is a single identity within all." Putnam would reply that in each case, even what the '*is*' means is relative to the scheme, and not a univocal '*is*.'[24] The Realist is clinging to the "naive idea that at least one Category—the ancient category of Object or Substance—has an absolute interpretation."[25]

VI. Conceptual Relativity

The ultimate relativity of truth, fact, and meaning to their use in particular languages, or conceptual schemes, is what Putnam has come to denote as a "conceptual relativity." In the above examples concerning the number of objects existing in W, there were at least several options for describing W. Choosing a particular option would be motivated by certain interests one had (for instance, showing a mathematical relation *vs.* finding out how much money you had in your pocket), and given a scheme, the correct answer was far from relative. The confusions arise in trying to ask the questions such as "how many objects are there *really*?" We are always describing the world for different purposes, and given those interests, our descriptions can be correct or incorrect. What we cannot hope to be given is some sort of God's-eye view, the world's *own* conceptual scheme, from which it is possible to say how the world is *in-itself*.

> To ask "How are things in themselves?" is, effect to ask how the world is to be described in the world's own language, and there is no such thing as the world's own language, there are only the languages that we language users invent for our various purposes.[26]

VII. Direct Realism Again

The Realist will complain as follows:

> You have said nothing decidedly 'realist' in your account of our relationship with the world. In fact, it appears to us as though there is nothing for your 'realism' but interest-based relativity all the way down. And we can even find solidarity with that debauchèd relativist Richard Rorty on this point: "if there are no objects which are what they are independent of our ways of talking, it is hard to formulate *any* distinctly realist, non-trivial, doctrines — even 'internal' ones."[27] Our interests, cultures, and desires have made up the world in our image; we have invented our languages. We judge the value of language-games on their adequate fulfillment of our needs. Where's the 'realism' in that? What can now be 'independent'?

In one sense, Putnam would agree with this Realist's (as well as with Rorty's) critique: "Our image of the world cannot be 'justified' by anything but its success as judged by the interests and values which evolve and get modified at the same time and in interaction with our evolving image of the world itself."[28] But there is another side to Putnam's anti-relativist agenda, one, which has been outlined above—his recovery of the doctrine of *direct realism*. Associating his own position with that of William James' direct realism, Putnam insists that in his own view of truth (like that James' own holistic theory), "our role as 'coefficients of the truth on one side' *is balanced by the insistence that we share and perceive a common world*, by the insistence that 'we register the truth which we help create'...."[29] Putnam sees the fact that we directly encounter the real world as preserving us from all forms of skepticism/mentalism/subjectivism. There is, after all, the world 'out there,' independent of all language-users: "the notion that our words and life are constrained by a reality not of our own invention plays a deep role in our lives, and is to be respected."[30] It is really the case that "if language-users had not evolved, there would still have been a world;"[31] the world is not ultimately and finally a *product* of our interests.[32] In fact, Putnam does agree with the Realist critic "that the world is as it is independently of the interests of the describers."[33]

VIII. Putnam's Realism and an Interpretive Metaphor

The resulting picture Putnam appears to offer is something like, "The world compels us, once we have given it a voice, to conceive of it in a certain manner relative to the concepts we have chosen, based on our interests. I am not denying that 'there are experiential *inputs* to knowledge; knowledge is not a story with no constraints except *internal* coherence.'[34] But what is important to remember is that there cannot be 'any inputs *which are not themselves to some extent shaped by our concepts*, by the vocabulary we use to report and describe them, or any inputs *which admit of only one description, independent of all conceptual choices*.'[35] For, 'even our description of our own sensations, so dear as a starting point for knowledge to generations of epistemologists, is heavily affected (as are the sensations themselves, for that matter) by a host of conceptual choices. The very inputs upon which our knowledge is based are conceptually contaminated.'[36] Perception itself, while at the heart of direct realism, is a possibility necessarily dependent upon 'a whole conceptual scheme, on a language [being] in place.'[37] 'We should accept the position that we are fated to occupy in any case, the position of beings who cannot have a view of the world that does not reflect our interests and values.'[38] The presence of constraint does not imply that our notions somehow are latching onto the way the world 'really is.' Constraint does not move us towards anything like an ideal one-to-one correspondence. And yet, we should not deny that there *are* these brute forces which the world exerts upon our lives, a world whose independence is made evident by 'looking at the ways in which we endlessly negotiate—and are *forced* to negotiate—our notion of reality as our language and our life develops.''[39]

Perhaps an example of this 'constraint without correspondence' would be in order. Imagine the typical perceptual puzzles you were given as a child. Take, for instance, the picture that has been drawn in such a way so that there appears to be both an old woman and a young lady present, depending upon how you look at it. Or picture the others, the champagne glass and/or two faces about to kiss, the box with no bottom, or even a Wittgensteinian duck-rabbit drawing. But what could we possibly be looking for when we feel the need to ask the following: "Which of our perceptions is *really* in the picture? Which is the thing *in the picture itself*?" How could we ever expect to answer this question? Well, we might begin by saying the answer depends on our perspective, so, in this case, both are in the picture. But, suppose this interlocutor is not satisfied and persists: "No, I don't want to know which is present to you, or to me. Tell me rather which one is present *in the picture itself*; is it the glass that is *really* there, or is it the faces who are *really* there? Which of our perceptions correctly corresponds to the picture?"

We might feel that our companion was trapped in a confusion. The whole point of these pictures is that there is no one thing in the picture, no one correct correspondence between the perception and the picture itself. The central theme in the pictures is their unavoidable ambiguity. This ambiguity leaves the picture open to be perceived in a number of different possible ways. The picture here is silent, only potentially perceived, until our minds have made the choice to see one thing rather than another. In simple examples such as these, we might then go back and see the picture in a different way. We are at a loss as to which is the more valid perception, because both seem equally 'true' to the picture, given their respective points of view.

Of course, there is always something perceived; it is not as if we can say we perceive nothing. In each case we perceived *something*, if we understood the picture to be meaningful at all. But, of course, it is not as if you could perceive just anything in these pictures—we would all want to say that there was most likely not an elephant looming in the glass/kiss drawing, nor would we want to say that someone's perception that the old/young lady was really a cantaloupe was probably not a correct one. The picture has constrained us in some sense. But what the picture did not do was force upon us One Fixed Precut Object to which any and all correct perceptions must correspond. There is only the possibility for objects, one of which our minds then choose to perceive.

These examples might seem a bit trivial, but suppose for a moment that the whole world was of this sort—an ambiguous picture, offering only blurred possibilities to be perceived relative to the choices of perspective of the perceiver, rather than One Fixed Totality of Objects to which our perceptions might correspond if they were to be true perceptions. Take Quine's suggestion that "we could reinterpret 'cat' as designating no longer the cat, but the whole cosmos minus the cat."[40] From what point of view can we say that this *Gestalt* switch of universal measure is somehow *less true* to the world itself? The only legitimate point of view would be that of the universe itself, but as in the trivial examples, this view is a "view from nowhere" which is never available to us. The thrust of Putnam's realism is that there is an inherent ambiguity in the world, which cannot force upon us any particular conception until we have chosen our point of view. For Putnam, these points-of-view are chosen on a basis of our interests and needs. We have decided throughout at each moment, perhaps less and less as we come to settle into a community of language, which perspective we will choose. And we come to choose these perspectives based on their coherence with our previous choices, as well as their successful use in the forms of life.

We have chosen 'cat' to mean cat is not because cat is somehow a metaphysically privileged being, or is as Haldane puts it, "more substantial than others,"[41] but because "we can see the cat, and pet her, and [do] many other things, and we can hardly see or pet the whole cosmos minus [the cat]"[42]—because this reference is more useful to us than the other. It is the function that 'cat' has come to hold in relation to the whole of our way of life that determines its reference.

IX. Conclusion

With the preceding discussion, I hope to have elucidated a possible explanation of perception, which is congenial to the rest of Putnam's work which, at the same time, escapes from any entanglement with the remainder of the Realist's metaphysical convictions. I would like to conclude by drawing on Thomas Kuhn's similar conclusions concerning the relationship between theory, perception and the 'independent world' in his study of the history of science. Kuhn suggests that "what a man sees depends both upon what he looks at and also upon what his previous visual-conceptual experience has taught him to see."[43] Consider the example of a contour map: "the student sees lines on paper, the cartographer a picture of a terrain."[44] Which is 'in' the picture? The possibility of perceptions are thus co-determined by both the world and the perceiver's particular conceptual scheme, determined by the *direct* perception of the *real* world *and* by the conceptual framework one has chosen for one's own purposes. Kuhn's conclusion that, in some sense, "the world itself changes"[45] when paradigms change dovetails neatly with Putnam's own saying that the "mind and the world jointly make up the mind and the world."

NOTES

1 Haldane, "On Coming Home to (Metaphysical) Realism," p. 388.

2 *Ibid.*

3 Haldane, p. 391.

4 For the actual account of the Brains in Vats experiment, see Putnam, *Reason, Truth, and History*, Ch. 1, "Brains in a Vat." For the remainder of the paper, I will use the following abbreviations: RTH—*Reason, Truth and History*; R&R—*Representation and Reality*; MFR—*The Many Faces of Realism*; RHF—*Realism with a Human Face*; P—*Pragmatism*; W&L—*Words and Life*; SNS—"Sense, Nonsense, and the Senses."

5 Putnam, "Truth, Action Vectors, and Possession Conditions for Concepts," p. 433.

6 Note that, *prima facie*, either route is amenable to a direct realism—if the mind plays a passive role in our interaction, then it *directly* receives the things already in the world; if an active role, it *directly* forms the things to be in the world (but not in an idealistic sense, as it is not causing them to exist—allowing for an equivocal sense of "exist" here, not causing the world's "existence" in the ordinary sense of "causing to exist" of sustaining, or of granting being, but rather "causing to exist" as defining, as causing to *exist-as some thing*).

7 RHF, 53.

8 Another way of phrasing this observation is by referring to the ubiquity of intentionality in our dealings with the world. We always orient ourselves *towards* something. We are always concerned *about* something. We are always directed *at* something.

9 Haldane, p. 391.

10 *Ibid.*

11 Russell, *The Problems of Philosophy*, p. 97.

12 *Summa Theologiae*, I.12.4; p. 27.

13 Thomas interprets Aristotle to accommodate direct realism even though his account contains language which might suggest otherwise, as is noted by Putnam who then interprets Aristotle's theory

as representational which would then succumb to the unintelligibility of "the way of ideas" epistemology the direct realist is trying to avoid. Cf. RTH, 57: "That Aristotle actually held [the representational epistemology] I am not sure; but it is suggested by his language."

14 *Summa Theologiae*, I.76.2; p. 114.

15 *De Anima*, Bk. III.4, 429a14-17; p. 217.

16 Cf. Haldane, p. 393.

17 *Summa Theologiae*, I.3.2; p. 14.

18 *Posterior Analytics*, 100a6-8; p. 107.

19 Putnam, "Aristotle After Wittgenstein"; p. 119.

20 R&R, p. 120.

21 SNS, p. 452.

22 MFR, pp.18-19; RHF, Ch. 6, "Truth and Convention," pp. 96-104.

23 SNS, p. 449.

24 For instance, in one scheme, 'is' refers to an abstract existence (limits), while in the other, 'is' refers to a concrete existence (the component parts of a plane). Cf. SNS, p. 450, n12—Putnam's discussion of why he views the similar move in Quine's "criterion of ontological commitment," which prescribes as necessary the commitment to the existence of a kind of object, as ascribing a meaning to 'existence' that is univocal and ultimately misguided for the same reasons above.

25 MFR, p. 36.

26 P, p. 29.

27 Richard Rorty, "Putnam on Truth," p. 414.

28 RHF, p. 29.

29 P, p. 20.

30 SNS, p. 452.

31 Putnam, "Truth, Activation Vectors, and Possession Conditions for Concepts," p. 433.

32 RHF, p. 28.

33 SNS, p. 448.

---

34 RTH, p. 54.

35 *Ibid.*

36 *Ibid.*

37 RHF, p. 28.

38 RHF, p. 178.

39 SNS, p. 452.

40 W.V. Quine, *The Pursuit of Truth*, p. 33. Quoted in W&L, p. 279.

41 Haldane, p. 395.

42 W&L, p. 284.

43 T.S. Kuhn, *The Structure of Scientific Revolutions*, 2nd edition. Chicago: U. Of Chicago, 1970. P. 113.

44 *Ibid.*, p. 111.

45 *Ibid.*

References

Aquinas, St. Thomas. *Summa Theologiae*. Translated and edited by Timothy McDermott. Chicago: Christian Classics, 1989.

Aristotle. *De Anima*. Translated by J.A. Smith, in *Introduction to Aristotle*, edited by Richard McKeon. New York: McGraw-Hill, 1947. Pp.145-238.

_______. *Posterior Analytics*. Translated by G.R.G. Mure, in *Introduction to Aristotle*, edited by Richard McKeon. New York: McGraw-Hill, 1947. Pp.9-109.

Haldane, John. "On Coming Home to (Metaphysical) Realism," *Philosophy* 71.276 (April 1996): 287-296.

Kuhn, Thomas S. *The Structure of Scientific Revolutions*, 2nd edition. Chicago: University of Chicago, 1970.

Putnam, Hilary. "Aristotle after Wittgenstein," in *Modern Thinkers & Ancient Thinkers*, edited by R.W. Sharples. London: UCL Press,1993. Pp.117-137.

_______. *The Many Faces of Realism*. LaSalle, IL: Open Court, 1987.

_______. *Pragmatism*. Cambridge: Blackwell, 1995.

_______. *Realism with a Human Face*. Edited by James Conant. Cambridge: Harvard, 1990.

_______. *Reason, Truth, and History*. Cambridge: Cambridge, 1981.

_______. *Renewing Philosophy*. Cambridge: Harvard, 1992.

_______. *Representation and Reality*. Cambridge: MIT, 1988.

_______. "Sense, Nonsense, and the Senses: An Inquiry into the Powers of the Human Mind," *The Journal of Philosophy* XCI.9 (September 1994): 445-517.

_______. "Truth, Activation Vectors and Possession Conditions for Concepts," *Philosophy and Phenomenological Research* LII.2, (June 1992): 431-47.

_______. *Words and Life*. Edited by James Conant. Cambridge: Harvard, 1994.

Rorty, Richard. "Putnam on Truth," *Philosophy and Phenomenological Research* LII.2 (June 1992): 415-8.

ASIAN AND COMPARATIVE PHILOSOPHY

GREAT PERFECTION: THE PRACTICAL PHENOMENOLOGY OF TIBETAN BUDDHISM

Daniel J. Bristol
SUNY Oneonta

Perhaps the most intriguing of the teachings of Tibetan Buddhism are the Dzogchen ("Great Perfection"). According to the Great Perfection teachings, the whole of phenomenal experience, including the basic nature of human awareness, is equal to the realization of the Buddha. Usually considered esoteric in nature, the Dzogchen teachings are a highly incisive form of phenomenology that combines theory and practice as inseparable elements. We will be examining three texts: Longchengpa's *Great Perfection: The Nature of Mind, The Easer of Weariness*, Namkhai Norbu Rinpoche's *The Cycle of Day and Night*, and the contemplative instructions of Padmasambhava as found in a collection entitled *Advice From the Lotus Born.*

It is said that the Buddha Shakyamuni gave three cycles of teachings during his lifetime. The first cycle, known as *Theravada* (Skt. "The Way of the Elders") is comprised mainly of a rigorous ethical training combined with basic, meditative practices. It focuses mainly on individual liberation from the woes of worldly existence. The second, known as *Mahayana* (Skt. "Great Vehicle") combined this ethical and meditative training with further developments on such themes as emptiness and universal compassion. The third, known as *Vajrayana,* which means "Adamantine" or "Lightning" vehicle, combined the teachings of the previous cycles of teaching with various doctrines widely considered esoteric in nature in as much as they were given only to a select few of Buddha's pupils. The Theravada taught that enlightenment is attainable only after many lifetimes, and existed as a potentiality to be developed. In the Mahayana, the potentiality of enlightenment was held to lie dormant within all sentient beings. In the Vajrayana, it was taught that enlightenment is the intrinsic nature of all sentient beings, or to refine it further, that sentience itself, is enlightenment. Furthermore, the Vajrayana cycle of teachings uphold that buddhahood can be attained in a single lifetime.

What is essential to the Vajrayana is an understanding of the phenomenal world of sensory experience and the mind. The noumenal is not so much rejected as subsumed within the phenomenal as an apparent aspect of it, devoid of inherent objectivity. The process of phenomenal arising, and its role in the arising and cessation of suffering are central to the Vajrayana Buddhism of Tibet, which upholds the non-dualistic belief that samsara (Skt. "running around"), the cyclical, conditioned realm of experience that is suffering, is of the same nature as nirvana (Skt. "extinction"), the liberation from the sorrows of conditioned existence. This idea is central to the teachings and practices of the Dzogchen (Tbn. "Great Perfection") lineage. The Great Perfection lineage, also known as Ati Yoga, is not a distinct school, but is encountered in all schools of Tibetan Buddhism, but is most commonly encountered among the lamas, lay-teachers and practitioners of the Nyingma (Tbn, "Old Translation") school, which is held to be the oldest. In a nutshell, the Great Perfection teachings uphold the belief that the whole of phenomenal experience is inseparable from the enlightenment of the Buddha. All its teachings and practices are thus aimed at the realization of this unitary essence.

Whereas it is common for theistic religions to construct an etiological account of the noumenal world, Dzogchen, which is non-theistic, focuses its efforts on an account of the phenomenal from which the notion of a metaphysical Supreme Being of primary causation is absent. Among the numerous works that provide such accounts is entitled *Great Perfection, the Nature of Mind, the Easer of Weariness*. This immense text, which has the shorter subtitle of *The Great Chariot,* is part of a trilogy, the subsequent installments of which deal with meditation and illusion respectively. The first installment deals with the nature of mind. The text was composed by the 12th century Lama Longhen Rabjampa, often referred to as Lonchenpa. This text is in thirteen chapters, each containing root verses and prose commentary.

Longchenpa opens his text in the manner traditional for Lamas of his school, the Nyingma lineage, with a short homage to Samantabhadra, the Primordial Buddha who is held to be the source of all the Buddhas, as well as the mind's natural state. The text reads

> The primordial lord; the great, full ocean of buddha qualities; Whose natural wisdom and kindness is limitless in its depth, Birthplace of the Victorious Ones and all their sons, Who emanates heaped up clouds of goodness and benefit, I prostrate to the one who is all that is desired. (p. 2)

Since the Vajrayana attempts to provide a non-theistic account of the phenomenal world rather than the noumenal, we would do well to try to understand this verse in such a context. Samantabhadra (Skt. "All-Good") does not occupy the role of a centralized, creator god, hence the phenomena dealt with in *The Great Chariot* and other Dzogchen texts are not held to be contingent to a necessary first cause. Instead, all phenomena are viewed as interdependent and spontaneously arising. We must also bear in mind Vajrayana's emphasis on *madyamika* (Skt, "middle way") a view expressed in many of the Buddha's discourses, and commented on and developed at length by the Patriarch Nagarjuna. According to madyamika, it would be a mistaken extreme to interpret Samantabhadra as some sort of supreme divinity existing independently of the world. It would also be a mistake to interpret Samantabhadra as a mere fabricated, ineffectual symbol. According to the middle way and Longchenpa's commentary, Samantabhadra is "the manifestation of enlightenment, whose place is the primordial ground" (p. 2). In other words, Samantabhadra is the enlightenment of all the Buddhas, which state according to the Great Perfection teachings is the basic, underlying wakefulness; the intrinsic awareness of the mind, not so much in the sense of the mind being aware of objects, but the actual principle of pure awareness in its original state.

After a detailed explanation of the reasons for practicing the buddhadharma and a series of lengthy chapters describing the Buddhist cosmology, Longchenpa proceeds with his description of phenomenal arising in the fourth chapter, entitled Karma, Cause, and Effect. Under the heading, The brief teaching of the essence, Longchenpa posits karma (Skt. "action") as the prime mover in determining the conditions of samsara, which term denotes the cyclical, conditioned existence of the phenomenal from which the enlightened person is liberated. He asks,

> Why do these lives of wandering in the sufferings of samsara, each with its own appearances of joy and sorrow appear? They occur because of karma . . . From the different conditions of beings, different fruitions of their associated karma exist. Many kinds of connection[s] with their happiness and sorrow ripen. (IV, A)

Thus, the phenomenal appearances of existence arise from action. From the conditions of beings arise various tendencies of action. These actions then determine the conditions of phenomenal existence.

Under the heading of *the extended explanation*, Longchenpa provides a more protracted and detailed explanation of this process. The first part of the extended explanation, called *the support*, begins with *the explanation of alaya and consciousness* (IV, b1a) the Sanskrit term *alaya* is defined by Herbert Guenther's translation of the same text as "and indeterminate stratum of all and everything" (BIb1a). Thus, this *alaya* is the "primordial ground" referred to in the beginning of the text, and it serves as a basis for the arising of the phenomenal world. The root verses begin,

> The supporting ground of these [actions] is the neutral alaya. As if on the surface of a mirror without reflections, Luminous awareness, without conceptual objects, produces a ground for such reflections to arise, It is like the luminous clarity of a mirror. (IV, b1a)

In the prose commentary, Longchenpa defines *neutral alaya* as "the suchness of space" (*ibid.*). This is a state often characterized by the term *sunyata* (Skt. "emptiness" or "no-thing-ness"), which represents a lack of determinative factors in phenomena. Longchenpa states that

> Emptiness expresses the idea that the apparent [phenomenal world], from the time it appears, is empty of complexities grasped as one and many, and empty of individual existences, like the reflections in a mirror, that all extremes are completely non-existent, and that non-existent now and primordially, things are not like their confused appearance. (*ibid.*)

Neutral alaya, as the suchness of space, is empty in the way described in this passage. According to Longchenpa, this empty alaya is "the ground of all that is divided; it is completely neutral and undistinguished" (*ibid.*). Hence, it is a basic ground of undifferentiated awareness, empty of phenomenal distinctions, which are conceptual aspects rather than inherent aspects of an objective noumenon.

The root verse continues,

> From that [neutral alaya] comes the consciousness of the five sense faculties. As the five senses fixate their objects, such as form. In its own nature this is not conceptual; rather they are like reflections in a mirror. (*ibid.*)

From the basic ground of undifferentiated awareness arises the differential consciousness appearing as the five senses. Each of the five senses then becomes fixed on the phenomena corresponding to them, as in the case of the eye seeing forms. This process does not involve conceptual, volitional action. According to Marpa Rinchen Choying Dorje's Singular Advice On The Essence of the Sutra and Mantra Paths, this stage in the arising of the phenomenal world adheres closely to the neutral alaya as "the mind that knows that manifestation is without acceptance, rejection, creation or change." In other words, in the early stages of phenomenal arising, the five senses fixate their objects, but there is no conceptual labor performed on these fixations. Hence, Longchenpa tells us these fixations "are like reflections in a mirror" because a mirror reflects objects without changing them. Thus, at this stage, we are in a state of unconditioned awareness that, like a mirror, reflects without bias whatever it encounters.

The root verse continues by detailing the next stage of the process:

> After that occurs, there rise the awarenesses of the divided objects of grasping and fixation. Within suc-

> cessive moments, as these are fixated or not, there may be conceptualization, or there may not. The former is klesha-mind, and mental consciousness. (IV, b1a)

Longchenpa refers to this stage as the *alaya of the various habitual patterns* (*ibid.*). He goes on to say that, "within this are supported all things of the compounded nature of good and evil, arising as various joys and sorrows" (*ibid.*). There now arises the awareness of dual objects as things grasped and fixed upon by the senses. Fixation is a process of determining an object to possess a given status, nature, or essence. Grasping involves holding an object in awareness, but this holding has a negative connotation that is not to be confused with the state achieved in various contemplations.

In this verse, Longchenpa seems to focus more on the process of fixation than of grasping. "Within successive moments," this process is not necessarily continuous. The conceptual fixation of the awareness upon objects does not occur in an unbroken flow. Hence, what we have is the primordial ground of neutral alaya covered by the alaya of the various habitual patterns, like a veil with holes in it covering a globe. Longchenpa refers to the fixation that results in this "veiling" of the primordial ground as "klesha-mind, and mental consciousness." "Klesha" is often translated as "defilement," "poison," or "obscuration". This should not be taken as referring to a state of sinfulness or ritual impurity as much as a condition that impedes clarity. Fixation as mental consciousness embraces the processes of acceptance, rejection, creation and change; the various conceptual modifications to phenomena mentioned by Marpa Dorje.

Earlier, I referred to a non-dualistic belief operative within the Vajrayana which states that samsara is of the same nature as nirvana. The very same processes of phenomenal arising that lead to bondage to the cycles of conditioned existence also play a very important role in liberation from those cycles. In the commentary following the early root-verses of Chapter IV, Longchenpa has occasion to quote from the *Sutra of the Immaculate Wisdom of Manjushri*. He quotes this short verse:

> Alaya is the ground of everything, the ground of both samsara and nirvana, and all the appearances of phenomena.

In this brief verse we have an exposition of this non-dualism. In the religious language of Vajrayana, every Budhha is held to simultaneiouly embody specific modes of realization as well as specific kinds of klesha. This is also applied in Longchenpa's phenomenology. In reference to the alaya of the various habitual patterns he states that "here all causes and fruitions in accord with merit and all goodness according with liberation are also supported." He goes on to say that "these ... are known as the basis, producer, and fruition of purification and that which is to be purified." Many texts within the tradition speak of purifying the kleshas. Hence, the habitual patterns of perception and thought are the basis not only of the obscurations that block the omniscience of buddhahood: they are also the very means whereby those obscurations are purified, removed, or rendered ineffectual.

This non-dualistic view is pervasive throughout the teachings of Great Perfection, and what is also striking about the teachings is that their content and the language in which those contents are expressed has changed little throughout the centuries. One text exemplifying this non-dualism and the apparent timelessness of the teachings is Namkhai Norbu Rinpoche's *The Cycle of Day and Night*, which was composed in 1983. In *The Cycle of Day and Night*, it is observed that, "without categorizing phenomena (as either good or bad), we find them present in the state of the real condition of existence" (p. 46). This is an extremely telling statement with regard to the view of non-duality. It emphasizes abstaining from making value judgements concerning phenomena. This is because, according to the teachings on emptiness, value judgements are projected conceptualizations that do not inhere in the phenomena being judged. The value is unfindable upon analysis. Also, since all phenomena are held to arise from the same, primordial ground of alaya, they share in its nature, which is value-neutral, or devoid of value. According to Namkhai Norbu's text, phenomena are present "in the state of the real condition of existence." This does not imply that phenomena inherently exist, as that would contradict the Buddha's essential teaching of emptiness. Liberation in no way entails an escape from the phenomenal world. Otherwise, what would be the case in consciousness is a state of mental blankness. Rather, what is the case according to the Great Perfection teachings is that the liberated or enlightened person remains a participant in phenomenal experience.

The text goes on to say that,

> Because all [phenomena] are present in total awareness, without there being any conceptualizing with regard to them, we recognize delusion (itself as being nothing other than) nondiscursiveness. *(ibid.)*

This "total awareness" is akin to resting the mind in its natural state; in achieving a meditative absorption in the primordial ground of alaya. Because this state is beyond the alaya of habitual patterns, and because this state in no way negates phenomenal experience, the mental consciousness does not activate the habitual patterns of conceptualizing about the phenomena it experiences. This conceptualization is held to be a mode of discursive thought. In this teaching, nondiscursiveness does not refer to the mental blankness of not thinking or not conceptualizing. Instead, it refers to a state where discursive thoughts and conceptualizations are allowed to arise and cease as they will, without the practitioner participating in them. Delusion belongs to the alaya of habitual patterns, which includes discursive thought and conceptualization. However, since all the different modes of alaya, including that of habitual patterns, are held to arise from the same primordial ground and share its nature, the nondiscursiveness of that ground is pervasive throughout all the succeeding alayas. Thus, the non-dualism of delusion and enlightenment is reiterated here.

This verse from *The Cycle of Day and Night* concludes, "phenomena manifest (nondiscursively) as the real condition of existence just as it is in itself" (*ibid.*). That is to say, the phenomenal world appears to the enlightened person, but without the conceptual overlay of the alaya of habitual patterns. The phenomenal experience of such a person is centered, or grounded, in the primordial alaya, which is often described as having the qualities of luminosity and clarity. Without this conceptual overlay, phenomena are then experienced as empty, which emptiness is "the real condition of existence just as it is in itself."

The Cycle of Day and Night goes on to say that, "all phenomena which appear as objects of the six sense aggregates are present in luminous clarity and lacking in any inherent nature" (p. 47). This statement is pregnant with information concerning the Dzogchen phenomenology. There are held to be six sense-aggregates, each of which consists of the organ or center of sensory consciousness, the consciousness appropriate to the specific sensory organ or center, and the object appropriate to the sensory-consciousness. These six are: eye, ear, nose, tongue, body, and mind. Mind is considered a sense aggregate because it is composed of the sensory center of mind, the mental consciousness, and the objects of mental consciousness such as thought and perception. According to Namkhai Norbu, these six sense-aggregates "are present in luminous clarity." In other words, just as the same phenomenal world is encountered upon realization of the real condition of existence, the same six sense-aggregates through which it is experienced are present in the luminosity and clarity of the nature of mind, which is the pure alaya.

Namkhai Norbu goes on to say that "we recognize *anger* to have the character of clarity and it manifests now as the primal awareness of clarity" (*ibid.*). Here, anger can be replaced with any of the emotions. The essential point is to demonstrate the non-dualism of samsaric and nirvanic phenomena as well as their non-separation from the nature of mind. Anger has the character of clarity because it arises from nowhere other than the mind, the true nature of which according to the Great Perfection teachings is centerless luminosity and clarity. Anger (or any other emotion or phenomena) is said to manifest in immediate experience as the primal awareness of clarity, but this should be understood as experiential. It manifests as this "primal awareness" within the context of Dzogchen's contemplative practices, a primary aspect of which is allowing the mind to rest as it is, without conceptual overlay or active participation in any of the habitual patterns of phenomenal process.

From here, our discourse should perhaps proceed from simply establishing that alaya is the mind's natural state to as thorough an examination of that state as possible. According to Longchenpa's commentary,

> The natural state is natural, complete purity, like space. Though described by the names markless, emptiness, completely uncompounded and so forth, it is not nihilistic empty nothingness; rather, it is realization of spontaneous presence, the luminosity of the kayas and wisdoms. It is empty in the sense of being completely liberated from all dharmas of samsara. (IV, A)

What begins to emerge is a picture of the mind that is actually rather hard to characterize as a picture. According to Longchenpa, mind is like space, which has the qualities of being pure and natural. *Pure* in this context is akin to the purity of the sky: it contains nothing that makes it sky apart from its spaciousness. Furthermore, when birds or clouds cross the sky, they neither mark nor effect the sky in its spaciousness. *Natural* in this context indicates that the mind's natural state, like the sky and space, cannot really be established nor said to have a place where it begins or where it ends. It is not exactly an ontic void, either. Since the phenomenal world is apparent to us, there must assuredly be a mind that ensures this perception. However, when we try to locate the mind within rigidly defined parameters, it eludes our grasp. Yet the perceptual experience of phenomena continues.

This is what Longchenpa refers to as the "realization of spontaneous presence, the luminosity of the kayas and wisdoms" (*ibid.*). The word kaya (Skt, "body") refers to the body of the Buddha. According to the Mahayana teachings, from which the Vajrayana and the Great Perfection teachings arose, a buddha has three bodies. First, there is the *dharmakaya,* (Skt. "Truth-Body") which is the formless principle of enlightenment held to pervade the universe, or in the context of Dzogchen, the phenomenal world. Second, there is the *sambhogakaya* (Skt. "Divine-Body"), which in some ways roughly corresponds to the Jungian notion of an archetype. It is a term which merits a discussion in itself. Basically, it is a kind of extra-temporal body, which can emanate in various, visionary forms. In Dzogchen, it is the mind's natural bliss. Finally, there is the *nirmanakaya* (Skt. "Manifestation-body"), which is the physical body of a buddha. In the Great Perfection, nirmanakaya is the mind's capacity to arise as phenomenal appearance and the perceiver which perceives it. Longchenpa also makes use of the term "wisdoms" to refer to the various modes of realization and enlightened activity embodied by the various buddhas, whom according to the Mahayana and Vajrayana, are innumerable. Hence, the mind's natural state is inseparable from the emanations and modes of realization that are the enlightenment of the buddhas.

Longchenpa states that the mind's natural state "is empty in the sense of being completely liberated from all dharmas of samsara." Here, the word dharma, which is frequently used to refer to the teachings given by the historical Shakyamuni Buddha, is used to denote *phenomena*. This is one of the reasons why Buddhism is often described as more of a science of mind than a religion. The goal of buddha dharma, the full realization of one's own essentially enlightened nature, is approached not by means of reliance on a deity, but rather through an introspective examination of the mind and senses. In any case, Longchenpa is here describing the mind's natural state of emptiness as one which is free from all phenomena of cyclical, conditioned existence.

Once the nature of mind is theoretically established, the matter of achieving this realization in actual practice remains. Some of the most lucid and compelling teachings connecting Dzogchen theory and practice can be found in the body of writings left behind by Padmasambhava, whose name means "Lotus Born", and who lived during the ninth century C.E. Padmasambhava, frequently referred to as *Guru Rinpoche* (Tbn. "Precious Teacher") is considered by Tibetans to have been the final reincarnation of Shakyamuni, who took birth one final time to develop on and propagate the Vajrayana teachings. His teachings, many of which appear in *Advice From the Lotus-Born*, are filled with detailed advice concerning meditative practice. Concerning the realization of the nature of mind, he says

> In this regard, 'mind' is that which thinks and cognizes; there is indeed something that experiences. Don't seek this mind outside, look within! Let mind search for itself! ... At first, from where does mind arise? Right now, where does it stay? At the end, look into where it goes! When your mind looks into itself, it finds no place from where it arises, remains, or goes to. There is no explanation of 'this is how it is.' 'Mind' is discovered to be without something outside or inside. (p. 36)

Identifying mind as "that which thinks and cognizes," Guru Rinpoche uses conceptualizations, which belong to the alaya of habitual patterns, to provide distinguishable characteristics through which the practitioner may recognize the object (for lack of a better word) of the meditation. He then eliminates the rigidly defined conceptual parameters within which mind is conventionally held to exist. By means of this combination of pointing out distinguishable characteristics, and eliminating the conceptual parameters to which these characteristics are connected, Guru Rinpoche introduces a subtle notion of mind as a formless essence.

Guru Rinpoche goes on to identify six central aspects of the teaching that join Dzogchen theory and practice. These six are:

1. To 'possess confidence'
2. 'possessing the experience of meditation'
3. 'possessing the equal taste of conduct'
4. To 'cross the dangerous defile of moving thoughts'
5. To 'gain the unchanging confidence of fruition'
6. To 'gain certainty'

Guru Rinpoche says that "to 'possess confidence' in this means to realize that like space, mind is spontaneously present from the beginning" (p. 36). Confidence in this context does not refer to faith in something outside oneself, nor reliance upon an ego. Instead, because mind is spontaneously present and spacious, it is a natural state in which one can be supremely secure because it never deviates from one's true nature. This confidence is not something which requires assertion, but a calm settling or resting the mind. Because mind does not require an assertion of oneself in order to exist, one can settle into this state and experience the confidence of being grounded in one's true nature, without having to make any inner assertions such as "I am such and such".

Guru Rinpoche goes on to say that

> ...to 'possess the experience of meditation' means to leave your mind uncontrived, uncorrupted and fresh... By neither placing your mind on something outside nor concentrating inwardly, you remain free of focus... Within this state, experiences can occur... Don't cling to or fixate on them at all! (p. 37)

Here, Guru Rinpoche focuses on practice and implies the theory. Mind, according to Great Perfection, is inherently empty of conceptual overlay. By simply letting the mind be as it is or appears, the parameters within which it is usually defined are not relied upon. One remains "free of focus" upon an object. Concentration is still cultivated, but it is not attached to anything in particular. Instead, a state of formless, centerless focus is called for, which according to the teachings is an expression of the mind's natural state. By not clinging to or fixating upon the experiences that occur, one allows them to arise and cease as they will. In this way, the mind's natural state is allowed to make itself apparent.

Concerning 'possessing the equal taste of conduct,' Guru Rinpoche says that this means "to be uninterrupted in meditation; without being distracted, even though there is no thing being meditated upon" (*ibid.*). In other words, a contemplative state is cultivated that is carried into post-meditation experience. Throughout all forms of activity, one remains calmly focused and grounded in the mind's natural state, devoid of fixation or center. Guru Rinpoche explains that

> Equal taste' means to embrace whatever you see, or whichever … sense pleasures occur, with the recognition of your innate nature, free from attachment or clinging. (*ibid.*)

This implies that, since the innate nature and phenomena are empty of inherent existence, there is really nothing to be attached to or to cling to. The conduct called for is based on a recognition of this emptiness.

Guru Rinpoche then explains what it means to 'cross the dangerous defile of moving thoughts.' He says that, "when conceptual thinking occurs while resting in meditation, whatever arises does so out of your own mind." This gives us a basis for crossing this defile. One need not be intimidated by the experiences of meditation, for they are none other than the mind's projections. They cannot be proven experientially to have any basis other than mind. Guru Rinpoche explains that "'Crossing the dangerous defile' means that when mind moves into a variety of thoughts, you should direct your attention into this mind itself." In meditation, as well as in post-meditation, thoughts will arise spontaneously and often unbidden. Rather than participating in these thoughts, the practitioner continually directs attention to the primordial ground from which they arise. In this way, thoughts lose their distracting power, and become transparent as it were. One becomes able to effectively 'see through' them to realize their source.

Concerning 'gaining the unchanging confidence of fruition,' Guru Rinpoche tells us that

> The awakened mind ... is not created through causes nor destroyed through circumstances. It is not made by ingenious buddhas nor manufactured by clever sentient beings. It is originally present in you as your natural possession ... since mind is the forefather of the buddhas, it is like the analogy of recognizing someone you already know. To awaken to what is spontaneously present from the beginning, free from fear and intimidation, is called 'possessing the confidence of fruition (p.38)

"Fruition" is traditionally synonymous with attaining the results of practice. Here, Guru Rinpoche explains the spontaneous presence of mind by describing it as something that is neither created nor destroyed. It has neither beginning nor end in the way a discrete phenomenon appears to have a beginning and end. Since the mind is one's own "natural possession", and since it is "the forefather of the buddhas," one's true nature does not deviate from the fruition of the path. Since mind according to the Dzogchen teachings is beyond the phenomena of fear and desire, settling into the realization of its nature is a kind of confidence, as discussed in the preceding section. Here, one is not confident that the aim of practice will be achieved. Instead, one settles into the confidence that it already has been achieved, or that it needs no achieving, since it is spontaneously present.

Finally, Guru Rinpoche explains what 'gaining certainty' means. He says,

> Gain certainty in the fact that since the very beginning your own mind is the awakened state of buddhahood. Gain certainty in the fact that all phenomena are the magical display of your mind. Gain certainty in the fact that the fruition is present in yourself and is not to be sought elsewhere. Gain certainty in the fact that your master is the buddha in person. Gain certainty in the fact that the nature of view and meditation is the realization of the buddhas. To gain such confidence you must practice! (p.39)

In this passage, not only is the non-dualism of mind and the phenomenal world reiterated; that of mind and buddhahood is mentioned as well. Here we have the Dzogchen phenomenology in a nutshell: the state of buddhahood, the phenomenal world, and the mind are a singular entity. That being the case, as this text points out, the fruition of practice is never separate from the practitioner. Because of this non-dualism, the master who teaches the path is viewed as the buddha himself. Furthermore, all such views arising from instruction and contemplation, as well as the states attained in meditative practice, are equal to the realized state of the buddhas. The non-dualistic phenomenology of the Great Perfection is therefore total. It embraces the primordial ground, which is Samantabhadra, the forefather of the buddhas, the phenomenal world arising from that ground which includes the practitioner and the teacher.

Since the realization of this non-dualism is experienced in the phenomenal world, and mind is one with that world, this certainty is based on empirical experience rather than doctrinal faith. The doctrine plays the role of a map, and practice is the means of making the journey. Since the fruition is inseparable from the practitioner, the implicit message is that enlightenment itself is a journey rather than a goal. Or to refine this analogy further, each step of the journey is the goal itself, yet each step is experienced as a unique and necessary stage of the journey.

In their religious aspect, the Great Perfection teachings of Vajrayana Buddhism introduce the practitioner to the enlightened state as an intimate and immediate experience. Buddhahood is revealed as an open secret into which anyone can enter through the realization that there is neither entrance nor egress, but that one has never parted from that state. The world of everyday experience is shown to be identical to the realm of Buddhism's continua of spiritual and religious experience. As a philosophy, the Great Perfection not only posits a unity of the ideal and the actual: it also offers a skillful melding of theory with practice by which this unity can be directly experienced. The perfect or ideal state of buddhahood is shown to be immanent and identical with the actual or natural. By focusing its efforts on phenomenology rather than metaphysics, it takes the notion of an absolute truth and removes its remoteness by showing that the truth it posits is not something to be sought for in the conventional sense. Instead, the Great Perfection upholds that the truth being sought for is none other than the seeker, as well as the search itself.

References

Longchenpa. *The Great Chariot: Great Perfection: The Nature of Mind, The Easer of Weariness*. Translated for the Internet by Rime Lodro Waldo, Ph.D. [*http://users. plinet.com /~rime/OpenTibetanBuddhistTexts.html*]

__________ *Kindly Bent to Ease Us. Part One: Mind.* Translated and Annotated by Herbert V. Guenther. Berkeley: Dharma Publishing, 1975.

Marpa Rinchen Choying Dorje. *Singular Advice On The Essence of the Sutra and Mantra Paths.* [*http://quiet-mountain.com/dharmacenters/heritage_trust/-liberate.htm*]

Namkhai Norbu Rinpoche. *The Cycle of Day and Night: An Essential Tibetan Text on the Practice of Contemplation.* Translated and edited by John Reynolds. Station Hill Press. 1987.

Padmasambhava. *Advice to King Trisong Detsen.* Appearing in *Advice From the Lotus-Born.* Translated by Erik Pema Kunsang. Edited by Marcia Binder Schmidt. Boudhanath, Arhus, Hong Kong: Rangjung Yeshe Publications, 1994.

COUNTER-INTUITIVE ETHICS

Meghan Tadel

George Washington University

This paper investigates the plausibility of conscience and intuitive thought as an epistemic foundation for ethics as proposed by Joseph Butler (1692-1752) and Wang Yang-Ming (1472-1529). It is found that although both philosophers offer significant contributions to the study of ethics, neither one succeeds in successfully and absolutely asserting conscience or intuition as the basis for ethical systems. Instead, both fail to clearly delineate intuition from other internal faculties and therefore allow for other internal ethical foundations such as sentiment or reason. Moreover, due to a lack of anchoring ethics in intuition and conscience, both philosophers leave open the possibility for an external source of ethical systems; in fact, their suppositions almost require such a source. Although this point is not argued as a more plausible solution, it is used to demonstrate the difficulty in locating a precise fundamental ethical principle.

One of the major difficulties facing the philosophers who take on the realm of ethics is and always has been the problem of locating a firm foundation for ethical principles. This investigation has interested many great thinkers from all cultures, backgrounds, and even eras in time. Possible elements for the framework of ethics have included ideas ranging from the consequences of actions, to the sentiments which stand behind them. However, although many viable conceptions have been explored, there still remains no firm resolution on the matter.

One such view, that of conscience or intuition as an epistemic foundation for ethics, was proposed by Joseph Butler, of eighteenth century Britain, and Wang Yang-Ming, who was born in 1472, during the late Ming dynasty in China. They both offer important contributions to ethical studies, yet in spite of their arguments, I find that neither philosopher manages to actually ground ethics purely in the intuitive faculty of conscience. This failure arises from two sources. First, we have no independent awareness of conscience which causes or even necessarily contributes to ethical action. Second, intuitive thought does not possess the authority required of an ethical foundation. Although both philosophers support an intuitive basis for ethics, the arguments of Joseph Butler and Wang Yang-Ming differ greatly in their choices of supporting evidence and necessary assumptions, and therefore, must be investigated and refuted individually.

There are several significant qualities of conscience which could distinguish it as a possible candidate for an ethical foundation. First of all, conscience is claimed to be present in all persons, that is to say, it is a universal quality; asserted to be an innate characteristic, it must be so. This is a necessary trait for recognizing what is right if people are expected to choose to behave morally.

Butler sets up his ethical system with a foundation that stands in opposition to the ideas of other ethical philosophers, who are as diverse as Meng Tzu, Thomas Hobbes, and Hsün Tzu, when he asserts that: “the very mention of deviating from nature would be absurd; and the mention of following it, when spoken by way of distinction, would absolutely have no meaning” (Butler 1873, 40). Rather, Butler wants to posit a more organic version of human nature that includes the whole of our motivations in a single system that allows for all desires and behaviors. Then, to keep his paradigm from slipping into absolute disorder, he proposes conscience as the keeper, or administrator of the system. This is an attractive solution in that it treats human nature in a real and naturalistic fashion, incorporating the complexities of humankind into a single integrated system rather than simply labeling certain aspects of human behavior as good or bad. This more realistic model of human nature is one possible reason for believing that an intuitive element, such as conscience, should be accepted as a possible foundation for ethics.

Another argument in favor of conscience as a basis for ethics, which Wang Yang-Ming points out, is that when one seeks the cause of behavior, he cannot look to the object of action but must investigate whomever committed the act. Wang offers the following examples:

> For instance, in the matter of serving one's father, one cannot seek for the principle of filial obedience in one's parent, or in serving one's prince one cannot seek for the principle of faithfulness in the prince, or in making friends or governing the people one cannot seek for the principle of sincerity and benevolence in the friend or the people (Wang 1964, 51).

Wang summarizes the point of his example when he states: "They are all in the mind, for the mind is itself the embodiment of principles" (Wang 1964, 51). It seems that Wang's convincing demonstration of the internality of principles should correlate with an equally strong conviction that only an internal element (or elements) can serve as a foundation for action, and therefore, as the basis for an ethical system. However, although I agree with Wang that there is a manifest necessity for an internal foundation for ethics, I do not think that intuitive knowledge conclusively establishes itself as such an internal system.

In order to establish conscience (or intuitive thought) as a foundation for ethics, it must be shown that conscience, and conscience alone, could serve as the basis on which all ethical actions are supported. Joseph Butler promotes this idea by setting up an internal system of checks and balances in which conscience acts as the final judge of actions.

> This principle in man, by which he approves or disapproves his heart, temper, and action, is conscience; for this is the strict sense of the word, though sometimes it is used so as to take in more. And that this faculty tends to restrain men from doing mischief to each other, and leads them to do good, is too manifest to need being insisted upon (Butler 1873, 30-31).

This conception of conscience as executive manager of our other faculties leaves it up to our hearts and tempers to actually promote the passions which they favor with conscience acting only to choose between the presented possibilities. Butler goes on to refer to conscience as "our natural guide" (1873, 49); however, this analogy is defective in that even a skilled guide can require a path to follow. Butler makes some attempt to reconcile this difficulty through his principle of self-love which he very nearly equates with benevolence.

> I must, however remind you that though benevolence and self-love are different; though the former tends most directly to public good, and the latter to private: yet they are so perfectly coincident that the greatest satisfactions to ourselves depend upon our having benevolence in a due degree; and that *self-love is one chief security of our right behavior towards society.* (Butler 1873, 27-28) (italics added)

As Butler says in the last part of this quotation, perhaps it is self-love that is to act as the 'path' along which conscience can follow.

It should be noted that Butler's conception of self-love varies significantly from the more common, egoistic view of self-love as self-interest. For Butler, self-love is akin to Aristotle's notion of virtue; it is a wholly internal pursuit of happiness and satisfaction in sharp contrast to passions or desires. For as Butler states quite clearly, "The principle we call self-love never seeks anything external for the sake of the thing, but only as a means of happiness or good: particular affections rest in the external things themselves" (1873, 126-127). Moreover, the idea of self-love as a guide for conscience is not inconsistent with Butler's repeated mention that, as we increase our level of self-love, it becomes easier to follow the dictates of our conscience. However, if that is truly the case, there is no need for a conscience at all, only for a more fully developed self-love and the more ethical behavior which follows from such development.

Another difficulty with Butler's proposed intuitive ethics is that he seems to wholly disregard the problem that is posed by the fact that any faculty that is to act in a superintendent fashion, as he supposes conscience to act, requires a referential framework upon which to base its governance. I would suggest that perhaps Butler expects his reader to accept the idea of a completely innate knowledge with which all humans are born by the grace of "our Maker's care and love both of the individual and the species" (Butler 1873, 30), as he refers to the gifts of the Christian God. In that case, I think one should note that it is not truly conscience which would serve as the foundation of Butler's ethical system, but rather the omniscience and eternal goodness of a God who thought to instill in humankind this capacity to recognize and choose what is good and right rather than that which is bad and wrong. This is a problematic solution because it inevitably moves the final source of ethics from an intuitive element to an external being, namely God.

Wang Yang-Ming may have recognized this need for a referential framework which would act as a basis for the discerning of right or wrong. I think that is what Wang was trying to provide when he proposed that ethics is based on intuitive knowledge of "heaven-given principles (natural law)" (Wang 1964, 52). Nonetheless, here I detect the same problem that was present in Joseph Butler's account of a foundation for ethics in intuitive knowledge—that is, the idea of intuitive knowledge necessitates something about which one must have knowledge. In other words, because knowledge is not a self-contained entity which can be possessed in and of itself, one must have knowledge of or about some entity. If, as Wang Yang-Ming supposes, this knowledge is an intuitive knowledge of right and wrong, then why does it become necessary for him to refer outside of the human mind and it's intuition and rely upon the idea of a natural law? And, if it does become necessary, it must be recognized that this natural law, as with Butler's Maker, takes on an external form.

Wang brings yet another problem into the argument. He wishes to posit that the "highest virtues are innate to the mind" (Wang 1964, 50), yet he continually stresses how much that knowledge must be put into action before it can be recognized and that, "it is necessary to develop the intuitive faculty to the utmost through investigation of things in order to overcome selfishness and reinstate the rule of natural law" (Wang 1964, 60). I mention this because it seems counter-intuitive to me that an innate knowledge should require such intense development. If an "intuitive knowledge of good" exists in humankind, which "is not attained through external investigation" (Wang 1964, 60) as Wang asserts, it seems inconsistent that such knowledge would necessitate development "through investigation of things" (Wang 1964, 60).

In the case of other kinds of *a priori* knowledge, it is plausible to accept this intermingling of preexisting ideas with knowledge which is dependent on a trigger provided by experience. However, in this case, I find it inappropriate to put forward ideas which require such development as a foundation for ethics and still refer to them as intuitive. Since, if it is experience and investigation that are required for development of these ideas, it could be argued that these experiences are truly the basis for the ethical system and not the "intuitive knowledge," after all. Once again, it is demonstrated that the supposedly intuitive foundations actually rely upon an external source in order to fully formulate the ethical systems.

Furthermore, neither Wang Yang-Ming nor Joseph Butler is able to convincingly pinpoint conscience or intuitive ideas as the specific foundation of ethics, separate from other internal sources. Their inability to do so is not only evident in the regressive nature of the arguments but also in the fact that they seem unable to cleanly cut conscience from the alternate possible foundations of ethics. Although Butler has a very distinct and well-articulated view of self-love and benevolence, his arguments about them can not help but mingle with those of the egoists on some level. Clearly Butler does not actually refer to the idea of self-interest when he describes self-love, but nonetheless, he is talking about events and actions which serve to please oneself, for as he states: "All particular affections whatever, resentment, benevolence, love of arts, equally lead to a course of action for their own gratification, *i.e.*, the gratification of ourselves" (Butler 1873, 133). Thus, regardless of how Butler names the feeling, it certainly seems to be that actions are motivated by some form of self-interest, as the term is commonly understood.

However, Butler will demonstrate a significant difference in his use of the term, "self-love" when he continually ties this is with his idea of benevolence. Butler claims that benevolence and self-love are not at odds, as some would have it, but instead are frequently coincident. But yet again he strays from his discussion of conscience as the authority of ethics when he further explicates this coincidence and states that "public affections or passions; have an immediate respect to others, naturally lead us to regulate our behavior in such a manner as will be of service to our fellow creatures" (Butler 1873, 28-29). Note that here Butler fails to even make mention of conscience in this description of moral behavior. Rather, in this case, the behavior occurs as a result of a human being's appreciation for the feeling of public affection and the coincident benevolence that is gratified by the good that is done to achieve public affection.

I can find little difference between this position and a consequentialist view of ethics which postulates that actions should be based on their anticipated reactions, or consequences, and which supports an epistemic foundation for ethics in sentiment. After all, as Butler explains, conscience does not actually motivate action but simply serves to judge which action is appropriate. Thus, I return to the dilemma: on what basis does conscience judge action? Given the above example, I would declare that conscience judges actions based on the consequences they produce. This leads to the root of the difficulties with an intuitive foundation for ethics as explained by Butler—he falls short of delineating whether or not conscience uses compassion, reason, or even self-interest as criteria in its ruling.

Yet this description of conscience as an overseer, could still be enough to warrant that it serves as a separate basis for ethics if conscience could be shown to be an autonomous faculty. However, Butler fails to grant it the strength or authority to override the motivations for action—it can only advise, not enforce. Butler argues that "how often so ever men violate and rebelliously refuse to submit to it, for supposed interest which they cannot otherwise obtain, or for the sake of passion which they cannot otherwise gratify; this makes no alteration as to the *natural right* and *office* of conscience" (1873, 46). I take exception to this point because it seems to me that a faculty which weighs the propriety of actions but can neither initiate them nor enforce its decision is no more than evidence of a specialized function of reason. How it is that the appetites, passions and even reason can be considered subjects of "the one supreme principle of reflection or conscience" (Butler 1873, 48) if conscience can not even definitively rule over them? Furthermore, if Butler wants to argue that conscience does provide a means for enforcing its verdicts by way of the resultant good that comes from following conscience and the guilt and shame which follow from neglecting to do as conscience dictates, then I must counter that this demonstrates conscience as merely a tool of reason which predicts the consequences of actions. Thus, we would once again revert to an ethical system which holds that consequences are seen as the ultimate foundation for ethical knowledge.

Recall Wang Yang-Ming's intuitive knowledge which acts as a mechanism that provides humans with a method to channel the natural law through them to return to the "state of equilibrium and harmony [that] is originally possessed by all men" (Wang 1964, 101 brackets added). Note that this is no more distinct than Butler's conscience. Upon interpreting Wang Yang-Ming, I envision intuitive knowledge as an internal agent which can merely assist in the process "to sweep out and wash out the every-day love of lust, fame, and similar things—a lot of passions—so that not the least bit will be retained. Then the mind will be completely fixed with unmixed heaven-given principles" (Wang 1964, 102). In this instance, intuitive knowledge is no different from reason: slowly, methodically, consistently, and efficiently recognizing and eradicating unreasonable wants or passions.

In conclusion, I think that although Butler and Wang demonstrate valuable insight into ethical studies, they do not provide a stable foundation for ethics in conscience or intuitive knowledge. Conscience is not provided with any valid distinguishing mechanism which separates it from the innate faculties of reason, self-interest or sentiment. Intuitive knowledge is not properly invested with the capability necessary to rule the passions but must instead rely on its ability to eventually 'sweep them out.' In the end, I think both Butler and Wang's arguments offer an ethical system which must reach outside the human mind for its absolute grounding. This sort of system is unstable because it ultimately requires that people accept on faith the idea of either a beneficent God or a set of self-creating, universal, external, natural laws. Eventually, it must be recognized that if either an external source or alternate mental faculties are necessary, then it is not actually conscience or intuition that serves as the foundation for ethics. Rather, it seems there exists a single faculty or set of faculties of the mind that can merely assist humanity in channeling and implementing those external sources of an imposed ethical system. Clearly, a system of imposed ethics is not the aim of either Butler or Wang's argument, nor is it a system I intend to defend. Instead, this criticism merely stands as a further example of how Wang and Butler's arguments for intuition as a foundation for ethics fall short of their goal in a significant fashion. Their defeasible arguments demonstrate the true difficulty in locating a definitive source for ethical systems and bring to light the need for any successful theory of ethics to be self-contained and explicable as such, a criteria which Butler and Wang both fail to meet.

References

Butler, Joseph. [1692-1752]. *Sermons*. New York: Robert Carter, 1873.

Wang Yang-Ming. [1472-1529]. *The Philosophy of Wang Yang Ming.* Translated by Frederick Goodrich Henke. 2nd Edition. New York: Paragon Book Reprint Corporation, 1964.

Poetry and Metaphor

THE THINKER AS POET

Robb Eason

University of New Hampshire

Martin Heidegger proposed in 'Being and Time' that we, in the Western Philosophical tradition, must again "raise anew the question of the meaning of being."[1] This question, since the ancients, has been forgotten, subtly put aside and has "ceased to be heard as a thematic question of actual investigation."[2] This 'forgotten question' has permeated all of Western Metaphysics, leaving it ultimately unsatisfying in portraying an accurate account of how it is that other beings and we are in the world. According to Heidegger, Plato plays a constitutive role in leading metaphysics into an ultimately problematic position. This paper aims to show that Heidegger's interpretation of Plato is, in fact, incomplete and thus inaccurate. A new interpretation of Plato's '*Symposium*' might reveal an understanding of Plato which reaches beyond the 'theory of the Forms,' beyond "metaphysical language," and beyond Heidegger's interpretation.

Introduction

In his essay "Plato's Doctrine of Truth," Heidegger illuminates Plato as that thinker who perhaps played the greatest part in laying the grounds for that which we now implicitly understand as truth. Truth, in Metaphysics, since Plato, according to Heidegger, has been a 'a mere variation on a theme' playing itself out through history. "What began with Plato—metaphysics as the errancy of the question about Being—comes to an end, according to Heidegger's interpretation, with Nietzsche."[3] According to Heidegger, Plato's thinking, in its sundry forms and interpretations throughout history has occluded the manifold meanings of truth by settling on one particular mode of truth. This mode of truth Heidegger terms 'truth as "permanent presence."' An investigation into just how Heidegger has reached this interpretation of Plato's doctrine of truth in 'Part I' of this paper will lay the grounds for yet another investigation of just how it is that perhaps this interpretation of the *Platonist* doctrine of truth does not itself measure up to or directly correspond with the full gamut of Plato's works. This will make up Parts II and III of my paper. Part IV of the paper, by revealing Plato's understanding of other modes of truth brought to light in the *Symposium*, aims to reappropriate Plato by means of another interpretation and to provide (via this interpretation) a valuable well-spring from which Heidegger himself might again take up Plato's thinking to further his own thinking. Here, I am referring not only to the thinking that Heidegger undertook immediately after "the turn," poetic thinking, but I am also referring to the "thinking" which Heidegger partakes of near the end of his career in his essay, "The End of Philosophy and The Task of Thinking."[4]

Part I: "He Who Thinks Greatly Must Err Greatly."
— Heidegger, *The Thinker As Poet*

In an analysis of Plato, Heidegger interprets the metaphor of the "cave" in Plato's *Republic* (514A-517A) as the site from which a process of education is revealed to that individual who is freed from her bonds and shackles within the cave. Heidegger understands this initial freedom as the first step in the process of an education (paideia) disclosed to the now free individual as a series of stages, transitions, and dramatic changes in the way in which the freed prisoner comes to understand her world. These stages within the process of education, according to Heidegger, consist in an initially painful reacclimation and re-orientation of the eyes to either a lighter or darker environment. This re-orientation process, the reacclimating of the eyes to the different light intensities in, through, and out of the cave; this slow painful, confusing, period of adjustment is, according to Heidegger, the process of education. "It is a periagoge holes tes psyches, a turning around of the whole soul, a leading of man out of his customary dwelling place and into another abode."[5]

It is not immediately evident from Heidegger's utilization of Plato's metaphor of the cave how it is that this interpretation necessarily or directly clears the grounds for what Heidegger refers to as Plato's theory or "doctrine" of truth. For this connection to be brought to light, we need to focus our attention on Heidegger's translations of two particular ancient Greek words. First, Heidegger translates "paideia" as "education."[6] As we have already seen, "paideia," as interpreted by Heidegger, carries with it more than our average and everyday understanding of education. "Paideia," as understood by Heidegger, in its richest sense is "a transition of man from one abode to another and a corresponding conversion of the soul from what had been apparent to it before, to what is now revealed."[7] This process of transition from one abode to another, this process of revealing what was once not revealed, that was 'concealed,' is interpreted as an "education" by Heidegger. "It shows how man must attain certain levels of an assent if he wants to come out of the enclosure of his accustomed abode, cave, and arrive at the open region of the light."[8] This ascent to the open region of light is an ascent to where beings, once hidden, are now brought clearly into the light of understanding. This ascent is an education in the disclosure of beings.

Second, in order to understand Heidegger's utilization of Plato's metaphor of the cave we must now turn our attention to another of Heidegger's translations. The ancient Greek "aletheia" usually is translated as 'truth.' However, the Greek "aletheia" also carries with it another connotation or interpretation of "unconcealment." Aletheia as unconcealment or unhiddeness, an ancient Greek understanding of truth, is necessary to Heidegger's interpretation of Plato's doctrine of truth, for Plato, as Heidegger shows us, has a different, more complex (more complex than aletheia), notion of truth. Unconcealment, aletheia, and paideia, a transition into another abode where the soul apprehends beings once concealed, are fundamentally connected or related. "There can be a parable of the cave only they're where the truth is thought of in terms of the contest between unconcealment and concealment."[9] This is to say that, according to Heidegger's interpretation, paideia leads to or allows a region of alethiea, or unconcealment, to be opened or cleared. Paideia, a turning of the soul, reveals what was once hidden or concealed.

As the cave dweller ascends from the cave into the light, beings, which were once 'concealed,' become revealed or unconcealed to the freed prisoner. Poggeler writes, "The different levels which man attains in his self-education are differentiated respectively to how they manifest beings, e.g., as the shadow of a copy, as the copy, as the reflection of beings, and the being itself."[10] For the freed prisoner, first, beings (in their truth) are revealed as the shadows of copies. The world on the wall on which the shadows danced for the chained prisoner now reveals itself to be a *mere* shadow of the figures or puppets obstructing the light from the burning fire to the wall. When the freed prisoner ascends from the cave, she realizes that the puppets, which she had observed as beings, were *merely* copies of reflections. Furthermore, these reflections gazed upon in the water reveal themselves from their concealedness to the freed prisoner as *mere* reflections of beings themselves. For the freed prisoner, each of these transitions in the apprehension of beings from their concealedness have been painful and confusing yet these transitions have also revealed something much more critical and fundamental concerning Plato's theory of truth. It is with this fundamental part of Plato's theory of truth that Heidegger constructs his indictment of Plato.

That fundamental part of Plato's theory of truth, which the cave metaphor has brought to light for Heidegger, turns on aletheia. "... Plato turns his attention not to the counteraction between concealment and unconcealment, that is the dialogical play of aletheia, but rather turns to unconcealment as *mere* 'unconcealment,' as *mere* revealing."[11] Disclosure, unconcelament, here is important only as it lays the grounds for how beings disclose themselves. And, although it is aletheia, this notion of unconcealment as truth, which Heidegger himself is interested in raising again, what matters, or becomes important for Plato and the metaphysical tradition is not aletheia itself, not the disclosure; rather what is of concern for Plato (and the rest of the history of metaphysics until Nietzsche) is that this disclosure serves as the way in which the essence of a form can "shine forth." Truth for Plato, according to Heidegger, does not find itself in the aletheia, in the unconcealment itself, but rather truth, and its subsequent interpretations throughout the history of metaphysics, has metamorphasized into something subtly different from its origins as "unconcealment." Although Plato employs the notion of aletheia as disclosure or unconcealment, truth, instead of aletheia, has become the relation of sight to the form. The emphasis for Plato has moved from the unconcealedness to, instead, a recognition of this accord. This relation for Plato we know as the "Good." "What the good itself is in the intelligible realm, in relation to understanding and intelligible things, the sun is in the visible realm in relation to sight and visible things"(*Republic* 508C). The Good, the form of forms, provides the light from which the other forms may shine. The Good is analogous to the sun and the sun, letting beings shine forth correctly in the light of day, is analogous to what is of importance in the notion of aletheia for Plato. Heidegger, in "Plato's Doctrine of Truth" writes, "To be sure, unconcealment is named in its various stages, but it is considered only in terms of how it makes what appears accessible in its appearance (eidos) and how it makes visible this showing of itself (idea)."[12] The idea, for Plato has thus taken primacy in a now formal conception of the truth. This is to say that the relation of sight to the form, terminologically the "Good", no longer finds itself as a disclosure (a way of disclosing), but rather it is the way in which disclosure itself is now construed as occurring. The Good, the manifestational 'form' of altheia, is the idea of all ideas. The idea, in place of unconcealment (disclosure, aletheia), now moves to take priority. According to Heidegger, Plato has made truth (aletheia) subordinate to the idea. Heidegger famously writes, "Truth (unhidden) has been brought under the yoke of the idea."[13]

Hence, Plato's system of education, one's coming into the light of the disclosure, into the light of the Good, into the light of the sun, is an education in the correctness of vision. Truth has been modified from the unconcealment of beings in their very nature to the correspondence between knowledge and its object as it disclosed itself. The essence of truth, according to Heidegger, has become the correctness of perception. And, rather than giving primacy to the understanding of unconcealment, Western Metaphysics has tended increasingly to focus on the securing of a judgement system guaranteeing a correspondence theory of truth. This correspondence theory of truth, according to Heidegger, has occluded both the original meaning of truth as unconcealment or unhidden and any other conceptions of truth which do not focus their efforts on securing an 'idea' which most closely resembles the 'outside' world.

According to Heidegger, Plato's transformation of the essence of truth transformed philosophy. Plato's emphasis on the form, the idea as truth, focussed philosophy on securing a position of knowledge on high, all the while setting aside, forgetting the original ancient Greek understanding of truth as aletheia. The disclosure and unconcealment of Being come to be forgotten tossed aside, and "man" and the primacy of his self-made challenge to demarcate the world with the most correct theory of knowledge became the task of Western philosophy. Might it be possible to now, in the light of the resurrection of the original meaning of truth, disclose perhaps new tasks for philosophy? Might it also be that a starting point to disclose these new tasks for philosophy can be found in Plato himself?

Any serious inquiry into Plato reveals Plato as essentially more than what we inherit through Platonism. Platonism, what we inherit from the ancient Greek thinker is necessarily part of Plato's thought. However, mere Platonism is not a sufficient explanation of the entirety of Plato's thinking. Mere Platonism, that is, the conception of Plato, which the history of philosophy most readily reveals, might tend towards an understanding of Plato's theory of truth as necessarily connected with the theory of the forms. However, is this the only way in which Plato presents truth? Can we find traces of an original conception of alethiea that still survives in our inherited Platonism?

Part II:
"... And What Are Poets For In A Destitute Time?"

— Holderlin, *Bread and Wine.*

Heidegger's project, his indictment of 'Platonism,' works in a two-fold manner. Heidegger's interpretation of Plato depicts that which we inherit as "Platonism" and Heidegger's interpretation allows us to look into the *origins* of that doctrine, that is, into Plato's doctrine. Heidegger's critique of Plato turns on the notion that aletheia, unconcealedness, is, forgetfully strewn aside. This forgetfulness, according to Heidegger, is a drifting towards metaphysics and away from the original conception of aletheia. Our inquiry, however, also reveals something different, that is, the poetic nature of at least one of Plato's dialogues. We might now continue this inquiry in the light of one fundamental question: "Might Heidegger's conception of the "thinker as poet," the conception of 'non-metaphysical thinking' find its grounding in Plato, that is, in the very character Heidegger also seeks to indite?"

"...And what are poets for in a destitute time?" asks Holderlin. For Heidegger, in his later works, after the 'turn,' poets, poetry itself, holds a vital wellspring, "a rich source for philosophy." Heidegger in the essay "What Are Poets For?" writes,

> But there would be, and there is, the sole necessity, by thinking our way soberly into what his [Holderlin] poetry says, to come to learn what is unspoken. That is the course of the history of Being. If we reach and enter that course, it will lead thinking into a dialogue with poetry, a dialogue that is the history of Being... Philosophers consider the dialogue to be a hopeless aberration into fantasy. But destiny pursues its course untroubled by all that.[14]

What has been "unspoken" is truth as aletheia, as unconcealedness. However, the poet, in this case Holderlin, speaks poetically of the history of Being, a history which finds its roots in the forgotten conception of aletheia as unconcealedness. Poetry unconcealed beings hidden by what the history of Being has forgotten. Simply, this is to say that poetry, for Heidegger, displays the 'forgotten history of Being.' It displays aletheia as truth. And, philosophy, still dealing with its self-made challenge to demarcate the world with the most correct theory of knowledge, considers a dialogue with poetry, a dialogue with the history of Being, according to Heidegger, to be "a helpless aberration into fantasy." Philosophy must now take up this aberration.

In order to find Heidegger's 'thinker poet' in Plato, let us turn our attention, specifically, to one of Plato's dialogue. The *Symposium* offers a rich source for thinking. And, perhaps in spite of Heidegger's interpretation (indictment) of Plato, this dialogue holds the possibility for an alternative interpretation of Plato that is not what we inherit as Platonism (i.e., that truth must concern itself with the correctness of the relation between knowledge and its object rather than concerning itself with aletheia or unconcealment itself). An interpretation of the *Symposium*, one that paints a "poetic" picture might help us in our task to locate Plato, the thinker poet. Martha Nussbaum appears to offer just such an interpretation in The Speech of Alcibiades: a reading of the *Symposium*.[15]

The *Symposium*, a dialogue rich in detail and atmosphere, presents Socrates as the member of a 'symposium', a dinner or drinking party attended by Phaedrus, Pausanias, Eryximachus, Aristophones, Agathon, and eventually Alcibiades. Throughout the night, each guest, in his own particular style, gives a speech regarding the being of 'love'. The two accounts Nussbaum focuses her interpretation on are those of Socrates and Alcibiades.

The first half of Nussbaum's interpretation of the *Symposium,* focussing on Socrates' speech, reveals the speech as one, which may or may not be his own.[16] The view of love that Socrates discloses is a view that he says he had originally learned from a teacher-priestess Diotima. Diotima's, or Socrates' view of love finds its fundamental momentum in, like Plato's metaphor of the cave, an ascent of the soul. "The young lover beginning the ascent—always under the direction of a 'correct' guide (210A6-7)—will begin by loving a single body, or, more exactly, the beauty of a single body: 'Then he must see that the beauty in any one body is family related (adelphon) to the beauty in another body; and that if he must pursue the beauty of the form, it is great mindlessness not to consider the beauty of all bodies to be one and the same' (210A5)."[17] From these words of Diotima it is clear that love, at least for a Platonically inclined Socrates, is an orientation of the soul towards the idea or the form and away from the particular being or instance of love. The love of one beautiful body is equivalent to the love of beautiful bodies and the love of beautiful bodies is equivalent to the love of the idea or the form of the beautiful. This ascending of the soul resembles, very closely, the ascending of the freed prisoner out of the cave in the *Republic* and perfectly falls prey to Heidegger's criticism that idea (the correctness of vision) has "yoked" truth. Nussbaum writes, "The lover's final contemplative activity meets the Republic's standards in every way".[18]Love is a turning away from the particulars to the form of love. It is a correcting of vision, a re-orientation, a turning of the soul, a paideia.

Through this, the first half of our interpretation of the *Symposium,* it is possible to clearly identify Heidegger's grounds for his indictments of Plato as, at least thus far, holding true or accurate. Certainly it seems that Socrates' speech concerning love is an account of the search for the correct view of knowledge. Indeed, in the light of this interpretation even raising questions concerning the unconcealedness of beings in their Being seems to philosophically miss the mark. May we now conclude from this 'evidence' that Heidegger's claims against Plato are wholly correct? If our interpretation were to stop at this point, a point in which we have merely extracted the Platonism (i.e., the theory of the forms as a pointing to the 'correct' view of knowledge) from the dialogue, then yes Heidegger would be, in his interpretation of Plato, wholly correct. However, our interpretation of the dialogue is only half-complete. The *Symposium* reveals another kind of knowing; a knowing which is not a form of positing a theory of knowledge which best hooks up with the world. The *Symposium* offers an interpretation of Plato which, unlike Heidegger's conception of Plato which depicts the thinker as drifting away from the original "Greek" conception of aletheia as unconcealment towards a more metaphysical conception, might depict quite the reverse—Plato as writing and thinking non-metaphysically, that is, poetically.

Part III: "What Is Spoken Is Never, And In No Language, What Is Said."

— Heidegger, *The Thinker as Poet*

If we read further into Nussbaum's interpretation of the *Symposium*, we find that a wholly different type of knowledge arises or comes into play, a knowledge that Heidegger does not cite Plato for having brought to light as a possible mode of disclosure. The second half of Nussbaum's interpretation of the *Symposium* points to a knowing which Heidegger, in making Plato primarily the site of the original forgotten conception of truth as aletheia, fails to bring to light.

> A moment later they heard Alcibiades shouting in the courtyard, very drunk and very loud"(221D). Alcibiades joins the symposium hunting for the beautiful Agathon only to find not only Agathon, but also Socrates with whom he is in love. Nussbaum interprets Alcibiades' entrance in this manner:
>
> Alcibiades the beautiful, the marvelous nature, presents himself to our sensuous imagination, an appearance bursting with color and all the mixed impurity of mortal flesh.... From the rarefied contemplative world of the self-sufficient philosopher we are suddenly, with an abrupt jolt, returned to the world we

> inhabit and invited.... To see this vision, too, as a dawning and revelation.[19]

Alcibiades is an "abrupt jolt" returning us to the world we inhabit from the world of the self-sufficient philosopher. We are returned from or brought out of our contemplative exercise demarcating the best theory of knowledge, of trying to apprehend the forms. Alcibiades brings us back into our life-world, that is our world where the lines between metaphysical contemplation and outrageous oration have become blurred. Alcibiades brings us in contact with the particulars, with the world.

Alcibiades, like the rest attending the symposium is called upon to give an oration concerning the nature of love. However, unlike the other guests at the drinking party, Alcibiades' speech comes not from a theoretical impetus, but rather his oration comes forth from his own experience. Alcibiades decides to speak on his experience of love, his love for Socrates. The impetus for this speech does not come from a desire to get us closer to the form of Eros, but rather the impetus of the speech is to get us closer to the experience of love, of this love. "And, what is more, this story conveys its truths using images or likenesses—a poetic practice much deplored by the Socrates of the *Republic*, since images lack the power to provide us with true general accounts or explanations of essences (cf. Interlude 1; Ch.7 S III)."[20] Alcibiades' speech, his poetic speech, moves and turns on constant images and references to Greek myth as well as to Greek poetry.[21]

What is the significance of bringing to light the ramblings of a drunk Alcibiades? Surely Heidegger's "Thinker as Poet," the powerful romantic vision, is not a description of Alcibiades the drunk. What then is the significance of the image that Plato has injected into the dialogue? The significance of the image of Alcibiades is the following: First, Alcibiades arrives and remains drunk throughout his speech. Alcibiades in making his speech, in his drunkenness, and in his love for the particular (Socrates), remains wholly enamored with images. Alcibiades remains without real understanding; understanding which penetrates the realm of the forms. Furthermore, it seems as though Alcibiades is the least likely ever to reach this understanding, this 'form' of knowledge. Alcibiades, the drunk is not the 'Thinker Poet' for which Heidegger searches. And, certainly, Alcibiades is not Plato's model of one who is partaking in an exercise concerning the correctness of vision. Alcibiades is neither Plato's or Heidegger's model.

However, the second, and more important question to raise in the light of a figure like Alcibiades is: What is the power of the Image of Alcibiades such that he might abruptly "jolt" us from our self-sufficient world of philosophy? Might we hear and take up Alcibiades words in such a manner that Alcibiades does not he understand them, so that we might go where he cannot? It is in the answer to this second question where we again might bring Plato and Heidegger into one discourse.

Part IV: Conclusion
Poetry, Language, Thought

"The time remains destitute not only because God is dead, but because mortals are hardly aware and capable even of there own mortality."[22] How can mortals not be capable of their own mortality? — When mortals cannot 'think' in terms of their mortality (their being human), then this is when such mortals are not capable of that mortality. The power of the image of Alcibiades such that it might serve to "jolt" us from philosophy is a power only in the sense that reflection on this image brings us closer to the image's creator, Plato, and his conception of poetry. The image serves to return us from "metaphysical Platonism," the Platonism we inherit, to Plato's own doctrine and the intricacies of his writing. Alcibiades serves as figure that we are forced to analyze and come to an understanding of in comparison or contrast to Plato's doctrine. Alcibiades' image serves the function of, once again, introducing the 'poetic' into the scene.

Whether it is in the *Symposium* or in the *Republic*, Plato finds himself addressing poetry. It is the power of poetry, poetry in contrast to strict metaphysics, always in a bothersome manner, which calls out to be dealt with. We find, that "if we reach and enter that course [the course of the history of Being], it will lead thinking into a dialogue with poetry, a dialogue that is of the history of Being". Poetry, for Plato as well as for Heidegger, shows itself, that is, it is in some manner always "there" to be dealt with. Heidegger's own efforts, which attempt to utilize the notion of unconcealedness, aletheia, as truth, focus on the many different modes through which beings in the world disclose themselves. For Heidegger, the dominant mode of the disclosure of being both in the traditional and in the everyday conceptualizations of our life lies in that mode first given primacy in Plato's Doctrine of Truth. This mode of disclosure is the mode, which seeks to match knowledge with its object most correctly, the correspondence theory of truth. The fundamental project, then, for Heidegger, after seeing how they have been occluded, is to bring once again to the fore those modes of disclosure which have receded out of the fore and to develop a way of post-metaphysical 'thinking' which would always work against any dominant mode of disclosure. This paper thus far has pointed to ways in which the dominant conception of truth has occluded the mode of disclosure that is poetic that remains open to whatever is unhidden. An in depth account of how poetry both needed to be addressed as a mode of truth, and how that mode could be occluded from the dominant conception. (I.e., how the 'drunk' poet is only a lover of fleeting experiential images, and will never comprehend the forms) has been brought to light via re-appropriation Nussbaum's interpretation of the *Symposium*.

How could we, with Heidegger, come to understand what poets do as a mode of truth? What is the nature of that which Heidegger terms "poetizing"? In order to understand the power of the poet for Heidegger we must understand that Heidegger does not consider his later thought to be 'philosophy' or even phenomenological ontological; that is, an account of the world which is metaphysical, but rather construes his thought as different, as "thinking". "Thinking," for Heidegger, can only arise after one has come to understand that metaphysics is fulfilling itself, that is, philosophy, as Heidegger construes it, is ending. Philosophy, Western Metaphysics, is culminating, according to Heidegger, in science. In "The End of Philosophy and the Task of Thinking," Heidegger writes, "The development of philosophy into the independent sciences that, however, interdependently communicate among themselves ever more markedly, is the legitimate completion of philosophy".[23] What then is "the task for thinking" reserved for the end of philosophy? Asks Heidegger. This task, in line with the fundamental task facing Heidegger throughout his career, is to begin to articulate or at least lay the grounds for the articulation of the many modes of Being that have been occluded by the dominant conception of truth. Heidegger's task is to be responsive to what becomes unhidden, unconcealed, so that these things might be given their due. The dominant conception of truth, truth as correspondence between the object of knowledge and the world, completes itself in the explanative and descriptive powers of science.

The task for what Heidegger calls 'thinking' can now is addressed in the light of philosophy's ending. Just what is left untouched by philosophy in its end? Heidegger asks, "But what remains untaught in the matter of philosophy as well as in its method?" It is in answer to this question that Heidegger takes up a dialogue with poetry. Poetizing for Heidegger, what all art does, does not refer only to poetry, but rather to the way in which all forms of art find their essences. "Poetizing" and "Thinking" for Heidegger are fundamentally related. In Holzwege, Heidegger writes,

> However, thinking is poetizing, and indeed more than just one kind of poetizing, more than poetry and song. Thinking of Being is the original way of poetizing. Language comes into word, i.e., into its essence, in thinking. Thinking says what the truths of Being dictates; it is the original dictate. Thinking is primordial poetizing, prior to all poesy, but also prior to the poetics of art, since art shapes its work within the realm of language. All poetizing in this broader sense, and also in the narrower sense of the poetic, is in its ground thinking. The poetizing essence of thinking preserves the sway of the truth of Being.[24]

Thinking and poetizing, for Heidegger, dwell in a relationship together necessarily. Heidegger, by choosing not to re-

read Plato in light of this relationship, but rather re-reading Plato as "Platonism" in order to push his thesis of the "history of being", has, in an incomplete interpretation of Plato, missed the poetic nature in Plato which might itself help Heidegger elucidate the relationship between thinking and poetizing. Furthermore, it only seems clear that at this pivotal time, at the birthplace of philosophy, that which was occluded and forgotten might make itself most manifest, not yet subject to generation after generation of rearticulating questions which searched for an answer in terms of only one mode of truth. Ultimately Plato might be more valuable to Heidegger, than Heidegger realizes. The poetic nature of Plato in the *Symposium* might serve to be the site from which another investigation into the meaning of truth as aletheia may find its grounds. Plato's dismissal of poetry and the unhidden, unconcealing nature of the poetic, the seeds of Western philosophy (of metaphysics) needed a soil out of which to grow. It is in Plato and in a dialogue like the *Symposium* where Heidegger might have the most luck in digging into the earth, into that soil in search for another "thinking."

NOTES

1 Heidegger, Martin. *Being and Time.* Trans. Joan Stambaugh. Albany: State University of New York Press, 1996. (Page xix).

2 *Ibid.* p.1.

3 From: Otto Poggeler, *Martin Heidegger's Path of Thinking*, Trans. Daniel Magurshak and Sigmund Barber. Atlantic Highlands, NJ: Humanities Press, 1987. (Page 100)

4 From: Krell, David ed. *Martin Heidegger Basic Writings.* New York: Harper, 1993.

5 From: Laszlo Versenyi, *Heidegger. Being and Truth.* New Haven CT: Yale University Press, 1965. (Page 54)

6 Note: Heidegger's interests in this particular Greek word "*paideia*" might, in fact, have been a result of his study of Werner Jager's work, *Paideia: The Ideals Of Greek Culture.* New York: Oxford University Press, 1939. On page v. Of *Paideia* Jager writes, "It is impossible to avoid bringing in modern expressions like *civilization, tradition, literature, or education* (to define or understand "*paideia*"). But none of them really covers what the Greeks meant by *paideia.* Each of them is confined to one aspect of it: they cannot take in the same field as the Greek concept unless we employ them all together".

7 From: Laszlo Versenyi, *Heidegger. Being and Truth.* New Haven CT: Yale University Press, 1965. (Page 55).

8 From: Otto Poggeler, *Martin Heidegger's Path of Thinking*, Trans. Daniel Magurshak and Sigmund Barber. Atlantic Highlands, NJ: Humanities Press, 1987. (Page 101)

9 *Ibid.* p.102.

10 *Ibid.* p. 101.

11 *Ibid.* p. 102.

12 See: Heidegger, Martin. *Plato's Doctrine Of Truth.* From: *Philosophy in the Twentieth Century: An Anthology*, 4 vols. ed. Wm. Barret and Henry D. Aiken. New York: Random House, 1962. Vol. 3, p. 261.

13 *Ibid.*, p. 265.

[14] From: Heidegger, Martin. *What Are Poets For?,* Trans. Albert Hofstadtrt from: *Poetry, Language, and Thought.* New York: Harper & Row Publishers Inc., 1971.

[15] From: Nussbaum's *The Fragility of Goodness*, New York, Cambridge University Press, 1986. (page 165).

[16] Note: it is controversial to historians as to whether or not Diotima was a fictional character of Plato's or whether Diotima actually imparted this speech to Socrates.

[17] From: Nussbaum's *The Fragility of Goodness*, New York: Cambridge University Press, 1986. (Page 179)

[18] *Ibid.* p.182.

[19] *Ibid.* p.184.

[20] *Ibid.* p. 184.

[21] Alcibiades' speech contains references to Homer's *Iliad* twice and his *Odyssey*. The speech also makes reference to Aristophones' *Clouds*.

[22] From: Heidegger's *What Are Poets For?* From: *Poetry, Language, and Thought.* New York: Harper & Row, Publishers, Inc., 1971.

[23] From Krell, David, *Martin Heidegger Basic Writings*. New York: Harper Collins Press, 1993. (Page 434).

[24] *Holzwege*, p.303 (19); cf. Richardson, *Heidegger*, p 522; Kelkel, *Legend,* pp. 501-503, 544-545, from: Joseph J. Kocklemans. *On The Truth of Being: Reflections on Heidegger's Later Philosophy*. Bloomington: Indiana University Press, 1984.

REFERENCES

Heidegger, Martin. *Being and Time.* Translated by Joan Stambaugh. Albany: State University of New York Press, 1996.

__________. *Plato's Doctrine Of Truth.* From: *Philosophy in the Twentieth Century: An Anthology*, 4 vols. ed. Wm. Barret and Henry D. Aiken. New York: Random House, 1962. Vol. 3.

__________. *What Are Poets For?* Translated by Albert Hofstadtrt, from: *Poetry, Language, and Thought.* New York: Harper & Row Publishers Inc., 1971.

Jage, Werner. *Paideia: The Ideals Of Greek Culture.* New York: Oxford University Press, 1939.

Kocklemans, Joseph J. *On The Truth of Being: Reflections on Heidegger's Later Philosophy.* Bloomington: Indiana University Press, 1984.

Krell, David ed. *Martin Heidegger Basic Writings.* New York: Harper, 1993.

Nussbaum, Martha. *The Fragility of Goodness*, New York, Cambridge University Press, 1986.

Poggeler, Otto. *Martin Heidegger's Path of Thinking*, Translated by Daniel Magurshak and Sigmund Barber. Atlantic Highlands, NJ: Humanities Press, 1987

Versenyi, Laszlo. *Heidegger. Being and Truth.* New Haven CT: Yale University Press, 1965.

NIETZSCHE'S USE OF METAPHOR

John R. Hartmann
Alfred University

This paper is an examination of Nietzsche's metaphoric style and thought, and the structure of the genealogy that maintains it. Perhaps the most interesting result of this line of thinking is the idea that post-metaphysical philosophy is indeed possible, insofar as post-metaphysical thought can generate interpretations that derive concepts from active metaphorizing. Epistemology is replaced with an economy of forces, with an aesthetic. In this light, our understanding of ideas like the Will to Power and the Eternal Return must be reinterpreted as metaphoric, and this reinterpretation has certain implications both for the scholarship surrounding Nietzsche's works, as well as our reading of the works themselves.

Perhaps no other recent thinker has been subjected to as much critical evaluation and interpretation than has Friedrich Nietzsche. Numerous books, papers, etc., have been written on various aspects of his thought, with an equally tremendous number of interpretations being exposed in these works. Walter Kaufmann, for example, found Nietzsche to be something of a radical empiricist, denying metaphysical truths but not empirically derived truths. Martin Heidegger's enormously influential interpretation named Nietzsche the 'last metaphysician' of the West, finding him to be battling metaphysics only to be trapped within metaphysics itself. And the explosion of French commentators on the scene, i.e. Deleuze, Derrida, Granier, Klossowski, and Kofman (to name but a few) have only further complicated the picture.

Despite these differences in interpretation, virtually all Nietzsche scholars would characterize Nietzschean thought as *perspectival*. The doctrine of perspectivism, that there is no Truth but instead truths, no privileged vantage point but simply different perspectives, has proven vexing for a number of scholars. After all, it does seem that Nietzsche falls prey to some sort of performative contradiction in the assertion of his brand of perspectivism—how can his view be true when all that exist are perspectives?

Is there a 'solution?' I think that the most fruitful inroads can be made through examining the issue of metaphor in Nietzsche's works. Perspectivism, I want to argue, requires metaphoric thought, and metaphoric thought requires genealogical analysis. This paper is an examination of that metaphoric style and thought, and the structure of the genealogy that maintains it. Perhaps the most interesting result of this line of thinking is the idea that post-metaphysical philosophy is indeed possible, insofar as post-metaphysical thought can generate interpretations that derive concepts from active metaphorizing. Epistemology is replaced with an economy of forces, with an aesthetic. In this light, our understanding of ideas like the Will to Power and the Eternal Return must be reinterpreted as metaphoric, and this reinterpretation has certain implications both for the scholarship surrounding Nietzsche's works, as well as our reading of the works themselves.

Why Metaphor?

Without a notion of a metaphysical, real world, the Nietzschean world-view must by necessity do without many of the traditional philosophic answers as regards truth, objectivity, etc. Yet, this does not seem to bother Nietzsche—in fact, he writes that "knowledge of [a metaphysical world] would be the most useless of all knowledge: more useless even than knowledge of the chemical composition of water must be to the sailor in danger of shipwreck."[1] The Kantian project of phenomenal and noumenal realms does not hold any value, as Nietzsche makes a quite Rortyian move in dismissing the noumenal—after all, if we can't access it, it isn't much good.

Due to this rejection of traditional notions of truth, Nietzsche instead explores a very different model—that of all concepts as essentially metaphoric. Nowhere is this view more eloquently described than in his early, unpublished *On Truth and Lies in a Nonmoral Sense*. In this essay, Nietzsche describes all the truths of man as being illusory, or, better still, metaphoric. "Truths are illusions which we have forgotten are illusions...metaphors that have become worn out and have been drained of sensual force."[2]

What exactly does Nietzsche mean by the term metaphor? Here, Nietzsche considers all conceptualizing to be metaphoric—it is an approximation, inexact, a convenient lie. In fact, Nietzsche writes that

> we believe that we know something about the things themselves when we talk of trees, colors, snow, and flowers; and yet we possess nothing but metaphors for things—metaphors which correspond in no way to the original entities.[3]

The concept (i.e. a concept of a tree) is thus found to be an abstraction three powers away from the original sense data, or nerve stimulus. This fundamental metaphorical position can be described via the three metamorphoses of the original stimulus:[4] first, the nerve stimulus is transformed into image (thus leaving dreams as originary writing?). Second, the images become sounds, or words. Language, which is so pervasive in our human existence, is thus the second level of metaphor. Finally, there is the transformation from the sonic realm back to the conscious, as the sound/word becomes the concept. Thus, there is no proper concept, or direct correspondence, but only figurative, metaphoric conceptualizing.

This is a non-Aristotelian notion of what a concept is, whereas metaphor refers to the concept itself for Aristotle. In this view, metaphor is dependent on the concept for material to utilize in the metaphoric event, i.e. the word play depending on the concept for its basis. Nietzsche reverses this by insisting that the concept refers to metaphor—seeing as all we have are metaphors in this human existence, there is no escaping this conclusion. As Sarah Kofman notes,

> Aristotle's definition of metaphor could not be retained as such by Nietzsche since it is based on a division of the world into well-defined genera and species corresponding to essences, whereas for Nietzsche the essence of things is enigmatic, so genera and species are themselves but human, all-too-human metaphors.[5]

However, one must not make the mistake of privileging metaphor at the expense of concept, or simply inverting the equation. To recognize metaphor solely falls into the same sorts of traps that does the privileging of concept—one forgets that metaphor is *only* metaphor, abstraction, a convenient lie, and metaphysical posturing returns. One must realize that metaphor is encased within concept, and that we have forgotten that concepts consist of varying metaphoric constructs.

So, in discarding traditional, correspondence epistemology and by uttering the now-famous "God is dead," Nietzsche plunges us headlong into a infinite system of metaphor. There is no truth *per se*, only illusion; there is no knowledge, but instead the knowledge that "a concept has no greater value than a metaphor and is itself a condensate of metaphors..."[6] Yet we still believe in the fictions that concepts create, i.e. the self, will, the 'thing.' How does/has this happened? Here we find ourselves moving into perhaps Nietzsche's greatest contribution to the Western philosophic tradition (in terms of sheer utility)—the genealogical method, and his historical analysis of how metaphors come to be 'mummified' into concepts, thus enforcing the forgetting of the true nature of the metaphor.

Genealogy

Nietzschean genealogy is inherently an *interested* process, for one does not seek out the (absolute) beginnings of things, but rather one looks to find the (relative) origins of concepts, and thus their position within the historical field. Genealogy is then somewhat unique as it recognizes the fluid movement of meaning within any given sign or concept. In *The Genealogy of Morals*, Nietzsche recognizes this fluidity of meaning when he notes the distinction between the

> two aspects [of any event or concept]: on the one hand, that in it which is relatively *enduring*, the custom, the act, the 'drama,' a certain strict sequence of procedures; on the other, that in it which is *fluid*, the

> meaning, the purpose, the expectation associated with the performance of such procedures.[7]

What Nietzsche means by this is that in any sign there are two elements: the first, which is static, enduring, i.e. the actual word, or action. The second is the element we find much harder to pin down—the actual meaning of the sign, or, perhaps better put, the current understanding of the sign or action in relation to the varying perspectives over the course of time.

To illustrate this point, Nietzsche examines our notion of punishment—a study which Michel Foucault, perhaps the most Nietzschean of the French Nietzscheans, himself undertook in his seminal *Discipline and Punish.* In *The Genealogy of Morals*, Nietzsche finds that our notions of punishment are not as clear cut as we might think. For example, we modern men like to think that punishment is a case of holding a wrongdoer responsible for his deed. And yet, when one looks at the history of the concept of punishment, this is not the case. Nietzsche, through his genealogical analysis, finds that the origins of punishment lie in the creditor-debtor relation. "Have these genealogist of morals had even the remotest suspicion that, for example, the major moral concept *Schuld* [guilt] has its origin in the very material concept *Schulden* [debts]?"[8] That a debt could be paid back in some way led to the cruel and barbaric practices of the Old Germans: stoning, breaking on the wheel, piercing, trampling by horse, boiling in oil, and flaying alive, to name but a few. If one looks hard enough, one may find elements of these practices in our modern, supposedly 'humane' methods of punishment. As John Gilmour writes,

> When we interpret our practices as governed by a higher moral purpose, Nietzsche immediately re-

> minds us that their meaning may be superficial, masking deep structures of cruelty that our rational purposes merely obscure.[9]

Our signs have long histories, the depths and importance of which we are only vaguely aware. Nietzsche lists in *The Genealogy of Morals* a tremendous variety of different 'motives' behind the practice of exercising punishment on wrong-doers, in order to "give at least an idea of how uncertain, how supplemental, how accidental 'the meaning' of punishment is, and how one and the same procedure can be employed, interpreted, adapted to ends that differ fundamentally..."[10] All of this leads us to ask the following: how is it that any one of these meanings comes to be 'truer' than any other? Why this meaning, and not that one? If we are to understand how metaphor becomes rigid concept, it is essential to comprehend this phenomenon.

Again, we must turn to Nietzsche's genealogical method to give us some sort of answers. Genealogical analysis, in tracing back meaning of concepts to varying origins, helps us to understand the twists and turns of any given conceptual meaning in a manner that traditional, 'linear' history never could. Yet, we discover in this analysis many different origins that we have 'forgotten,' meanings which have been subsumed within the greater signification. This forgetting, and the creation of a memory which incorporates these collective forgettings, are the key issues for understanding how concepts become absolutes, how we forget that they are "truths...we have forgotten are illusions..."[11]

Deleuze and Guattari write,

> Nietzsche says: it is a matter of creating a memory for man; and man, who was constituted by means of an active faculty of forgetting (*oubli*), by means of a

> repression of biological memory, must create an other memory, one that is collective, a memory of words (*paroles*) and no longer a memory of things, a memory of signs and no longer of effects.[12]

What is at stake in this passage is not only understanding of how metaphor becomes rigid concept, but also as to *why* this phenomenon occurs.

Klossowski says that "a sign traces the fluctuation of an intensity."[13] In light of previous analysis, what does this mean? Signs, while designating nothing in themselves (i.e. no correspondence to a 'reality'), nevertheless do change. They 'trace a fluctuation,' meaning in this case (and in this post-modern reading) that signs are the external marker of changes in meaning—changes that are constituted by and affects of varying intensities and fluctuations of different *forces*. Forces, for Nietzsche the totality of all that exists, come together, create intensities, dissolve... all having an effect on our realities. We ourselves are temporary unities of differing forces, the notion of a 'self' being only a useful metaphor. However, these changes do not occur randomly, as one might be led to think. The forgetting of certain meanings immanent within signs, and the valorization of others is sheerly due to the qualities of the different forces that affect the change. In other words, there is a social element to this 'creating of a memory.'

Nietzsche makes a distinction between forces; there are active forces, those that are life-affirming, and there are reactive forces, or those that are life-denying. What defines these qualities of forces will be discussed later, but for now, it is enough to say that these differences exist. Certain metaphors become taken as 'truths' due to the power of the different forces/intensities that create them. In *The Geneal-*

ogy of Morals, Nietzsche outlines just how such changes in conceptual content occur on the social level. At one time, with the pattern recurring at different spots in history, the ideals of the noble classes (strength, beauty, wit, power) were considered good, and anything else (plainness, dullness, etc.) were deemed bad. Ascetic priests reversed this, so that first 'cleanliness' and purity became the good, then ideals such as humility, meekness, and so forth. Pride, strength, and beauty become evil. This reversal, noble 'bad' becoming herd 'good' and noble 'good' becoming herd 'evil,' affects itself through the exertion of a reactive Will to Power (*ressentiment*), creating a herd mentality and morality such that the defining characteristics of the majority of humanity, or the herd, becomes the most valued characteristics, and thus are deemed good. Thus, political superiority (a means of gaining social power) transforms itself into superiority of personal soul, or personal identity. As Nietzsche writes,

> [t]he slave revolt in morality begins when *ressentiment* itself becomes creative and gives birth to values: the *ressentiment* of natures that are denied the true reaction, that of deeds, and compensate themselves with an imaginary revenge.[14]

What is true on the macro-level is also true on the micro-level. As Klossowski says, a sign traces a fluctuation in intensity, or a change in forces. Our current, 'herd' morality is a result of re-active forces becoming powerful enough to overwrite the previous morality. The social context of this *ressentiment*, the social importance of forgetting certain meanings, cannot be missed. For example, Nietzsche believes that consciousness is a direct result of such re-active forces. He writes,

> consciousness has developed only under the pressure of the need for communication... it was only as a social animal that man acquired self-consciousness ...[as] required by social or herd utility. Consequently...each of us will always succeed in becoming conscious only of what is not individual but 'average.'[15]

In this view, not only is consciousness unnecessary, but it also drags us into the realm of the herd, through the powers of re-active forces. Consciousness, far from being life-affirming, reduces all of our experiences to linguistic constructs—the second abstraction of metaphor. (To be fair, however, we should note that Nietzsche also deemed consciousness, the creation of an interiority, and even the advent of Judeo-Christian metaphysics as events which gave us 'depth' and made us 'interesting animals.')

The import of this may seem distant and uninteresting, but it is through genealogical analysis that Nietzsche allows us to see how meaning becomes hidden within concepts, concepts in which (due to social need) meaning is either glorified or pushed aside. It is due to the relative standing of different forces at different times that signs receive the signification that they do. This leads us into a fundamental criticism of Martin Heidegger's reading of Nietzsche's works, and the interpretations of Heidegger's followers (e.g. Jean Granier). Heidegger posits Nietzsche as the 'last metaphysician' of Western philosophy/metaphysics, in no small part due to his use of the concept Will to Power. Heidegger, viewing the Western tradition as being a progressing whole, sees Nietzsche as falling into the same traps as did Leibniz, Kant, Hegel, Schelling, and especially Schopenhauer—for, Heidegger believes, all of these thinkers incorporate a metaphysical notion of the will. Yet, keeping in mind the above analysis, it is surprisingly easy to dismiss this portion of Heidegger's reading.[16] Nietzsche did not utilize a notion of a metaphysical will; will, like all other concepts, is a metaphor, and a poor one at that. It is a notion born of re-active thought, due to social necessity. Thought requires a subject to think thought: thus the notion of self, and of will, are born. The self is simply a locus of forces, a synthetic unity that is momentary, fleeting. The will is a similar fiction. It is, to bastardize a very famous phrase, metaphor all the way down.

So, we have seen that the forgetting of metaphor is due to social need, and more precisely, to the domination of forces by other forces. Genealogical analysis gives us the tools to sift through the rubble of the ages and find origins for most all our modern concepts—often, very surprising and disconcerting origins. Yet, many questions remain. What is it that decides which forces dominate, and when? What does this metaphoric reading of Nietzsche's texts imply for some of his most difficult concepts, i.e. the Will to Power and Eternal Return? Both questions require a starting point, and there can be no better origin for this part of the discussion than that of the Will to Power.

Re-explaining Nietzsche

If we accept the above analysis as being true to the spirit of Nietzsche's writings, then we are placed in something of a bind—many of the traditional interpretations of his works, especially those of Kaufmann, Danto, Heidegger, etc., are lacking. A new analysis of Nietzsche's thought is thus required. In this section, I wish to undertake the beginnings of this by viewing a number of Nietzsche's main concepts as metaphoric; that is to say, not only being metaphoric in nature but also having certain implications due to this status. In her book *Nietzsche and Metaphor*, Sarah Kofman undertakes much of this task, especially as regards Nietzsche's re-appropriation of certain metaphors found in the Western tradition, for example, metaphors found in the works of Plato, Descartes, Spinoza.[17] Her claim is that Nietzsche does not coin new metaphors, but re-interprets old ones, thus reviving them. I do not wish to rewalk her paths, for a number of reasons, originality being one of these, but there is another which is more forcing. If Kofman is right in saying that Nietzsche only re-interprets existing concepts and metaphor, it seems as if her reading might be open to a criticism characteristic of the Heideggerian: that inversion does not imply overturning. This is the crux of Heidegger's pronouncing Nietzsche to be one who inverts Platonism, and thereby does not escape Platonic/Western metaphysics. Instead, I argue that while Nietzsche does occupy himself with re-working existing metaphor at certain points, he is a creator of new metaphor at other (strategic) points. Two of these, and certainly two of the most important for the Nietzschean tradition, are the Will to Power and the Doctrine of Eternal Return.

The framework within which we have been working has been one of *forces*. In many passages Nietzsche reminds us of this notion, most glaringly in the famous (infamous?) section 1067 from *The Will to Power*, where he writes that the world is "force throughout... a play of forces and waves of forces, at the same time one and many..."[18] We ourselves are comprised of forces, part of the world in this regard. Yet Nietzsche continues in this passage by saying that the name for this world might best be put as follows: "*This world is the will to power—and nothing besides*! And you yourselves are also this will to power, and nothing besides!"[19] What could Nietzsche possibly mean by this?

In his essay "Active and Reactive," Gilles Deleuze offers us a rather interesting interpretation, reminiscent of Derrida's conception of *différance* in some ways.

> [W]hat the Will to Power is is the genealogical element of force, at once differential and genetic. *The Will to Power is the element out of which issue both the quantitative difference of related forces and the quality that, due to this relation, devolves to each force.*[20]

What Deleuze is after is deceptively simple—the Will to Power is not a force in itself, but is instead the synthesizing element of all forces. It is what gives forces their active or re-active characters, and 'decides' how effective these intensities or loci of forces will become. It is determinant, yet fleeting, for it does not exist in itself except as an explanatory principle of sorts, differentiating between forces, within forces. All force exemplifies Will to Power, for all force relies upon Will to Power, co-exists with Will to Power. It is metaphoric in that it does not 'exist,' yet it is true because it is apt, useful. It is true because it is the product of an active willing, itself (the metaphor) a product of Will to Power.

A number of commentators, including Deleuze, Lingis, Klossowski, and even Heidegger, have made a connection between the Will to Power and the notion of the Eternal Return. Heidegger went so far as to call the Will to Power the *essentia* of Being, and Eternal Return the *existentia*. And I am of a mind to concur with this thought, although for very different reasons than those of Heidegger. If we view Eternal Return as we have viewed all of Nietzsche's concepts, as metaphoric in nature, we must wonder why Nietzsche would clutter his thought with such a difficult topic. But if we are being consistent in our interpretation and our understanding of Nietzsche's thought, we must abandon any metaphysical interpretations of Eternal Return and concentrate solely on its metaphoric status. We have found the Will to Power to be useful as an explanatory tool; what can we say about Eternal Return?

As a metaphoric conception, my reading of Eternal Return suggests that due to Nietzsche's idea that all is becoming and fluctuation of forces, the phrase 'return of the same' does not, and cannot, imply an exact return of all events in sequential and unveering order. Instead, I believe that by Eternal Return Nietzsche wished to convey the eternal becoming of our world—*the return of the similar* instead of the same. All that exists is becoming, fluctuation, difference. Could not Eternal Return be a metaphor for the ever-present blur of appearances that make up our human reality? Or, to put it more succinctly, could Eternal Return be designed to be a test, an affirmation of the human condition, a test of our bond to the earth, to this body, to this human life?

We are perhaps in a better position now to describe this metaphor—Eternal Return is a metaphoric/existential concept, just like the Will to Power, in that it is useful, born of active forces and active willing. Eternal Return should be understood in this context as a transformative notion; a theory that, regardless of its truth or falsity, transforms man into the Overman. Can you affirm that all there is is difference, becoming, the moment, from now into eternity? Can you be strong enough not to will away your past,[21] strong enough to affirm all that is? Can you affirm your human life? Here we can understand the link between Eternal Return and the Will to Power—affirmation is an inherently creative process, depending on the Will to Power as affirmation is found to be transformative, and increasing our power. Affirmation is an ultimately active willing.

Final Thoughts

Having completed most of the goals I outlined in the introduction to this paper, there remain a few loose ends to be tied up. The natural question to be raised after a discussion like this involves Nietzsche's choosing of these 'new' metaphors—why are they better than any others? After all, Nietzsche's perspectivism could be read to imply that no perspective is inherently better than any other.

Yet Nietzsche does privilege his metaphors over those found unworthy, and for good reason. Perspectivism does not imply an inability to decide relative value between perspectives. Rather, Nietzsche demands that we look to find the origins of any concept to discern its worth, to note what aspect of the Will to Power caused it to be born. And, Nietzsche would argue, the two metaphoric concepts I discuss above are better than other conceptual notions, because they both are children of active forces, active willing. Will to Power is co-existent within the field of forces, and an active exercising of the Will to Power is life-affirming, creating a new health, a new strength, a new power.[22] The notion of the Eternal Return has its transformative power due to its affirmative necessity, for affirmation requires an active willing via the Will to Power.

NOTES

1 Nietzsche, Friedrich. *Human, all too Human: A book for free spirits*. trans. by R.J. Hollingdale, intro. by Erich Heller. USA: Cambridge University Press, 1993 (1986). §16.

2 Nietzsche, Friedrich. "On Truth and Lies in a Nonmoral Sense," in *Philosophy and Truth: Selections from Nietzsche's Notebooks of the Early 1870's*, edited and translated by Daniel Breazeale. New Jersey: Humanities Press International, Inc., 1979. p.81. Hereafter TL.

3 TL, p.82-3.

4 *Ibid.*

5 Kofman, Sarah. *Nietzsche and Metaphor*. trans. by Duncan Large. Great Britain: Stanford University Press, 1993. p.15.

6 Kofman, p.3.

7 Nietzsche, Friedrich. *On The Genealogy of Morals*. trans. Walter Kaufmann and R.J. Hollingsdale. New York: Vintage, 1989 (1967). II, §13. Hereafter GM.

8 GM II §4.

9 Gilmour, John C. "Genealogy, Interpretation, and Historical Masks." *Historical Reflections*, Vol. 21, No. 3. p. 499.

10 GM II §13.

11 TL, p.81.

12 Deleuze, Gilles, and Felix Guattari. *Anti-Oedipus: Capitalism and Schitzophrenia*. trans. Robert Hurley, Mark Seem, and Helen R. Lane. Minneapolis: U. of Minnesota Press, 1983. p. 142.

13 Klossowski, Pierre. "Nietzsche's Experience of the Eternal Return." *The New Nietzsche*. ed. by David B. Allison. Cambridge: The MIT Press, 1995 (1985). p.111.

14 GM I §10.

15 Nietzsche, Friedrich. *The Gay Science*. trans. Walter Kaufmann. New York: Random House, 1974. §354.

16 I think it is important to make a note here, for the above text is quite damning of Heidegger's reading as a whole, and this is unfair to Heidegger's interpretation. Rather, I find that Heidegger's various texts on Nietzsche are not as misinformed as they have been made out to be. Certainly, when Heidegger plugs Nietzsche into his schematism of Western metaphysics one feels as if some sleight-of-hand has been performed, but there are other aspects to his reading

which are quite suggestive—especially in sections where Heidegger exposes the existential side of Nietzsche's work. To quote Jacques Derrida from his book *Spurs*, "The thesis of Heidegger's *grand livre* (i.e. *Nietzsche*) is much less simple than people have generally tended to say."

17 See Kofman, pp. 59-80.

18 Nietzsche, Friedrich. *The Will to Power*. ed. by Walter Kaufmann, trans. by Walter Kaufmann and R.J. Hollingsdale. New York: Vintage, 1968 (1967). §1067. Hereafter WP.

19 *Ibid.*

20 Deleuze, Gilles. "Active and Reactive," *The New Nietzsche*. ed. by David B. Allison. Cambridge: The MIT Press, 1995 (1985). p. 87. Hereafter AR.

21 See WP 557 for Nietzsche's belief in the complete interdependence of all that is.

22 One might argue that this is tautological in some way, and thus an impotent argument, but, as Nietzsche says, nihilists (meaning himself) require no logic.

REFERENCES

Deleuze, Gilles. "Active and Reactive." *The New Nietzsche*. Edited by David B. Allison. Cambridge: The MIT Press, 1995 (1985).

Deleuze, Gilles and Felix Guattari. *Anti-Oedipus: Capitalism and Schitzophrenia*. Translated by Robert Hurley, Mark Seem, and Helen R. Lane. Minneapolis: University of Minnesota Press, 1983.

Gilmour, John C. "Genealogy, Interpretation, and Historical Masks." *Historical Reflections* 21.3: 493-514.

Klossowski, Pierre. "Nietzsche's Experience of the Eternal Return." *The New Nietzsche*. Edited by David B. Allison. Cambridge: The MIT Press, 1995 (1985).

Kofman, Sarah. *Nietzsche and Metaphor*. Translated by Duncan Large. Great Britain: Stanford University Press, 1993.

Nietzsche, Friedrich. *The Gay Science*. Translated by Walter Kaufmann. New York: Random House, 1974.

________. *Human, all too Human: A book for free spirits*. Translated by R.J. Hollingdale, introduction by Erich Heller. USA: Cambridge University Press, 1993 (1986).

________. *On The Genealogy of Morals*. Translated by Walter Kaufmann and R.J. Hollingsdale. New York: Vintage, 1989 (1967).

________. "On Truth and Lies in a Nonmoral Sense," in *Philosophy and Truth: Selections from Nietzsche's Notebooks of the Early 1870's*. Edited and translated by

Daniel Breazeale. New Jersey: Humanities Press International, Inc., 1979.

________. *The Will to Power.* Edited. by Walter Kaufmann, translated by Walter Kaufmann and R.J. Hollingsdale. New York: Vintage, 1968 (1967).

Textual Analysis

WITTGENSTEINIAN HERMENEUTICS? PRELIMINARY SKETCH OF A READING OF WITTGENSTEIN'S *ON CERTAINTY* IN COMPARISON TO RICOEUR'S *FROM TEXT TO ACTION*

Kevin Goetz
SUNY Oneonta

On Certainty is a compilation of a number of the personal notes of Ludwig Wittgenstein. The notes found were written towards the end of his life, and center on the difference between the common use and the proper use of the word "Knowledge." To say, as some do, that the work is addressed only the positivists of the day is to leave out many incidentals. Many of these "incidentals" (the ideas and arguments which are passed through on the way) form a philosophy which takes its place in a larger community.

The thesis of this paper is that one of the traditions which may also be addressed in Wittgenstein's notes, though it remains fairly underdeveloped, is the Hermeneutic tradition. As a result of this possibility, there is a place for a non-positivist reading of Wittgenstein's work. The arguments for the thesis will be drawn from the similarity which Wittgenstein's writings and method shared with the thought of some of the ideas which are important in the history of the hermeneutic tradition.

Published in 1969, *On Certainty* is a compilation of a number of the personal notes of Ludwig Wittgenstein. The notes found in this edition were written towards the end of his life, and center on the difference between the common use and the proper use of the word "Knowledge," especially in the form of knowledge claims.

The readings of these notes which is generally accorded to the book are well summed up by British philosopher, A.J. Ayer, who wrote:

> In the notes collected... (Wittgenstein) bases his arguments upon G.E. Moore's celebrated defense of common sense.[1]

Along with sharing a number of assumptions with the common sense philosophies of G.E. Moore,[2] Moore is also addressed by name a number of times, a rarity in Wittgenstein's work, and certain of his assertions addressed.

The readings of the book, which address *On Certainty* in this manner, carry out a useful exegesis of the text. Many commentators find the book to be a commentary (as Ayer believes) on the logical positivism, which was fashionable at the time in Cambridge, where Wittgenstein held a chair in philosophy. There is some difficulty with such a reading of the book. To say that the work addresses only the positivists of the day is to leave out many incidentals—those thing which are found on the way to the ascribed end—which are also dealt with in the collection.

An assumption of this paper is that many of these "incidentals," the ideas and arguments which are passed through on the way, form a philosophy which takes it's place in a larger area than only the logical empiricist community, which positivism was a part of. That, along with the empiricist reading of Wittgenstein (along with, and certainly not instead of, or exempting), there are also other traditions which find themselves addressed in the text of *On Certainty* in specific, and Wittgenstein's philosophy in general.

This opening of the notes of Wittgenstein to different traditions has some amount of support by some Wittgenstein scholars. In *Wittgenstein's Vienna*, the claim that "analytic philosophers have systematically misread and misunderstood Wittgenstein..."[3] is put forth by the authors, Janik and Toulmin. Some part of Russell Nieli's *Wittgenstein: From Mysticism to Ordinary Language* is spent speaking about Wittgenstein, not only in relation to the group of positivists known as the Vienna Circle, but also in relation to Martin Heidegger, a popular German philosopher who was engaged in a different tradition than the logical empiricists.

The thesis of this paper is that one of the traditions which may also be addressed in Wittgenstein's notes, though it remains fairly underdeveloped, is one which had developed as a philosophical tradition a century earlier, and was one of the aspects of philosophy which was being addressed during Wittgenstein's life by Martin Heidegger; the Hermeneutic tradition, and that as a result of this possibility, there is a place for a non-positivist reading of Wittgenstein's work.

The arguments for the thesis will be drawn from the similarity, which Wittgenstein's writings and method shared with the thought of some of the ideas, which are important in the history of the hermeneutic tradition. A comparative view will be taken to determine the extent of the possibility of a hermeneutical reading.

***

One of the prevalent themes in modern philosophical inquiry is the push to transcend subjectivity and the question of what method would allow such a thing to be accomplished. There are any number of reasons why such inquests are popular, such as: the grounding of statements, satiation of curiosity, or presence.

Recently the natural sciences, through the scientific method, have laid popular claim to this ability, and have backed it up with results. The scientific method, or so some claimed in the last century, gave the natural sciences something which the humanities were without: an objective footing. To address this difficulty in the humanities, a hermeneutical project was begun. "The proper task of hermeneutics," writes Paul Ricoeur about the field's founders, was to reach the subject of a speaker, and to dispose of the language which had gotten the subject of a listener there.[4]

This proper task is 'positive' as opposed to the 'negative' task of the natural sciences. This means that unlike the natural sciences, which may only establish boundaries, indicating where the end of a universal lies, hermeneutics "reaches the act of thought which produced the discourse."[5]

It is the attempt here to address the ideas of two of the people who have set their shoulders to the task of moving past a subjective discourse for the humanities. The first, Ludwig Wittgenstein, felt that what he called 'knowledge' was the state in which subjectivity was overcome. 'Knowledge' "...properly means 'There is no such thing as doubt in this case' or 'The expression "I do not know" makes no sense in this case.'" [6]

'Knowledge,' however, is a term, which is often used during times when a person does not possess such objective ability as the proper usage of the term would suggest. 'Certainty' serves as one of the words, which can easily be used to replace 'knowledge' in situations where the latter is commonly used outside of the definition given above. Circumstances which 'certainty' would be more properly used under,[7] to resolve conflict which may occur, are while supplying empirical testimony: as in a courtroom,[8] or during description of an experiment, or on occasions where one is attempting to establish an agreement that one has "proper ground for their statement"[9] to another.

The essential difference between the two is that while in possession of knowledge, a person is in relation not with "the sense of a proposition,[10] but (with) a fact."[11] Statements of knowledge describe not merely a persons relations with himself, as in the case of his perceptions, thoughts or beliefs, but instead lay claim to a place in the world, allowing for an objective description.

The prompting of the Wittgensteinian work of differing 'knowledge' from 'certainty' lies within the activity of questioning. Whenever there is a form of questioning undertaken, either by physical or semantic means, certain processes come to the fore. Two possibilities exist at this point, the respondent either answers the question based on some automatic response,[12] or undergoes what might be described as a series of unobservable processes, "follows a rule," to generate a product.[13] The rule, the manner in which any solution is learned or gotten to, is learned through processes of interaction.[14] Continued events refine and develop the rule, so that versions which are defective (not working, or bringing up dispute) are no longer used when that rule is called for, though they may prove fit to be used on other occasions.

The second figure, Paul Ricoeur, uses the phrase 'explanation' to refer to "the claim of non differentiation, of the epistemological continuity between the natural sciences and the human sciences,"[15] which is to say "the mode of being of nature,"[16] wherein the methodology of the natural sciences, and of object/nature oriented criticism dominate.

Ricoeur opposes 'understanding,' the mode of being of mind, to the universal amalgamation of all disciplines under the methodology of the physical sciences. This understanding, as typified in the writings of Wilhelm Dilthey, a German representative of such a theory of understanding, creates a science of the mind, "reintroduces the...objective mind in a philosophy that none the less remained romantic, to the extent that it is life that expresses itself within signs, and therefore interprets itself."[17] This science of the mind maintains humans ability to "project (itself) into an alien mental life" through the usage of perceptible signs, but also 'fixes' certain of these as 'mental inscriptions' (a text of the mind), so as to allow the objectivity of the explanation of the natural sciences. This allows the mind to be viewed as a form of writing, of signs inscribed in the same manner as 'all of the inscriptions which human reality leaves in it's wake'[18]—all of which would grant the human sciences the same stability, through foundation, that the 'genuine knowledge' of the natural sciences found.

While Dilthey's interest in his enterprise was the formation of a psychology—a discipline of the human sciences which would possess the special methodologies of the human sciences, along with the claim to "objectification required by science,"[19] Ricoeur's concern lies in bringing the lessons of the expanded textual world into ethical discussion, and takes as assumption that psychology has been thus formed.

The description, which Wittgenstein gives to 'knowledge,' as stated earlier, is that it is a relation between a person and a fact, rather than a proposition. Since the relation between a person and nature is the providence of the natural sciences, which Wittgenstein felt to be the disciplines which held an ability to speak 'sensically,'[20] the relation of the process of explanation to 'knowledge' seems to be one of product.

Because this would leave statements which are unconfirmable scientifically 'cut out' of language, through a lack of production, we see a division in Wittgenstein's work which was similar to one in the work of the forerunner to Dilthey's philosophy, the division which Friedrich Schleiermacher proposed that languages, as understood, hold: grammatical interpretation, and technical interpretation.

Schleiermacher's distinction here indicates the two ways in which language can be interpreted, and interpreting in one way admits to ignorance of the other interpretation of the statement. Grammatical interpretation "is based on the characteristics of discourse which are common to a culture." This style of interpretation is both objective, concerned not with any author of a statement, and negative, establishing only errors of usage. The technical interpretation does away with commonality, and listens directly to the author of the words.[21]

While 'knowledge' appears to fit well the first method of interpretation, being the material which is interpreted here, both the input and output of the natural sciences, the second method of interpretation causes a problem. There are times when statements which only call for certainty, and not knowledge, are necessary: a court of law, interpersonal relationships, or any time where testimony is called for, for example. If these occasions call for the doing away of objectivity, how can there be a method, which allows for transmission of the subject's equivalent of datum in an understandable fashion?

This is why Dilthey's psychology project received so much attention. The possibility of developing a technology of interpretation of the subject also indicates the possibility of an assured understanding of 'genuine knowledge' in the humanities, which has unchanging roots that may be pointed to in text. The text grants 'Certainty,' logical form, which does not verify an objective answer, but verifies an answer according to the framework, which forms the text. This framework is a framework of explanation, which is given as a paradigm or story by the speaker, and accepted (taken as though it were a written book), by the listener.[22]

This textuality and Wittgenstein's notion of 'rules' bear extreme similarities. Wittgenstein believes that knowledge is passed on through teaching of these rules, and presents the performance of such rule teaching as being similar to explanation. The negative nature of the task—establishing boundaries through 'mistakes' or answers which generate results other than those which are desired, set the boundaries by establishing both a space in which to stay during usage, and the 'outside' which clearly defines it.

When the interpretive space which is being inhabited is less clearly defined, as it would be in the case of 'certainty.' This is not a rule system which has not properly been formed yet, but can instead be thought of as merely being statements formed without the technology with which to contrast them with other, similar, statements having already been built in. The formed stories of the given text help to establish this technology. They provide a background against which statements can be viewed, and the means for comparing the statements for value, by supplying standardizing rules.

Sharply differing is the end of these two figure's thoughts. Ricoeur states that his interest in a certain end—the bringing of the methods of textual interpretation into the field of action, and establishing a firm foundation for a paradigmatic ethical thought. Wittgenstein makes no statement of his end, but does call for the end to philosophy through the cleavage of problems which different methods afford him.[23]

These ends are vastly different. To expand upon one of Wittgenstein's metaphors,[24] Ricoeur's end has him examining books laying about a room with partially empty, partially messy, shelving, and conceiving of an order in which to place all of the books, and noticeably beginning the work so that it should be apparent to all who examine the same information which he takes in, what order the rest of the books will be placed in.

Wittgenstein's neatening of the room, however, is dealt with through any number of an innumerable set of moves. He places books on shelves where they will not find themselves in the end "for temporary storage" cantankers about, and does not admit himself to be following the shelving style of anyone else, nor does he appear to admit of a shelving style at all—all of the shelves are subject to change.

This irregularity, the valuation of methodical development over systematic theorizing, ensures that Wittgenstein has place in hermeneutical discourse. The skepticism which he utilizes, often at the surety of the method of the sciences[25] is too continual to formalize into a formed system or refined 'proper' hermeneutics; the subject is always either not private in the first place, or not within the bounds of speech. Wittgenstein's skepticism is not interested in achieving the stability within the realms of action and history which concern Ricoeur and many of the prominent figures in hermeneutics; skepticism appears to maintain it's own stability by utilizing one aspect of that which it is skeptical of against another aspect. Since this would be possible until *all* problems are dealt with, Wittgenstein's skepticism has a great deal of room in which to exist, outside of formal 'proper' hermeneutics.

Informally, however, the aspects of hermeneutical thought which Wittgenstein brings to his work are fairly rich. His idea of 'rules,' and the tremendous amount of his work and collected notes attesting to his attempt to interpret, describe and explain the idea, serve as one of the more complex examples of textual interplay which can be found. Besides this, Wittgenstein's skepticism, a skeptical movement which constantly points back at itself, as well as in directions away from it, may help to provide an examination of many of the problems which hermeneutics may face in the future. Viewing 'rules' as a metaphor for 'text,' and examining the workings of Wittgenstein's 'rules,' may find many involved in hermeneutical work not only more ready to handle skepticism, but also the handle skeptics.

NOTES

1 A.J. Ayer. *Wittgenstein.* Chicago: University of Chicago Press, 1985, p. 110.

2 Ayer describes three of them: "that there are in the universe enormous numbers of material bodies," "that men, and perhaps some other animals, have minds," and that people do know both of these to be true. The first two of these are not addressed in *On Certainty*, merely forming an underlying assumption.

3 As retold by A.C. Grayling in his *Wittgenstein* (New York: Oxford University Press, 1988, p. 117). Grayling brings up this point in discussion of what some scholars consider a badly formed view of Wittgenstein's place in tradition: The context in which this is brought up is Grayling's statements to the end that: if, indeed, Wittgenstein is deserving of a place among the most influential philosophers of the century, as some apparently assert, then the misreading of Wittgenstein as less influential has not yet ceased.

4 Paul Ricoeur. *From Text To Action.* Chicago: Northwestern University, 1991, p. 57.

5 *Ibid.*, pp. 57.

6 Ludwig Wittgenstein. *On Certainty.* New York: Harper & Row, 1968, paragraph 58.

7 "The difference between the concept of 'knowing' and the concept of 'being certain' isn't of any great importance at all, except where "I know" is meant to mean: I *can't* be wrong" (Wittgenstein, 1969, paragraph 8).

8 *Ibid.*, paragraph 8.

9 *Ibid.*, paragraph 18.

10 A broad set of terms which are inter-translatable / interchangeable in their usage, to some extent. For example, the group of propositions, among which are "I believe/surmise/doubt/(am) convinced" (*Ibid.* paragraph 21) "I am certain of" "It is my unshakable conviction that..." (*Ibid..*, paragraph 103), etc.

11 *Ibid.*, paragraph 90.

12 Like that of a light bulb being switched on and off, for instance. This is the example of 'Drill teaching' found in the Blue Book area of Ludwig Wittgenstein, *The Blue and Brown Books* (New York: Harper & Rowe, 1958, pp. 12).

13 As exemplified in his famous 'Lecture on Ethics,' where, to indicate what he means by 'ethics,' he engages in a replacement game

using an "Ethics is..." motif, and eventually culminating in the statement that "... if you look at all of these phrases, you will get a rough idea as to what ethics is." (Oliver Johnson. *Ethics.* New York: Harcourt Brace, 1994, p.358).

14 "For a large class of cases... the meaning lies within the words use in the language." (Ludwig Wittgenstein. *Philosophical Investigations*. Englewood Cliffs, NJ: Prentice-Hall, 1958, paragraph 43).

15 Paul Ricoeur *From Text To Action,* p. 125.

16 *Ibid.*, p. 126.

17 *Ibid.*, p. 127.

18 *Ibid.*

19 *Ibid.*

20 "The Proposition is a picture of reality. The proposition is a model of reality as e know it." (Tractatus, 4.01) and actually shows reality (4.12 & 4.121), but the world, the reality, which such propositions make up has no visible subject, only perceivable objects (5.632 & 5.633), which it was the natural sciences' job to verify.

21 Ricoeur 1991, p. 57.

22 *Ibid.*, p. 130.

23 *Philosophical Investigations,* paragraph 133.

24 *The Blue and Brown Books*, pp. 44-45.

25 As when doubting that repetition creates veracity, c.f. *On Certainty*, p. 118.

References

Ayer, A.J. *Wittgenstein.* Chicago: University of Chicago Press, 1985.

Grayling, A.C. *Wittgenstein.* New York: Oxford University Press, 1988.

Johnson, Oliver. *Ethics.* New York: Harcourt Brace, 1994.

Ricoeur, Paul. *From Text To Action.* Chicago: Northwestern University, 1991.

Wittgenstein, Ludwig. *Philosophical Investigations.* Englewood Cliffs, NJ: Prentice-Hall, 1958.

________. *The Blue and Brown Books.* New York: Harper & Rowe, 1958.

________. *On Certainty.* New York: Harper & Row, 1968.

"HEAR SAY YES IN JOYCE": OTHERNESS, GENDER, AND DERRIDIAN REPETITION

Litia Perta
Vassar College

The paper, written as a response to a piece by Jacques Derrida entitled "Ulysses Gramophone: Hear Say Yes in Joyce," focuses primarily on the role of affirmation in communication, and on the role of communication within human reality. The question of self-hood is raised, and whether or not this self is compromised by the necessary externality surrounding linguistic communication. The mechanization of communication in the age of technological convenience is also explored, with particular focus on the absentminded repetition of the affirming Yes.

Yes.

Yes I am writing? Or: Yes you are reading? Or: Yes I am writing some thing, which you did not expect, Yes, you are right, this is unexpected. Yes, capitalized because it is the beginning of something. Beginning of writing, of being; of being a writing, and of writing a being. If I am writing I must be being and if you are reading you must be being, yes? So: Yes I am writing, Yes I am expecting that you will read. First, Yes: Yes I, Yes You. The problem of first, second is whether the yes first says I, or, in saying it, first assumes you.

In the early part of "Ulysses Gramophone: Hear Say Yes in Joyce," Derrida explains that the yes comes always as an answer. If the yes is always an answer, an answer to the summons of an other, is there not already a yes in the presupposed being of the other? The yes is then a constant answer to a constant question, the affirmation and necessity of reaffirmation of being. Its structure is always *a priori*: containing within it the necessity of affirmation as a verification of the fundamental lack in our being.

Derrida speaks of Joyce's Bloom as a being at the telephone, a being at the distance-voice. Bloom is all humankind. A being at the one side of a distance-voice: both the expectation and the being of a voice, always across an unfathomable distance. The distance is that of the perpetual separation of all *I*s from all *You*s. The very notion of I presupposes a You, always confirming the distance, the separation of each entity, and always placing one's self in necessary relation to the other. The being at the telephone becomes a symbol of the constant and primordial awareness of the self, of the other, and of the difference between them. To exist at the telephone is to wait for, and then answer Yes to, a calling from the outside. Acknowledging the distance at each moment, and the necessity of a communication, which might reach across it. To answer yes to a telephone call, one has acknowledged one's own need to be responded to at the same time as fulfilling the need of an other's seeking of a response. To be prepared to respond is to mark an other's being with the acknowledgement that they have called to you from an outside, which is their inside, and to which you are responding as their respective outside. We understand the distance but can not fathom its implications because we can never live, from experience, the existence of an other. We can only witness and affirm their being as one separate, but somehow similar, to our own.

Within this system of distance between You and I, there is a potentially more disturbing possibility that within the supposedly singular I there also exists an other. If the Yes on the telephone implies within it "Yes I can hear," it affirms something to an other outside the I, and becomes a response. In the very act of voicing the affirmation that "I can hear," in pushing it outward, a distance is established between the I of the inside and the I of the outside. An other is set up within the self. This becomes a further acknowledgment that what is accessible to me, of me, within me, is always different from what is accessible to you of a me, which, in being accessible to you, on my outside, is already a kind of outside me. An other is set up within the self. If this is disturbing, is it because there might be something foreign, inaccessible, in us? Or is it because this means that, despite our systems of language and of communication, what we are sending out and making available to the others around us remains eternally different from what exists inside our selves? If the other within, in setting up a difference between the realm of the inside and that of the outside, implies an I which is more me and a You which is more You, it also implies that the communication we experience is fundamentally lacking. Or, rather, that the communication, instead of diminishing the space between us, becomes another example of it. The I that is truly I can never speak to the I that is truly You, even when we are speaking.

Derrida explains that in what is referred to as Molly's monologue, "... she starts or finishes by saying yes to the other in herself..."[1] Who is the other in her self? Is this other the one identified above, the one who is her self, but her outward self, the self-available to others? Is she affirming the existence of this self in relation to her more inward self? Is her yes an acceptance of the distance and difference between the self she knows and the self others can know, both of which are in fact her self? It seems that her yes can be identified as a self-yessing, an affirmation of the self that others will relate with and respond to, one that is always apart from the self which is her constant experience. The yessing of this outward-bound self draws it closer to the inside being. Perhaps this yes is the attempt to bring the other further in, attempting to bring it ever closer to a merging of the two. A merge which is impossible. Her yes is possibly an affirmation and an acceptance of the distance between the beings of her one self. At the same time, it is an attempt to erase the difference, to erase the space, which allows for miscommunication with other, outside beings; to erase the inevitable distance, which causes us to feel always alone.

Perhaps, however, this yes to the other in her self is something very different. As it comes within the context of her remembering the marriage proposal of a lover, perhaps the yes means the acceptance and affirmation of the literal other which has made its way (or has been drawn?) inside her self. Perhaps the other is actually the incorporation into her being of the one she loves. Or, is it possible to understand it as a yes to the outward bound self of an other which has found its way into her self? This then would be the acceptance of the distance between the two different people; the acceptance within each person of two different beings, or modes of being, and the acceptance that the level of communication that two people can share is always one which occurs between the modes of being within each respective person which are least true to their actual selves. That is to say that if the outward-bound being is at some distance from the inner (and, thus, more real?) being, it is only the outward-bound beings which can communicate with each other; the intermediaries of the truer self. Thus, the other within her which Molly says yes to is possibly a literal other in her. The yes that she yesses to it is seems to be one of acceptance by way of sharing the space of her self with this other, or the acceptance that this is as close to sharing being/existence with someone as is possible. The acceptance that the outward being of someone is all she will ever know, but that her call for response is always directed toward the being of the inner self, the being of the first hand experience. The being of the other she will never hear from.

If Molly is saying yes to some form of her lover's being which has constituted an other inside her, is there also the possibility that the yes of Molly, of a woman, is distinct from that of a man? Derrida notes at one point that "...in Blanchot's *La folie du jour*, the quasi-narrator attributes the power to say yes to women, to the beauty of women, beautiful insofar as they say yes..."[2] Which power to say yes is being referred to? Does the sentence speak of man's specific power to say yes to woman because of a certain beauty she possesses? Or is it implying that the ability to say yes is exclusively a power of woman? What is special about woman which makes her capable of saying a yes which accepts, affirms, calls, and responds? Is it that she is readier to admit to the incompleteness of being, the necessity of the other for existence? Is this the beauty of the woman identity? That she accepts her lack, her need for the other, and thus, is able to call to it: offering the affirmation of her need, the purpose of the other, and thus, the being of both? Within this structure, the calling of woman allows man to be brought into being, at the same time as it assures that his importance will supercede her's. Her summons affirms the being of both, and affirms for both beings her need, and her incompleteness. Man takes on the role of entering and completing woman; and both parties, because of her admittance to the desire for completion, assume her to be the weaker sex.

Is there, then, the possibility that the Yes of which I have been writing, the Yes which is the presupposed necessity of our existence, the primordial yes, is engendered? Consider Derrida's idea that the Yes always contains within it the possibility of repetition, that the Yes is gramophonic. Taken literally, this implies that the Yes is a writing of voice, an inscription. In Judith Butler's essay "Phantasmatic Identification and the Assumption of Sex,"[3] the idea is put forth that a subject is constituted through the act of inscribing, through the writing of something into a being. Is it possible that if the gramophonic yes is the writing of voice, and a subject is created at the moment of inscription, then the moment of yes, being the moment of the inscription of voice onto a subject, the utterance of a simultaneous call and response, is also the moment in which gender is affirmed? If I as woman say yes to an other, and in my yes is a summons to the other to complete the incompleteness I feel, a call to have my being reaffirmed (through the response and through the call itself), the distinctive identity of woman as being the one who lacks has already been incorporated into the yes that I utter. Is your yes, as man, very different? If you, man, say yes to me, is your yes more of an explicit affirmation of our beings than it is a call for me to join you because you need me, because you need the other? Is gender present from the moment of the first inaugurative yes?

If gender is present from the beginning, does it have something to do with the intrinsic need for repetition found within the structures of both gender identity and the yes? In Derrida's text, he says that, "In order for the yes...to have the value it has, it must carry the repetition within itself."[4] Part of the essential structure of the yes lies in its reiterability, and in its previous reiteration in the memory of itself, *a priori*. In a similar way, the power of gender identity arises from its structural reiteration: it requires repetition in order to become an identity at all. Is it possible that the assigning of gender occurs within the first yes we are exposed to? Does the first yes occur seconds after a baby is born, at the moment someone cries, "it's a girl?" This is possibly the first affirmation of being we know as living creatures, it is the first moment in which we are spoken of as having traits, as having subjectivity. It is the first moment of the inscription of our beings. The inscription is one of voice, of the yes, and also one of gender, of the sex. Perhaps this is why even the inaugural first yes carries with it already the weight of gender. Perhaps it is as early as this moment when the repetition of each phenomena begins; when we hear for the first time what will be eternally repeated afterward of what sex we are, and when we first know the meaning of the ever calling yes. Perhaps it is this first time when we begin to understand whether we are the beings who admit to the incompleteness, or whether we belong to those who will constantly try to fulfill it. Perhaps it was in the hospital as a newborn baby when Molly was first taught that she would say yes to an other which was already inside her, inside her as a space, a space that asked to be filled. Perhaps she was always told she would say yes.

The structural reiterability of the yes, apart from any gender formation or speculation, presents itself as an anxiety throughout "Ulysses Gramophone." It is always possible for the yes to become a parody, to become mechanic, automatic, unfelt. This possibility lies in the same quality, which allows the yes its value in the first place: its *a priori* reiterability. This repetitive/inaugurative structure is what Derrida names the "gramophone effect." What causes the fear and disdain for this more robotic yes? Why is it that "...the most serious of all prayers...should never be allowed to become mechanical, to be gramophoned...?"[5] In what way does this automaticity lessen the importance of the yes? Is it because one or both parties involved are taking the fundamental affirmations of being for granted? Is it because it implies a lack of caring for the other, perhaps a lack of need, or at least a comfort in not having an other? Or is it best exemplified in the deceit of the answering machine? The machine that says, "Yes, I am here," that you speak to, but that can never respond, because you are deceived, there is nobody there. There is nobody across the distance-voice, nobody on the telephone. Does it frighten us that we might in fact be alone in our lonesomeness? Does the mechanical yes mark, or perhaps even widen, the space which is between us, which is always in the middle of us, separate and contained beings that we are? It seems our aversion to the mimetic parody of the otherwise initializing and beautiful yes is not dissimilar to the contempt we have for the parasitic citationality of gender identity as explained in Butler's *Bodies That Matter.*

Within the programming and adoption of gender identity, it is absolutely necessary to constantly reaffirm which gender one has, which gender one has been given. The reaffirmation occurs through speech, clothing, dress, expectations, perceptions, etc., and is perpetual. There is no one signifying moment in which gender is wholly and totally adopted, and as of yet, no one moment in which it is abandoned either. This is the structure of identity in general. An identity must be constantly repeated, and reaffirmed if it is to truly be an identity. This necessity of repetition implies a fundamental instability within the framework of identity and its operation. As Butler points out, the fact that gender can not be given in one moment, or determined in one defining act or instant, suggests that it is neither intrinsic, nor essential. The fact that identities often seem unshakable in their naturality reinforces their fundamental deception: they must seem strong and immutable in order to attract and function. The more they are adopted and reiterated, the stronger they become. Is our disdain for the automatic yes associated with our disdain for the falsity encountered in the identity structure's need for reiterability?

If it is precisely the need to be constantly reiterated which makes us aware of the fundamental weakness of identities, does the structural necessity of the reiterability of the yes make us skeptical of the yes also? What are the implications of a mechanical yes? What does it mean that the yes also requires repetition to function? Does it too contain a fundamental weakness? It seems we may be frightened of the possibility that our being, and the system we have for the reaffirmation of our being by and through others, is possibly as weak at its core as the constructions of gender identity. The yes as affirmation and reaffirmation, as call and response, does take place in one act, in one moment, but it also takes place in many. It takes place in one moment, defined by the telephonic hello, or the telephonic yes. A call is sent out and the being of the sender is affirmed, simultaneous to the expectation of response affirming the being of the other, and the openness of both entities affirms the possibility of alliance and togetherness, the possibility of communication with each other. This happens all in one instant, in the very utterance of yes, the Yes which contains already within it both memory and futurity. Despite this, however, despite the fact that the yes can yes in the one singular moment of saying yes to an other, it does not eliminate the necessity of repetition. This one singular yes is not enough. Another moment and another yes is to follow. The yes is the precondition for responding or reacting or interacting at all with any other being outside the self. So, the yes, as found with identity, is also not a singularly definable, and therefore immutable, structure. When we consider that the sincerity of the call, of the yes, is always already in question because we are forever removed from the other, it becomes obvious that to mechanize the voice only intensifies the distance between us. The mechanical yes is the materialization of the fears inherent in a system of affirmation of being which is fundamentally based on the sociality of others; others of whom, in their distance, one can never be certain.

Does it frighten us that the patterns and systems we have developed to try and overcome the inevitable distance between us and the other are fundamentally unstable? Are they truly unstable? Is it possible that any system, which asks us to move outside the self and interact with others, is predestined to be uncertain? Is this why there is the constant need to repeat the yes? Is this why the yes contains already within it the promise of its own repetition?

Within the realm of identity, and its structurally necessary repetition, Butler points out a freedom insofar as the need to reiterate demonstrates the insecurity of the supposed power of a given identity. When identities, particularly those of sex or gender, become confining, it is important to be aware that an identity is inherently collapsible. This awareness opens up a space of new identity, perhaps intermediary identity, standing in until there is the possibility of no necessary identity at all. Is the loss of identity the fathomable ideal in terms of communication with the other? Do we try so desperately, through discourse and theory, to define the parameters of identity, in order to escape from them? What is this attempt at escape? Is it possible that we try to escape from our given identities for the same reason that, many paragraphs ago, Molly said yes to the other in her self? If we understand Molly's other to be her outward bound self, the foreign of her within her, this is, in some sense, Molly's identity. She says yes to it, admits it, affirms it, accepts it and responds to it, in hopes of lessening the distance between this self, her identity, what is available to others, and the self which holds her always conscious being, *her* self. Is our deconstruction of identity through discourse a similarly motivated action, carried out differently? By shedding our prescribed identities, we open up the possibility of feeling more "real," perhaps truer to ourselves. When we attempt to understand and thus abandon our identities, we are attempting to decrease the distance within our own beings between the outward-bound self and the inner self. If it is possible to decrease this distance within the self, a new kind of security in the communication we can have with the other, a new kind of security in the yes, might arise. If the distance between the selves within each person is diminished, then it becomes possible that the distance between the I and the You might also be diminished, offering a more complete communication. Offering the lessening of the space between the I and the other, a lessening of the difference of beings. Offering, ultimately, the possibility of a truer, clearer Yes.

"Here Say Yes in Joyce"

NOTES

---

[1] Derrida, p. 66.

[2] *Ibid.* p. 53.

[3] Chapter 3 of *Bodies That Matter,* pp. 93-122.

[4] Derrida. p. 43.

[5] *Ibid.* p. 38.

References

Butler, Judith. *Bodies That Matter.* New York: Routledge, 1993.

Derrida, Jacques. "Ulysses Gramophone: Hear say yes in Joyce," in *James Joyce: The Augmented Ninth*, edited by Bernard Benstock. Syracuse, NY: Syracuse University Press, 1988. Pp. 27-75.

A CRITICAL RE-EVALUATION OF THE ESOTERIC CHARACTER OF MAIMONIDES' *GUIDE OF THE PERPLEXED*

Michael L. Frazer
Yale University

It is impossible for the modern student of the *Guide of the Perplexed* to escape the esotericist school of Leo Strauss. Maimonides' philosophical opus is now widely agreed to be a work meant for a learned elite that can only be understood if one, to use a dead metaphor, is willing to read between the lines. This view has in the past few decades led to a full reappraisal of almost all of Maimonides' treatise. Strangely, however, one essential section of the *Guide* has not been critically re-evaluated—those very passages dealing with the esoteric nature of the work itself. After discussing the nature of an esoteric text and examining a number of rival esoteric interpretive techniques, this paper will apply these techniques to passages in the *Guide* which discuss the treatise's "secrets." When interpretive techniques based on the assumption that the *Guide* is an esoteric work are applied to Maimonides' description of his work as esoteric, one must confront the possibility that the work may not be esoteric at all. It will become evident that to solve this scholarly liar's paradox will require an examination of the subtle conflict between religious law and philosophy in the Middle Eastern Jewish communities of Maimonides' day.

It is impossible for the modern student of Maimonides to escape the influence of Leo Strauss. Over the past fifty years, the Straussian methodology has led to a nearly full re-examination of *The Guide of the Perplexed* in light of the treatise's status as part of an esoteric tradition outlined in Strauss's *Persecution and the Art of Writing*. Maimonides' *Guide* is now almost universally seen as a work meant for a learned elite that can only be understood if one, to use a dead metaphor, is willing to read between the lines. Strauss could hardly be said to have discovered this essential truth of Maimonidean interpretation, however. The twelfth-century thinker makes the esoteric nature of his treatise explicitly clear within the treatise itself, most notably in the introduction instructing all on the proper manner of studying the *Guide*. Commentators as early as Samuel Ibn Tibbon, the translator of the *Guide* into Hebrew and a proponent of an esoteric reading of the work, had focused on these introductory passages even as their author was still living. Strauss can legitimately be credited, however, with sparking renewed interest in this fascinating aspect of the treatise, leading to a full scholarly re-appraisal of the passages in the *Guide* on such fundamental aspects of Maimonides' thought as prophecy, providence, and the creation of the world. Strangely, however, one essential section of the *Guide* has not been re-evaluated using the techniques developed by Strauss and his followers—those very passages dealing with the esoteric nature of the treatise. While undermining the apparent meaning of the text repeatedly with regard to religious and philosophical doctrines, the esotericists refuse to question the truth of Maimonides' declarations concerning the character of his work. There is no reason why the methodology used for analyzing the rest of the *Guide* cannot be used for analyzing these passages, however. The Straussian project can only be completed when its techniques are carefully applied even to the texts that form the basis for undertaking this project; such scholarly self-criticism is bound to have profound repercussions.

Before any self-criticism can begin, however, it is first necessary to clarify what exactly is meant when the *Guide* is referred to as an esoteric work, for Maimonides himself never uses the term. A work may be esoteric in terms of the audience for which it is intended, that is, if its proposed readership is limited to a select circle based on interest or ability. A superficial reading of the *Guide* makes it clear that the work is esoteric in this sense, for Maimonides time and again insists that his work on the true science of the law is designed only for those who are thoroughly prepared for that difficult discipline. A work may also be esoteric, not in terms of its intended audience, but in terms of the method of its composition. Such a text functions simultaneously on two levels—with a superficial meaning accessible to all and a hidden, inner meaning accessible to only the very few capable of a properly close reading. For the medievals, Maimonides included, the classic example of a compositionally esoteric text *par excellence* is the Bible. Indeed, Maimonides seems to make clear in his introduction that the very purpose of the *Guide* is to explain the ambiguous terms and parables that hide the inner meaning of the Law and Prophets. This esoteric interpretation, not "the legalistic study of the Law" (*fiqh* in Arabic or *halakhah* in Hebrew), is "the science of the Law in its true sense."[1] While the Bible is by no means an esoteric work of the first type (its regular reading is obligatory for all), it is of course possible for a work to be esoteric in both senses of the term. It is Strauss's insistence that the *Guide* is an esoteric work in terms of its method of composition as well as its intended audience (that is, an esoteric work in the manner that the Bible on which it is a commentary is an esoteric work) which is the basis of his technique for interpreting the true teachings of Maimonides. "The Guide is, then, devoted to the esoteric explanation of an esoteric doctrine," Strauss concludes. "Consequently it is a book with seven seals. How can we unseal it?"[2]

It is this methodological question which is the central problem of the Straussian interpretation of the *Guide*, and it is this question which must be answered before any analysis of the text's claims about itself can be made. Strauss is provided with a good starting point for his methodological investigation by the fact that Maimonides held the Bible not to be just one of many esoteric works, but the most perfect esoteric work possible. It would be illogical, then, not to model the esoteric compositional techniques used in the *Guide* on the esoteric techniques used in the Bible. "Therefore," says Strauss "if we wish to understand the *Guide*, we must read it according to the rules which Maimonides applies in that work to the explanation of the Bible."[3] The main problem with this starting point, however, is that the Bible and the *Guide* use very different means of masking their hidden teachings. The Bible, as has already been discussed, uses ambiguous words and parables to present deep truths to the elite while simultaneously hiding them from the vulgar. While the *Guide* certainly could be seen as using ambiguous terms, and perhaps even parables (such as the education of Joseph ben Judah or the aborted composition of the exoteric treatises), they are not the work's primary compositional tools. The primary esoteric technique of the *Guide* is instead contradiction, as is made clear when the subject of contradiction is suddenly and unexpectedly raised at the end of the Introduction. Leaving the reader to determine the connection between this discussion and the discussion of his work's esoteric character, which has come before, Maimonides abruptly announces that "one of seven causes should account for the contradictory or contrary statements to be found in any book or compilation."[4] He attributes the divergences in his treatise to the fifth and seventh causes, with the former requiring contradiction for pedagogic purposes of gradually revealing the truth to the ignorant and the latter requiring contradiction for hiding that which must be hidden from the vulgar but can be revealed to men of wisdom. "Know this, grasp its true meaning, and remember it very well," Maimonides admonishes his reader, "so as not to become perplexed by some of its [i.e., the *Guide*'s] chapters."[5] Strauss takes these words on face value, seeing them as a clear declaration that Maimonides has turned away from the parabolic language of the Bible to use his own esoteric technique of contradictions, contradictions hidden among an overwhelming quantity of enigmatic or even false non-parabolic statements.

There is widespread agreement that Strauss has correctly identified the primary task of an interpreter of the *Guide*, the task of identifying the treatise's contradictions and determining which of its contradictory assertions are the author's true opinions. His method for accomplishing this task, however, strikes many as overly mechanical and arbitrary. Since the true teaching of an esoteric work must be hidden to all but the most careful reader, the preponderance of false or exoteric statements must overwhelm the isolated moments when the inner truth is revealed. "We may therefore establish the rule that of two contradictory statements in the *Guide* or in any other work of Maimonides," Strauss reasons, "that statement which occurs less frequently, or even which occurs only once, was considered by him to be true."[6] Such a view is suggested by Maimonides' statement in the Introduction to the *Guide* that the truth will be revealed in his treatise like flashes of lightning. Strauss himself points to the Biblical exegesis in Maimonides' *Essay on Resurrection,* since it has already been established that the same techniques used by Maimonides to interpret the Bible should in turn are used to interpret Maimonides. In this essay, the author accepts the truth of two verses in Daniel supporting bodily resurrection over countless Biblical passages that seem to reject the very possibility of such a miracle. Strauss's analysis, however, implies a shockingly superficial reading of both the *Guide* and the *Essay*. It seems very odd that Strauss, the great advocate of esotericism as the only response to the persecution of philosophers, bases his methodology on the literal meaning of an apologetic essay Maimonides was forced to write to defend himself against charges of heresy. Even accepting the literal text of the essay as reflecting a true teaching of the accused author, Maimonides never rejects the Biblical passages which seemingly deny the possibility of resurrection as false and exoteric teachings designed to hide the divine truth of Daniel. Instead, they are descriptions of "the customary, familiar pattern of existence" which are true insofar as the miracle described in Daniel violates all of the laws under which nature usually operates.[7] Indeed, the truth of resurrection is not esoteric at all, but a basic principle of the Jewish faith, and Maimonides seeks in his essay to make the truth of this dogma so clear that "even women and ignorant folk will understand."[8] While Strauss is correct in noting that the rarity of a Biblical statement makes it no less true, it also makes it no more true. Maimonides must have other grounds for determining whether a Biblical verse is literally true as stated or figuratively true as a parable. The reader of Maimonides must therefore also look for other grounds to determine which of any pair of contradictory statements in the *Guide* is the author's genuine view. While the rarity of a contradicted statement might be a clue that such a statement is preferable to its more commonly mentioned contradiction, it cannot be the final word on the subject. Indeed, Strauss makes it clear that his rule is not the only possible method for an esoteric reading of the *Guide*, filled as the treatise is with ambiguous words and enigmatic sentences.

In his relatively recent book *Interpreting Maimonides*, Marvin Fox presents one of the most systematic critiques of Strauss's superficial method for reading the Guide. Fox bases his criticism on Strauss's failing to make use of the categories of Aristotelian logic with which Maimonides was most surely familiar, not only as a medieval Aristotelian, but as the author of a respected treatise on logic. According to Aristotle, contradictions are statements that cannot both be true or both be false. Contraries, on the other hand, cannot both be true but may both be false, and subcontraries (often included under the larger umbrella of contraries) cannot both be false but may both be true.[9] While Strauss speaks generally of "contradictions," the seven causes discussed by Maimonides at the end of the introduction are specifically causes of "contradictory or contrary statements," and these terms carry a very precise meaning. Most importantly, they apply only to statements, and any inconsistency between a statement and an action or a statement and a normative law is not technically a contradiction. These formal, logical terms suggest a formal, logical method for determining which of any two contradictory statements in the *Guide* one is to accept as the author's true opinion. Maimonides provides such a technique, in a later chapter in Book I, by railing against those who "hasten to pronounce false, assertions the contradictories of which have not been demonstrated."[10] That is, when faced with two contradictory statements in his or any other work, the wise reader will reject one of the two statements if and only if its contradictory has been logically proven true. Rather than a mechanical analysis of how often statements are repeated, it is this technique that Maimonides uses in his esoteric analysis of the Bible. The literal meaning of a Biblical passage is rejected and its inner meaning is analyzed (for no Biblical passage is merely false) only when the contradictory of the literal meaning of the passage is indubitably demonstrated. "I fall back on interpreting a statement only when its literal sense is impossible; like the corporeality of God," Maimonides explains in the *Essay on Resurrection*. "The possible however remains as stated."[11]

Note that Maimonides does not hold that a statement should be accepted as true only if it is demonstrated to be so, but that it only should be dismissed as false if its contradictory is so demonstrated. This begs the question of how one should treat a statement in a work which has neither been demonstrated true nor proven false through the demonstration of its contradiction, let alone how one should treat two contradictory statements within a work, neither of which can be demonstrated. This is especially troublesome if Fox is correct in positing that Maimonides held that no singular proportions (statements with a proper or particular noun as their subject) could be demonstrably true under ordinary logic.[12] Much of the *Guide* (as a work of divine science) consists of statements with "God" as their subject, and many of these statements are contradictory. The particular subject of this essay consists almost entirely of singular propositions, many of which have "*The Guide of the Perplexed*" as their subject. Since it leaves the reader uncertain as to so many contradictories, logical demonstration is an insufficient tool for determining the true meaning of Maimonides' esoteric writing. While perhaps useful in isolated instances, it cannot be the primary means of determining how to treat contradictory or contrary statements in the *Guide*.

Aside from contradictory statements, however, there are a great many inconsistencies in the *Guide* which Strauss referred to loosely as "contradictions" but which are not so strictly speaking. Fox notes that Maimonides does something curious concerning the terms used to describe these inconsistencies in the final section of the Introduction. While the seven causes therein are introduced as offering explanations for "contradictory or contrary statements," when the causes are applied to the particular cases of both philosophical works and the *Guide* itself a new term is introduced, that of "divergences," *ikhtilaf* in Arabic.[13] "As for the divergences occurring in the books of the philosophers, or rather those who know the truth, they are due to the fifth cause," Maimonides explains. "Divergences that are to be found in this treatise," he says later, "are due to the fifth cause and the seventh. Know this..."[14] Fox notes that, unlike contradictions, divergences have no formal meaning under Aristotelian logic, suggesting that this term might refer to all types of inconsistencies, including contradictions and contraries but in no way limited to them. In this subtle way, Maimonides may have alerted the reader that divergences generally (such as between statements and actions, or statements and laws), rather than only contradictions and contraries, are the keys to unlocking the secrets of the *Guide*. Indeed, Fox notes that many of the "contradictions" discussed by Strauss and his followers are in fact other types of divergences, and thus cannot be analyzed through the processes of logical demonstration. Fox suggests the only possible approach to such divergences, especially those between philosophical truths and religious commands, is to learn "the great art of balancing," rejecting neither of the alternatives as false or exoteric.[15] The divergences would then be of no help in discovering the esoteric teachings of the *Guide*, however, reflecting no meaning deeper than their very inconsistency. While Fox may be an astute reader of the *Guide* in demonstrating that Strauss' methodology was far too simplistic, one must look elsewhere to discover an acceptable technique for analyzing the divergences (as it is now clear they are properly called) in Maimonides' work.

The nature and purpose of esotericism suggest one such attractive technique, for one does not hide a truth as "secret" unless there is a need to conceal this truth from all but a select few. The author may be acting from fear of persecution (as is discussed at length in the titular essay of Strauss's *Persecution and the Art of Writing*) or from pedagogic or political concerns for the well-being of the ignorant (as must be the case with the Bible, for none could persecute its author), but he must always have some compelling reason to write esoterically. If a statement were fully consistent with the common beliefs in the author's community at the time of his writing, to hide it with parables and contradictions would be entirely pointless. Although the task of determining the common beliefs of Plato's Athens or Confucius' China might be difficult work best left to historians familiar with the period, there is a simple way to determine what beliefs predominated in the Jewish community of Maimonides' day. The vast majority of medieval Jewry was governed absolutely in both thought and action by the dictates of Talmudic Law. Schooled thoroughly in the *fiqh* as outlined in the Talmud and codified in Maimonides' popular legal opus the *Mishneh Torah*, they were almost all wholly ignorant of philosophy or the "science of the Law in the true sense." The obvious response to a divergence in the *Guide* is thus to reject as exoteric the statement (or action or law) which is consistent with the Talmud and the *Mishneh Torah* and accept as the author's true opinion the truth which stands in opposition to these works that were commonly accepted as authoritative. This technique was adopted as early as Ibn Tibbon, who, as one modern commentator explains, understood that "the interpreter need not be troubled by contradictions when one assertion is consistent with the 'philosophic view' whereas the other is completely satisfactory to 'men of religion' (or 'men of religion of our time')."[16] The latter are clearly "said truly" while the former are "said for purposes of concealment."[17] Problems arise when there is a divergence between views that strike middle positions that are neither clearly Talmudic nor clearly philosophic (one of which is the subject of Ibn Tibbon's famous unanswered letter to Maimonides on providence), or when there is no definite Talmudic principle for the subject matter in question. Nonetheless, the interpretive method suggested by one of the first of Maimonides' commentators would be the primary technique adopted by this essay in its analysis of the *Guide*'s claims about itself.

The main advantage of such a methodology is not that it has a wider range of applications than the virtually unusable technique suggested by Fox, though this is indeed important. Instead, note that Ibn Tibbon's methodology, unlike those of Strauss and Fox, is arrived at independent of any particular methodological statements made within the *Guide*. These assertions ought not to have been accepted unquestioningly by those who maintain that the *Guide* is an esoteric work. To base one's methodology on "what Maimonides made explicit to his readers"[18] or "the method that Maimonides himself set forth"[19] is to assume that the passages so discussed reflect true and not merely exoteric teachings, an assumption one should not make until after having developed an interpretive methodology. Only when Ibn Tibbon's technique fails or is inapplicable should one turn to less well-established techniques whose validity depend on the superficial truth of certain statements in the *Guide*.

Of course, there is much more required for discovering the inner truths of the *Guide* than merely a method for resolving divergences. An acceptably close reading will also be on the watch for ambiguous terms or parables, indeed, for any literary or philosophical device that might be used to hide the author's actual intention. While one should not naively accept Maimonides' claim that "the diction of the Treatise has not been chosen at haphazard, but with great exactness and exceeding precision,"[20] every word must be scrutinized as if this were the case. Different techniques may therefore be required to resolve different divergences; other divergences may have to remain unresolved, but may point to a larger truth; many other puzzles will have to be left unsolved entirely. Remember as well that there are two different questions to be answered when analyzing the treatise esoterically to determine its true character, one corresponding to the two possible meanings of the term esoteric. First, what is the intended audience for the work? Second, is the work composed so as to conceal a "secret" truth?

Throughout this analysis it is critical to keep a certain critical fact forever at the front of one's mind: The Talmud prohibited revelation of the Bible's divine secrets to the masses. In the injunction most commonly quoted by Maimonides, an injunction which he repeatedly praises as quite sagacious, these secrets are loosely grouped into two categories, the Account of the Beginning (*ma'aseh bereshit*), and the Account of the Chariot (*ma'aseh merkabah*). The former literally refers to the secrets of Genesis and the latter to the secrets of Ezekiel, but Maimonides identifies them with the secrets of the natural and divine sciences respectively. "The Account of the Beginning ought not to be taught in the presence of two men," the Talmud commands. As for the Account of the Chariot, it must not be taught "even to one man, except if he be wise and able to understand by himself, in which case only the chapter headings may be transmitted to him."[21] Maimonides understands that "if someone explained all of those matters in a book, he in effect would be teaching them to thousands of men."[22] The divine Torah is not guilty of violating this precept, however, for it always speaks of such matters "in riddles and parables,"[23] that is, esoterically. Maimonides, however, seems to write quite clearly in the *Guide* about the Account of the Beginning and the Account of the Chariot. Not only does the *Guide* consist of virtually nothing but discussions of natural and divine science, but Maimonides also engages in extended commentaries on Genesis and Ezekiel 1. Any discussion of the *Guide*'s true character must be informed by the fact that, if it is not an esoteric work in at least one of the two senses of the term (or preferably both), the very composition of the work is a direct violation of Talmudic law.

From the words of the dedicatory epistle of the *Guide*, it might seem that Maimonides is following the Talmudic law concerning the Account of the Chariot to the letter. This would only be the case if the intended audience for the treatise consists of one man, a man who is already "wise and able to understand by himself." Luckily, the *Guide* in its entirety is addressed solely to one such man, a certain Joseph, son of Rabbi Judah. Great pains are taken to show that this Joseph meets the *halakhic* requirements for a student of the Account of the Chariot. Maimonides recounts in this opening letter his time spent with this particularly eager and gifted student, a student who had traveled great distances to study with the Master after having demonstrated his ability in eloquent letters of rhyming prose. Maimonides first systematically tutored the youth in all the disciplines of medieval philosophy, and only then began to reveal to him "certain flashes" of the secrets of the divine books. As Joseph learned of philosophy and the *Kalam* in a disorderly manner from men other than Maimonides, however, he became increasingly perplexed. At this time, Joseph was forced to leave his teacher, but Maimonides was determined not to let his education end while the boy was still in such a state, arousing in the Master "a resolution that had slackened."[24] He therefore began to compose a treatise, or perhaps worked to complete a treatise earlier left unfinished. He is now sending the work to Joseph in "dispersed" chapters, which will reach the student, "one after the other,"[25] a quite literal transmission of the "chapter headings." As a private correspondence between teacher and student, the *Guide* in no way violates the commands of the Talmud.

Of course, the very fact that one can now read the *Guide* is evidence of a divergence from the *Guide*'s status as a private letter to a qualified student. Not only did Maimonides make the work public, but there is also evidence that he fully approved of Ibn Tibbon's translation of the *Guide* into Hebrew, an act that made the treatise available to all of world Jewry. This is a perfect example of a divergence between a statement and action, with the statement consistent with Talmudic Law and the action in violation of it. It is therefore safe to conclude that the *Guide* is not a private letter to Joseph.

This view is supported by Maimonides' statement to Joseph that the treatise is composed "for you and for those like you, however few they are."[26] This might be taken to mean that the story of Joseph's education is to be read as a parable, a parable illustrating the type of reader Maimonides intends for the *Guide*. While the Master cannot guarantee that only his pupil Joseph will read the treatise, he has written it with Joseph in mind, and holds that the work is only appropriate for those with all his student's qualifications. While this may not be obedience of the law to the letter, it is certainly in keeping with the spirit of the law, and absolves the author of responsibility when those prohibited from doing so read his work. Here too, however, there is an inconsistency, though one far more subtle and ambiguous in its implications. His account of Joseph's studies makes clear that Maimonides first taught Joseph mathematics, then astronomy, and then finally logic. It was when he was studying logic that the Master determined that flashes of the divine secrets could be revealed to the successful student. In a later chapter, however, Maimonides says "it is necessary for anyone who wishes to achieve human perfection to train himself at first in the art of logic, then in the mathematical sciences according to the proper order, then in the natural sciences [including, but not limited to, astronomy], and after that the divine science."[27] That is, accepting Strauss's dictum that there are no mistakes in the *Guide*, Maimonides' program of study for Joseph was not the same program of study he feels is necessary in preparation for the divine science. The discipline of logic, which convinced Maimonides that Joseph was at last ready to learn the Torah's secrets, is the most preliminary of disciplines in the usual program of study. While Joseph learned only astronomy, the usual program of study requires familiarity with all the natural sciences. In short, Joseph did not conduct his preliminary philosophical studies "according to the proper order." Might this suggest that Joseph is an exception to the norm, and that no conclusions about who is prepared to read the *Guide* can be drawn from his example? Perhaps, and this would mean that the secret of the intended audience for the treatise must be discovered outside of the confines of the dedicatory epistle.

The Introduction to the *Guide* notes quite early on that "it is not the purpose of this treatise to make its totality understandable to the vulgar or to beginners in speculation." Maimonides continues by insisting that the work is instead written for "a man perfect in his religion and character, and having studied the sciences of the philosophers and come to know what they signify." [28] More specifically, it is a few pages later made clear that the treatise is directed "to one who has philosophized and has knowledge of the true sciences, but believes at the same time in the matters pertaining to the Law and is perplexed as to their meaning because of the uncertain terms and the parables."[29] That is, it is written for one in the position of Joseph ben Judah. After only a few more pages, however, Maimonides greatly qualifies this view. He notes that "among men generally, every beginner will derive benefit from some of the chapters of this treatise, though he lacks even an inkling of what is involved in speculation. A perfect man, on the other hand… will benefit from all its chapters."[30] This must mean that the initial statement as to the *totality* of the *Guide* being unavailable to the vulgar means that, while some passages will surely baffle the mass of mankind, others sections will benefit even the most foolish. The study of the *Guide* would thus be useful for the vast majority of humanity, though, as with any book, the wise will benefit more from their more enlightened reading. There is a further clue that the *Guide* is not an esoteric work of the first type in the epigrams that begin the Introduction. The second of these three epigrams, the quotation most likely to be ignored by a careless reader, reads "Unto you, O men, I call / and my voice is to the sons of men."[31] These (literal) words of wisdom from Proverbs address the *Guide*, not to Joseph ben Judah or to only those who are already wise, but to every son of man.

An even more radical view is suggested by Maimonides' discussion of why he is entering into the dangerous project of explaining the secrets of the Torah, considering that he is at great risk of violating Talmudic Law. The second of his justifications, a Mishnaic quote declaring that his actions are for the sake of heaven, is relatively self-explanatory. The first justification is less clear, however, for the quote on which it is based is cut off halfway through. Maimonides announces that he will act according to the dictum "It is time to do something for the Lord, and so on," with the conclusion of the verse reading "for they have infringed Thy Law" strangely left out of the text.[32] While the first half of the verse alone could suggest that Maimonides is justified in his actions because he is acting for the sake of the Lord, this would mean the two distinct justifications are nothing more than repetitions of one another. The whole of the verse, however, implies that the treatise is necessary because of violations of the divine commandments, and that the knowledge contained in the treatise will lead to greater obedience of God's Law. This would mean that it is the sinful who need to come to know the truth of God's reign and the secrets of the Bible through the *Guide*, not the wise and virtuous who are already obeying His Law. This is the exact opposite of the view previously considered; while all men may benefit from a study of the *Guide*, including the wise and virtuous, it is designed primarily for those who falsely deny the validity of God's Law. That Maimonides repeatedly describes the *Guide* as a work only for a pious and learned elite by no means refutes such a view; for the true Straussian, it can only make this position even more convincing.

Under either the more radical or the more moderate of these two scenarios, one is left with the conclusion that the *Guide* is most certainly not an esoteric work in terms of its intended audience. Though Maimonides is now dangerously close to a violation of the Law (as is evidenced by the need he feels to justify his actions based on pious aphorisms) he is not truly guilty under the *fiqh* if his treatise is at least an esoteric work in terms of its composition. After all, the Bible itself is a work of this sort, with a superficial meaning beneficial to the vulgar and an inner meaning revealing the truth to the wise. While Strauss and Fox hold fast to Maimonides' assertions that his treatise is indeed compositionally esoteric, the passages in the *Guide* on this subject are riddled with ambiguities, divergences and even outright contradictions.

Perhaps the most obvious of these, a contradiction in the technical sense of the word, is to be found in Maimonides' analysis of the relative worth of the external and internal meanings of a parable, and by implication the external and internal meanings of any compositionally esoteric work. This is not a contradiction concerning the esoteric nature of the *Guide* as such, but a contradiction about the nature of esotericism generally which can illumine the nature of this allegedly esoteric work in particular. The contradiction stems from two seemingly inconsistent parables on the nature of parables. The first of these, from the Midrash, reads, "A man who loses a *sela* [a valuable coin] or a pearl in his house can find the pearl by lighting a taper worth an *issar* [1/96 of a *sela*]. In the same way this parable in itself is worth nothing, but by means of it you can understand the words of the Torah."[33] The second, from the Proverbs, reads, "A word fitly spoken is like apples of gold in settings of silver."[34] From the first of these, Maimonides concludes "the external meaning of all parables is worth nothing;" from the second, "Their external meaning contains wisdom that is useful in many respects, among which is the welfare of human societies... Their internal meaning, on the other hand, contains wisdom that is useful for beliefs concerned with the truth as it is."[35]

This contradiction, occurring as it does within the course of two pages, is one of the most obvious in the entire *Guide*. Fox's technique for determining which of the true is of no help here, for neither the proposition that "the external meaning of all parables is worth nothing" nor its contradictory is amenable to logical demonstration. Nor do either of the two contradictories superficially seem to coincide with or violate Talmudic law. It has already been established, however, that the *Guide* is not an esoteric work in terms of its intended audience. A reading of the treatise will therefore be of worth to even the vulgar and ignorant. It has not yet been made clear, however, whether the *Guide* is a compositionally esoteric work. If the treatise were such a work, the vulgar could not be expected to discover its secret teaching, so any value they might derive from its reading could only be a result of the worth of its external meaning. Were the external meaning of the esoteric work to be entirely worthless, the only value to be derived from any text would be its true teaching. This would mean that the vulgar would have to be able to understand the true teachings of the *Guide*, thereby proving it is not a compositionally esoteric work. If the external meaning of a parable is worthless, in other words, the *Guide* would have to be in violation of Talmudic Law. Ibn Tibbon's technique would thus imply that the true teaching of the Guide is that external meanings of parables are indeed worthless, and hence the *Guide* in violation of the *fiqh*. The exoteric statement that external meanings of parables are of worth is included so that the vulgar will not believe that Maimonides has violated the Law. There are problems with such an interpretation, however. First, the quote from the Midrash clearly misinterprets itself. The external meaning of a parable is not worthless under its pearl/taper trope; it is worth an *issar*, and an *issar* saved is an *issar* earned. Second, the contradiction seems far too obvious to be a valid esoteric teaching. Might not Maimonides have included such a blatant inconsistency so that those with only a minimal degree of philosophic training would jump to the conclusion implied by Ibn Tibbon's technique, while the truly wise would understand that the opposite was intended? There are no easy answers here, but it is clear that further investigation of the inconsistencies concerning the question of whether the *Guide* is a compositionally esoteric work is necessary.

While Maimonides indeed insists that his is an esoteric work of this type, it is notable that his discussion of contradictions and divergences is not presented as a discussion of the esoteric method used in his work. Indeed, by introducing this discussion as an explanation of "contradictory or contrary statements" but then discussing the "divergences" in his own work, Maimonides brings into question the centrality of inconsistency as a compositional technique in the writing of the *Guide*. Rather than divergence, Maimonides asserts that his treatise hides its inner teaching through its organizational structure, or, more properly, its lack thereof. Immediately after noting the Talmudic prohibitions concerning the Account of the Beginning and the Account of the Chariot, Maimonides asserts he will obey the prohibitions by not including anything in his work on these prohibited subjects other than the "chapter headings." Moreover, to insure that even these fragments of truth are inaccessible to those unqualified to learn of them, the chapter headings "are not set down or arranged in a coherent fashion in this treatise, but rather are scattered and entangled with other subjects that are to be clarified."[36] The esoteric method of the *Guide*'s composition is to be found in the treatise's lack of a systematic organizational structure, with the secrets of the Torah randomly scattered among its hundreds of pages. This position would justify the *Guide*'s obvious lack of organization, an apparent fault when contrasted with the brilliant schematization of the commandments in Maimonides' *Mishneh Torah*. Only a few pages after this assertion, however, Maimonides claims that in his work "nothing has been mentioned out of its place, save with a view to explaining some matter in its proper place."[37] The latter statement serves as the basis of Strauss's reading of the *Guide* in his introductory essay to the Pines translation. The esotericist herein turns away from his methodology based on "contradictions" and devotes himself primary to an arcane analysis of the complex and numerologically significant hidden structure of the apparently haphazardly constructed treatise.

Note, however, that these two assertions of the *Guide*'s esoteric organization are inconsistent with one another. The first proposition states that the secrets of the Account of the Beginning and the Account of the Chariot are scattered with genuine randomness throughout the work, requiring for their discovery a close reading of each and every passage in the *Guide*. The work's apparent lack of structure is then real, but the work is disorganized intentionally so that the vulgar will not discover the secrets hidden therein, and the Talmud's commands may be obeyed. The second proposition states that the work's lack of structure is only an illusion, and that one of the keys to discovering the hidden truths of the *Guide* is to discover its hidden organizational structure. Strauss's complex outline of the *Guide* with which he begins his introductory essay is a powerful tool for an analysis of the work under the second proposition, but it will only serve to further obscure the treatise's secrets under the first. So which of the two contradictory propositions is the *Guide*'s true teaching? Fox's methodology is of no use here, for both the statement "*The Guide of the Perplexed* lacks a coherent organizational structure" and its contradictory are singular propositions, and thus neither is demonstrably true under rules of ordinary logic. Nor is Strauss' methodology helpful, for the work's discussions of its own structure are confined almost exclusively to this introductory section and these two inconsistent statements within it. Even Ibn Tibbon's technique is inapplicable in this instance, for the *Guide* remains a compositionally esoteric work whether its secrets are hidden through a secret organization or through intentional disorganization, and thus both statements are equally compatible with Talmudic Law. One could attempt to harmonize the apparent contradiction, perhaps interpreting the phrase "save with a view to explaining some matter in its proper place" as referring to the fact that while the exoteric teachings of the *Guide* are well-organized, the secret teachings are kept in their proper (secret) place through their random dispersal amongst this organized whole. Another possibility is that the statements could be harmonized because they are not truly contradictory, but instead contrary. The first statement should be formulated to read "*The Guide of the Perplexed* hides its secret teaching through the lack of a coherent structure," while the second should be formulated to read "*The Guide of the Perplexed* hides its secret teaching through a secret coherent structure." While these two statements cannot both be true, they can both be false if the *Guide* has no secret teaching, that is, if it is not an esoteric work of the second type.

There are countless "flashes" indicating that the treatise is not esoteric in this sense. One of the clearest of these is based on the fact that, if the *Guide* is indeed a compositionally esoteric work, then it is critical that its secret teaching, once discovered, is not made plain to the masses. Maimonides (at least superficially) accepts the Talmud's injunctions against revealing the secrets of the Torah to the vulgar as wise and just; the story of his aborted attempt to write exoteric commentaries explaining these secrets reinforces this view. The same rule must therefore prohibit exoteric commentaries on the *Guide* itself. If the *Guide* is indeed a compositionally esoteric commentary on the Law and Prophets, which are themselves also esoteric works of this type, then the secret teaching of the *Guide* is identical with the legally protected secret teaching of the Torah. Maimonides therefore vehemently ("by God, may he be exalted!") admonishes the reader "not to comment upon a single word of it [the *Guide*] and not to explain to another anything in it."[38] As has already been discussed, however, the author is known to have been quite satisfied with Ibn Tibbon's translation of the *Guide*. As his discussion of Onqelos' Aramaic *Targum* demonstrates, Maimonides understood that translation is a form of commentary. His letters also make clear that Maimonides happily answered some, but not all, of his translator's stylistic and philosophical questions about the treatise.[39] Here there is a divergence, not between a statement and an action as such, but between an imperative and an action. The position of the Law, and hence the conclusion to be drawn from this divergence, is clear.

There are many other "flashes" alluding to the possibility that the *Guide* might not be an esoteric work in either of the two senses of the term. They come, as Maimonides said they would, scattered throughout the treatise. Here and there, chapters arise which discuss the Talmudic prohibitions of teaching the secrets of the Torah, interrupting other thematic units in the *Guide*. In the first book, for example, a chapter (I: 17) devoted to the wisdom of the law prohibiting the teaching of the Account of the Beginning to the vulgar appears to have no connection to the so-called lexicographical chapters (Strauss's term for chapters devoted to the explanation of a particular ambiguous word in the Bible beginning with a statement of that word in Hebrew) surrounding it. Yet the chapter immediately following this one is devoted to the terms "to approach [*qarob*], to touch [*nago'a*]" and "to come near [*nagosh*]."[40] Is one to accept this as merely a result of the *Guide*'s random structure, or, following Strauss's methodology in his introductory essay, is Maimonides suggesting that the prohibited study of the Account of the Beginning is indeed approachable? Five later chapters (I:31-35) on the limits of the human mind and the need for the majority to refrain from studying divine science are placed between a lexicographical chapter on the words meaning to eat (which Maimonides sees as symbolic of knowledge) and a non-lexicographical chapter discussing what it means to say something pleases or angers God. Might this not suggest that all having knowledge of the divine science is pleasing to God, while a human mind that is content to stay within meager limits angers him? None of these hints is definitive, and this issue merits a thorough study beyond the scope of this essay. The possibility that the *Guide* may not be intended as an esoteric work at all, however, must be considered by any who wish to interpret the work esoterically.

How can such a possibility be conceived? The *Guide* is by no means a simplistic work, one whose every teaching is easily accessible to all who might read it. There are many ways, however, to view the work as fundamentally exoteric. A traditionally pious option, one called the "Moderate-Harmonistic Interpretation" by contemporary scholar Aviezer Ravitzky,[41] might choose to see the work as compatible on all possible levels with the religion of the Jewish community. Any divergences could then be harmonized, and any ambiguous terms explained away, such that the true meaning of the text is the same as its superficial meaning, both of which are identical with the Talmud's traditional teachings. While the vulgar might not understand all this, the more they study the *Guide*, the stronger their humble piety will become. All of Maimonides' talk of esotericism becomes nothing more than further evidence of his piety, reflecting an excessive scrupulousness in observing the law at the expense of misguiding some as to the true nature of his work. A far more radical alternative is that the *Guide* is a fundamentally incoherent and misguided work, attempting to unite Jewish piety with Aristotelian philosophy when the two are wholly incompatible. Its contradictions are nothing more than contradictions; its ambiguities reflect not profundity but uncertainty and ignorance. Claims of esotericism reflect not so much a desire to obey the Law as a need to mask the work's unavoidable flaws; they can make sloppy thinking look like the key to a hidden truth.

Neither of these alternatives is acceptable for the modern student of Maimonides, however. The former denies the obvious inconsistencies within the *Guide*; the latter denies its obvious genius. Perhaps the answer lies in Maimonides' insistence that human perfection can only come through the true science of the Law, and that the truths of God's unity and incorporeality "ought to be made clear and explained to everyone according to his capacity."[42] If Maimonides' goal was to bring about the perfection of all his fellow Jews, then he must have desired that they become students of the divine science, more specifically, that they "constantly study this [his] treatise" on the subject.[43] This study need not, indeed, ought not, be limited to only a small elite. A tradition had already been established of mass education in the medieval Jewish community, centuries before most of their gentile neighbors even considered literacy worth attaining. This tradition, however, was limited to the legalistic study of the law, the *fiqh* of the Talmud as summarized in Maimonides' *Mishneh Torah.* Since it is the true science of the law, however, which leads to human perfection, Maimonides' conviction that the study of the *Guide* would be of benefit to all must be interpreted to mean that he wished the divine science to take its place alongside the *fiqh* in the education of the mass of world Jewry. The author's treatise would then take its place next to his law code in synagogues and study halls across the face of the earth.

There were two great obstacles that prevented Maimonides from achieving his goal, however, one legal and the other sociological. As has already been seen, the *fiqh*, desiring to maintain its hegemony over the Jewish mind, had prohibited the mass study of the true science of the Law. Maimonides knew he could not blatantly violate a Talmudic prohibition, nor did he have any desire to do so. He sought to supplement the *fiqh* with the divine science, not replace it, for central to his thought was the importance of *halakhic* obedience for both societal harmony and individual perfection. It has already been shown that a claim of esotericism allowed Maimonides to avoid violating this prohibition while at the same time teaching the true science of the Law to thousands. The Talmudic prohibition, however, reflected a more general feeling of hostility toward the divine science (and the Aristotelian philosophy with which it is intimately related, if not identical) within the Jewish community. "Whoever considers four things does not deserve to have come into the world," said one popular Talmudic aphorism, "[namely, he who considers] what is above, what is below, what is in front, and what is behind."[44] Maimonides would have to overcome this bias against speculation in order to encourage widespread study of the divine science.

A claim that his work was esoteric could be understood as Maimonides' primary technique in carrying out this difficult project. Only by suggesting that divine secrets were hidden amongst its discussions of Aristotelian philosophy could Maimonides convince a pious student of the Law to read the long passages of seemingly gentile thought contained in the *Guide*. Only the search for such secrets could lead such a man to spend great stretches of time, time which could otherwise be devoted to the *fiqh*, poring over the treatise's every word. The ambiguities and inconsistencies within the *Guide* would lead to further study, as the student wrestles with the perhaps unachievable task of resolving the work's divergences and piecing together its dispersed chapter headings. In order even to be deemed worthy of reading the work, however, he would also have to study all the disciplines of medieval philosophy, disciplines such as the natural sciences, which he would otherwise have neither the need nor the inclination to learn. In this way, the divergences in the *Guide* would indeed have the pedagogic value that Maimonides ascribes to them under the fifth cause for contradictions, though not quite in the way Maimonides describes. Rather than gradually revealing the truth to ignorant students, the *Guide*'s supposedly esoteric nature acclimates first individuals and then whole communities to the enlightenment brought by philosophy, a field of study which before the appearance of the *Guide* they had treated with outright hostility.

As might have been expected, this re-evaluation of the *Guide*'s esoteric character has raised more questions than it has answered. It has been made clear that the work is not esoteric in terms of its intended audience, but the more important issue of whether the treatise is esoteric in terms of its method of composition remains unresolved and, perhaps, unresolvable. There is no reason, however, to begin addressing the secrets of the *Guide* by ignoring what is perhaps the greatest mystery of all, that of the true nature of the work.

***Note**: Every word in this essay has been chosen with great exactness and the utmost care, and nothing has been mentioned out of its place, save when the need arose to do otherwise. Any contradictory or contrary statements can be ascribed to a need to gradually reveal the truth to the ignorant, and any divergences ascribed to a need to hide this truth from the vulgar. Anyone will derive some benefit from reading this essay, though only the wise and virtuous will understand all its paragraphs. It is not the purpose of this essay to make itself understandable to everyone, but rather to provide occasional flashes of insight to those who are already knowledgeable in all the sciences. These flashes will be scattered haphazardly amongst its pages. I beg of you, neither judge my work nor comment on a single word of this essay. Above all, do not hasten to refute me, for the way in which you understand me may be contrary to my intention.*

NOTES

1 Maimonides, *The Guide of the Perplexed,* I:Intro. Translated with an Introduction and Notes by Shlomo Pines with an Introductory Essay by Leo Strauss. Chicago: The University of Chicago Press, 1963, p. 3.

2 Leo Strauss, "The Literary Character of the *Guide for the Perplexed*," in *Persecution and the Art of Writing*. Glenco, Illinois: The Free Press, 1952, p. 55.

3 *Ibid.*, p. 61.

4 *Guide,* I:Intro, p. 17.

5 *Ibid.*, p. 20.

6 Strauss, p. 73.

7 Maimonides, "The Essay on Resurrection" Translated by Abraham Halkin in *Crisis and Leadership: Epistles of Maimonides.* Discussions by David Hartman. Philadelphia: The Jewish Publication Society of America, 1985. p. 226.

8 *Ibid.*, p. 219.

9 Marvin Fox, *Interpreting Maimonides: Studies in Methodology, Metaphysics and Moral Philosophy.* Chicago: The University of Chicago Press, 1990, p. 68.

10 *Guide*, I:32, pp. 68-69

11 "Essay on Resurrection," p. 228.

12 Fox, p. 72.

13 *Ibid.*

14 *Guide*, I:Intro, pp. 19-20.

15 Fox, p. 80.

16 Aviezer Ravitzky, "Samuel Ibn Tibbon and the Esoteric Character of the *Guide of the Perplexed*," in *History and Faith: Studies in Jewish Philosophy*. Amsterdam: J.C. Grieben, 1996. P. 214.

17 *Ibid.*

18 Fox, p. 5.

19 *Ibid.*, p. 55.

20 *Guide*, I:Intro, p. 15.

21 Babylonian Talmud: Hagigah 11b, 13a. Quoted *Ibid.*, pp. 6-7.

---

22 *Guide*, I:Intro, p. 7.

23 *Ibid.*

24 *Ibid.*, I:Epsitle Dedicatory, p. 4.

25 *Ibid.*

26 *Ibid.*

27 *Ibid.* I:34, p. 75.

28. *Ibid.*, I:Intro, p. 5.

29 *Ibid.*, p. 10

30 *Ibid.*, p. 16.

31 Proverbs 8:4 Quoted *Ibid.*, p. 5.

32 Psalms 119:126 Quoted *Ibid.*, p. 16.

33 Midrash on the song of songs 1:1 Quoted *Ibid.*, 11.

34 Proverbs 25:11 Quoted *Ibid.*

35 *Ibid.*, pp. 11-12.

36 *Ibid.*, p. 6.

37 *Ibid.*, p. 15.

38 *Ibid.*

39 Ravitzky, p. 214.

40 *Guide*, I:18, p. 43.

41 "The Secrets of Maimonides: Between the Thirteenth and the Twentieth Centuries," in Ravitzky, p. 256.

42 *Guide*, I:35, p. 81.

43 *Ibid.*, I:Intro, p. 15.

44 Babylonian Talmud, Hagigah, 11b Quoted *Ibid.*, I:32, p. 70, note.

References

Fox, Marvin. *Interpreting Maimonides: Studies in Methodology, Metaphysics and Moral Philosophy*. Chicago: The University of Chicago Press, 1990.

Maimonides. *The Guide of the Perplexed*. Translated with an Introduction and Notes by Shlomo Pines with an Introductory Essay by Leo Strauss. Chicago: The University of Chicago Press, 1963.

Maimonides. "The Essay on Resurrection." Translated by Abraham Halkin in *Crisis and Leadership: Epistles of Maimonides*. Philadelphia: The Jewish Publication Society of America, 1985.

Ravitzky, Aviezer. "Samuel Ibn Tibbon and the Esoteric Character of the *Guide of the Perplexed*," in *History and Faith: Studies in Jewish Philosophy*. Amsterdam: J.C. Grieben, 1996.

Strauss, Leo. "The Literary Character of the *Guide for the Perplexed*," in *Persecution and the Art of Writing*. Glenco, Illinois: The Free Press, 1952.

Human Nature

APOLLONIAN, DIONYSIAN AND SOCRATIC VIEWS: A NIETZSCHIAN EXEGESIS

G. J. Schwenk
Nazareth College

In his *Birth of Tragedy Through the Spirit of Music*, Nietzsche describes the two basic impulses of human psychological behavior in relation to the world, as well as art's role in that dichotomy. This monumental work gives us revolutionary insight into Greek Attic Tragedy (470-410 BCE). For the Apollonian, life is an illusion; for the Dionysian, Reality is warded off by an intoxicated state of revelry and Bacchic ritual. But, this work does not just explain the audience's role throughout sixty years in Greek theatre; it gives us a glimpse into the mind of the ancient Greek, as well as ourselves. What do we learn about the Greek gods by understanding this theory? What psychological significance does this have for us? Who is the theoretical man—represented in the text by Socrates—whom Nietzsche speaks of, and what connections can we find between this aspect and our own scientifically oriented 20th-21st century world?

During the years 470 to 410 BCE, Greek tragedy, as noted by the German philosopher Friedrich Nietzsche, ascended, reached its peak and declined into anonymity. According to Nietzsche, Attic tragedy is a combination of both Dionysian and Apollonian forces of the universe into a singular event, resulting in theater which is not merely an imitation of serious action having magnitude and significance—Aristotle's own words from the *Poetics*—but rather a culmination of mythological, religious, spiritual and psychological forces within the very human beings who experience it.[1]

However, Nietzsche needs to define exactly what the Apollonian and Dionysian forces at work are before he can explain how they are united in tragedy, much less relate it to the idea of a 'Socratic man.' Essentially, the Apollonian view is personified and grounded in the post-chthonic Greek deity of Apollo, who stood for sculpture, art and the sun:

> *Apollo, als der Gott aller bildnerischen Kräfte ...Er....die Lichtgottheit ist, beherrscht auch den schönen Schein der inneren Phantasie-Welt. Die höhere Wahrheit, die Vollkommenheit dieser Zustände im Gegensatz zu der lückenhaft verständlichen Tageswirklichkeit, sodann das tiefe Bewu(stein von der in Schlaf und Traum heilènden und helfenden Natur ist zugleich das symbolische Analogon der wahrsagenden Fähigkeit und überhaupt der Künste, durch die das Leben möglich und lebenswert gemacht wird. Aber auch jene zarte Linie, die das Traumbild nicht überschreiten darf...darf nicht im Bilde des Apollo fehlen...*[2]

This is the very heart of the Apollonian view, contrasting directly with the Dionysian. The very idea of illusion is at the heart of the Apollonian belief; concealing behind an illusion the primitive brutality and chaotic horror of nature and Reality is the heart of the Apollonian *weltanschauung*. This *Traumerfahrung* (dream-experience) of which Nietzsche speaks is directly associated with the Apollonian perspective and envelops *all* the experiences of life:

> *Nicht etwa nur die angenehmen und freundlichen Bilder sind es, die er mit jener Allverständlichkeit an sich erfährt: auch das Ernste, Trübe, Traurige, Finstere, die plötzlichen Hemmungen...*[3]

Despite the supposed ignorance one may logically associate with any psychological process involving illusion and/or the removing of one's self from true reality, there is a certain understanding and attraction to us for this veneer of structured and purposeful ignorance. As this second quote illustrates, the Apollonian is not completely ignorant of the Horrible, which underlies all existence. It is only because the truth drives men mad, as the sun blinds those who look at it, that the Apollonian shield themselves behind an aura of pleasant illusion personified in what Nietzsche calls *grichischen Heiterkeit* ("Greek cheerfulness").[4] This carefully fabricated illusion disguises multiple horrors from the being to whom identity and individualization are central: the realization that we shall someday die and become nothing; the truth that the world is brutal, horrible and uncorrectable; and the fact that there is no cosmic or ultimate justice. These are all aspects of Reality hidden behind the Apollonian's shield: illusion.

Similarly, it is the horror of

> *...das ungeheure Grausen geschildert, welches den Menschen ergreift, wenn er plötzlich an den Erkenntnisformen der Erscheinung irre wird, indem der Satz vom Grunde, in irgendeiner seiner Gestaltungen, eine Ausnahme zu erleiden scheint...*[5]

which is the foundation of the fear at the heart of the Socratic, or theoretical man. As a variation of the Apollonian worldview, the Socratic man fears only this: something unexplainable by whatever system of values he or she holds to be evident. Scientists, scholars, philosophers and theologians all try to explain the universe, it is when some bit of data or truth that we have collected lies outside our realm of understanding that the fear begins to take hold and we depend even more heavily upon the falsities upon which organized existence is based.[6]

Consider the last line of the first quote above: "that delicate boundary, which the dream-picture must not overstep." The fact that in each and every one of us is that suppressed urge for Ultimate One-ness and wild, intoxicated reverie where, as Nietzsche so brilliantly puts it "*...gerade die wildesten Bestien der Nature wurden hier entfesselt, bit zu jener abscheulichen Mischung von Wollust und Grausmkeit...*" and "*jene Erscheinung, dass Schmerzen Lust erwecken, dass der Jubel der Brust qualvolle Töne entreisst...*" is an ideal from which the Apollonian and the theoretical man willingly alienate themselves by means of selected ignorance and the construction of a pleasant illusion.[7] This pleasing facade supports the very sanity within which the Apollonian finds beauty, and is the tool for the theoretical man's hunt for answers. But what lies behind this shield? A vicious, maddening truth: the chaos of the cosmos; the true nature of the abyss; the central understanding of the Apollonian fear of death: *that individuality is fleeting*

And for the Apollonian this is the ultimate horror, which simply *must* be concealed behind this veneer of "pleasant illusion" and "Greek cheerfulness." The theoretical man may explain away death with hopeful yet unconsciously desperate theories about afterlife, the eternal nature of the soul and so forth. But to the Apollonian himself, individuality is the ultimate value, the greatest prize and quality which separates man from beast. Individuality and the idea of "I"—Freud's concept of the ego and super-ego fit in brilliantly here—are essential and paramount to life and existence for the Apollonian.

The loss of this quality is incomprehensible and maddening. And this view is understandable, for who has a correct and accurate answer as to what death is? Birth, in contrast, is the holy and wonderful process of individuation. It is sacred and ultimate, with each day a step towards the loss of the self, the loss of "I." Understanding this is essential for our comprehension of the Apollonian, which appears at first as a contradictory myriad of illusion and reality; understanding the horror in the chaotic madness of nature and purposely constructed ignorance of that very same horror go hand in hand, working in a delicate co-existive state. It is when Berkeley says that without the existence of the self which is necessary to perceive the world, the world and all inanimate objects there cease to exist: "*...esse est aut percipi, aut percipere...*" we can finally grasp the rationale behind Apollonian thought from a more contemporary viewpoint and begin to understand these views, not dimly, as if we perceived them from the far shores of a distant beach, but more personally and individually.[8]

Conceptually, this statement represents the necessary and significant relation between the individual human being and the entire world/universe, in that without the human to perceive it, the universe does not exist. A plastic and artificial view, this statement allows the Apollonian thinker to believe that life as an individual is good and free, and that as an entity unique and separate from all others he may strive for greatness and achieve better and grander results than his peers: the Greek competitions are excellent examples of this blind hope in physical excellence, paralleled with the symposiums of the philosophers as a place to prove one's superior intellect. It seems to say to us, this Apollonian statement, that without us, or the individual—the "I"—the world would somehow become less significant or worsen in some manner—perhaps even so much as to cease to exist altogether when we leave it, as Berkeley seems to imply.[9] To the Apollonian, life is sacred. On the other hand, death—the ultimate eliminator of life or even the "great equalizer"—is to be feared and denied as long as possible. It was a purposeful corruption of the satyr-deity Silenus' words when the Apollonians believed him to have said that living forever was best and living long, second. This is the exactly opposite of what his words truly entailed. As he was a satyr (that is to say, a demi-god, part of nature, or more distinctly, part of "reality") and therefore an embodiment of Dionysian values, nothing could have been a greater or more contradictory corruption of his words. The very idea of individual life is fearful and painful to a Dionysian.

To emphasize the influence and importance of the Apollonian view, we would do well to examine the deities of Greek religion and its development. Originally the gods of ancient Greece were those of earth, wind, water and fire, and they ruled haphazardly. These 'chthonic' or earth bound elementals were given names by the cultures in the hopes that naming would make them more understandable. Naming, one must realize, is an Apollonian characteristic. A proper name—being unique to a person, place or thing—is therefore a further catalyst as to his/her separate identity. On the other hand, the ultimate unity of Nietzsche's Dionysian perspective has, at best, the ominous and vague description of *Ur-Einen*: "all-oneness." *Gaia, Ouranos, Oceanos, Chronos*: these are all names provided by the Greek Apollonian (even theoretical man's) impulse to understand and clarify the haphazard quality of nature. As with any beginning or primitive religion, these deities were revered and sacrificed to in addition to the regular practice of Greek ancestral worship. But nature is an abstract, chaotic being that something far removed and orderly—such as a human being—cannot begin to comprehend. And because these names did not provide enough comfort or "controllability," they were discarded. In order to try and explain the unexplainable and anarchistic forces of the cosmos, these chthonic gods—faceless elementals of earth and water—were not enough to satisfy human desires for explanation.

It was an Apollonian view and fear of uncontrollable nature that carved from the elemental, chaotic and incomprehensible chthonic gods the anthropomorphized and "comprehensible" Olympian figures so familiar to us in Greek mythology. Why? In order to perpetuate this "pleasant illusion." And how did this filter through the ages, this paradigm shift in religion?[10] It was explained in a rarely heard myth of Zeus killing his father, who was one of those very chthonic representational god-elements, while the once central elemental constructs faded into anonymity through disuse, persevering only in such vague terms as Atlas, Prometheus and Chronos.

As believers in the individual nature of things in a primordial 'Nature', the Apollonians could only create gods who were in control of singular aspects of that 'Nature': Zeus of thunder and lightning, Athene of wisdom, Poseidon of the ocean...etc. These were very human-like (and therefore comprehensible) deities to whom the Greeks could more readily relate than the earth (Gaia) or the ocean surrounding creation (Oceanos). In reality however, these newly constructed Olympian artifices still could not completely subvert the inherent values of Dionysian culture, as is clearly evident in the few remaining works we have from ancient Greece, especially Hesiod's *Theogony* and Aeschylus' *Prometheus Bound*.[11]

In contrast with an Apollonian attitude, the Dionysian perspective is one that seems wild and base—feral and primitive. Drunken anarchistic orgies leading to unity and a community of one with the "Ur-Einen," though central to the Dionysian view, seem horrible and manifestly dangerous to our Apollonian selves.[12] Compared with the seemingly aesthetic Apollonian appreciation of beauty in symmetry and order, the Dionysian intoxicated state in that drunken revelry as evident in the Bacchic rituals and influences from "barbaric" cultures adjacent to the proper Hellenic society *does* seem wild and primitive. For ourselves as "rational beings" of the 20th century trying to cure diseases and thwart nature's omnipotence through rational thought processes that attempt to explain—such as science and philosophy—this obviously can not be seen as anything *but* an evil to the Dionysian.[13] The very crux of Dionysian belief is the opposite of the Apollonian: birth, or the process of individuation, is terrible and frightening, as terrifying as the thought of death is to the Apollonian. What Silenus really said when he was captured by Midas before it became corrupted by Apollonian individualism and romanticism was this:

> *Elendes Eintagsgeschlecht, des Zufalls Kinder und der Mühsal, was zwingst du mich dir zu sagen, was nicht zu hören für dich das Ersprie(lichste ist? Das Allerbeste ist für dich gänzlich unerreichbar: nicht geboren zu sein, nitcht zu sein, nichts zu sein. Das Zweitbeste aber ist für dich—bald zu sterben.*[14]

This horrible realization of the hell of solitude—ultimate ostricization from all true contact with the Universe, the primordial quality of chaotic existence: solitude and isolation for all time—is displayed quite brilliantly and powerfully by Nietzsche's words. And does it not immediately repel us? Have we not been taught that life is a sacred bounty? The voice that responds to this with "what horrible pessimistic words" is that of our theoretical man selves, as derived from our Apollonian impulse. The fear of the Dionysian aspect is eternal or long-lived life. Complete isolation from the instant of birth and revered by the Apollonian mind-set is the greatest fear for and most horrible thing imaginable to a Dionysian. It is this source of suffering and anguish which Nietzsche so brilliantly relates back to his understanding of Greek Attic tragedy. It is best never to be born, second best to die soon thereafter and end the nightmare of individuation. We, as rational beings (and therefore, instances of the theoretischen Menschen which I shall momentarily explain) see this idea as unpleasant. It goes against the very zest and love for life which our society has indoctrinated us to appreciate, ennoble and love. This is for us, grim and morbid, but for the Dionysian it is his center of oneness with the Chaotic-Allness. Why does Œdipus suffer? Yes, he has committed the greatest Greek sin: Pride in Accomplishment, but why do we feel for him so? Remembering the true nature of Greek drama, one can only suddenly come to this horrible conclusion: the dramas were celebrations of religious festivals. To whom? Dionysus. Œdipus is Dionysus forced into the form of the individual. And not only does he suffer because he lives, he suffers because as an *individual* he has accomplished great things—the very antithesis of Dionysian existence.

By its very nature, the Apollonian view can be just as horrible as that of the Dionysian forced to exist—and even worse, as with Œdipus, exist well—if we just carefully examine it. As mentioned above, the Apollonian views nature from behind a veil, a veil it must be careful never to overstep for fear of falling into the horrible abyss of the Dionysian world. Humans are wonderful creations, but they are *individual ones*. Here lies the heart of Dionysian terror: the loss of contact with the great wholeness and community of Nature. This ostricization from true contact with a collective drives him mad. It causes him as vicious and real a terror as we feel when in the middle of the night we awake, sweaty and frightened, from a dream and realize that someday we will cease to be—we will become nothing. As just recently stated, being[15] (and existing, furthermore, as an *individual*) is essential to our sanity. Our minds and separate identities determine who we are and what we do; death erases that identity, which is the reason it is so feared by "rational men of science." But of even greater importance (if only because it is not as well recognized or as often considered as death) is the true horror innate in complete solitude that we often enough do not recognize as a source of much of our own misery. For the Dionysian in all of us, being alone is a horrible fact, for community and the spirit of losing one's self into the many is central to that part of us.[16]

Yet in being an individual and consciously taking a step back from the illusion and the world we live with and in by means of the Apollonian view, we separate ourselves from each other by that very same step. Poetry by that of renowned individuals and of the teenage population often deals with feelings of loneliness and solitude. This can be seen as the denial of the Dionysian element intrinsic to ourselves. Being alone is quite often a subject of teenagers' poetry and juvenile writing: they feel the need for and want of acceptance. Therefore it is clear that this isolationism is certainly a concern worth examining.

Every rational mind—because it is rational and therefore grows and learns from the experiences it has—develops differently because no two people can have the exact same experiences all the time. As a result, two rational beings cannot truly and completely understand what each other is thinking of and as a result, human beings become isolated creatures that desire a sort of conformity through means by which it is not possible to conform. Conformity, in this case, is to be understood as a Dionysian value of desiring to be with the Primordial Unity or Chaotic oneness from which we have been separated since birth. An excellent modern illustration of this would be the philosophical system of solipsism. This belief system understands that the "I" or the self is the only true creation in the world and that everything and everyone else is but a creation of the "I," be it conscious or unconscious, pleasant or harmful. Being a believer of this leads to a lonely, secluded life where the real world becomes something from which one shrinks. This is the Apollonian view of mastery and self-individualization taken to an extreme such that it terrifies us. Why? Because deep down, human beings want to be wanted and they desire not to be alone, whether it be because of us originally existing as Androgens as Plato relates or some other, related cause.

Having thoroughly and painstakingly established this dichotomy, we must now examine the only view not yet considered seriously. What remains to be explained is Nietzsche's understanding of the "theoretischen Menschen" and how it pertains to the aforementioned dichotomy, as well as the modern world. Here is its keystone, in Nietzsche's own words:

> *...so werden wir jetzt dem Wesen des ästhetischen Sokratismus schon näher treten dürfen, dessen oberstes Gesetz ungefähr so lautet: "Alles muss verständig sein, um schön zu sein"*[17]

This is the grounding of the Socratic/theoretical man. Related to the Apollonian understanding of beauty in the world, it takes one more step and declares that in order for something to be beautiful, it must be intelligible. As a result, because the world is beautiful, it is ultimately understandable.[18] This beautiful view of the world as proportional and somehow ultimately "orderable" is, like the Apollonian perspective it is so closely associated with, an illusion. But here, it is an illusion that leads to an attempt at explaining and predicting the way in which the world works, which seems to us as if it may be more noble than a mere retreat from the veil of truth which Apollonian thought results in. The theoretical man, epitomized in the person of Socrates (hence, Socratic-man) rationalizes and explains away the once chaotic aspects of the world that the Apollonian merely placed behind a thin veil of self-constructed fantasy. As a result of this beauty through understanding, Socrates feels no need to fear death; for him it is merely the joining of the immaterial spirit with the spiritual world. Because he has discarded the Apollonian fear of losing one's self in exchange with the Dionysian view of collective existence, he can very calmly and with his last breath remind his companions of something so unprofound as "remember to sacrifice a rooster to the gods."[19] Unfortunately, this exchange of ignorance for ignorance is something that we have not fully recognized. In placing our somewhat blind trust in science, technology, and philosophy as vehicles towards and explanation of the cosmos, one might argue that we have overlooked this duality within ourselves.[20]

In our modern society, science has generally replaced religion in explaining a majority of events. Through science we have come to the understanding of multiple phenomena once superstitiously associated with spirits, elementals and daemons. However, with the increase in understanding and the growing influence of science and scientific thought, realms have been discovered which science is unable to explain away. Quite often, these areas are seen as taboo by the proper, sophisticated society of scientific thought and even looked down upon as deviants from proper research. Individuals researching spiritual phenomena such as apparitions, psychology, metaphysical or spiritual occurrences, etc. have all been looked down upon, and still are. They are mocked as "ghost-hunters," "montebancs" and "shrinks."

Whether or not their research is ethical, viable or even noteworthy is not important. What is important is that there are many things that, despite our scientific leaps and bounds over the last two centuries, we are unable to understand, much less control. That which we do not understand, we fear. This is the epitome of a theoretical man view and is so inherent within our modern day view that often enough we do not recognize it.

It is here—at the border between understanding and chaos—when science begins to fail us with its explanations that humanity can fall into the abyss of reality and see the Dionysian truth and its contradictions. Is it purely coincidence that the two extremes of existence—such as the movement of sub-atomic particles and the ultimate order of universe and god's place in it—that they are, to science, inexplicable, either alone or together? Does it not seem odd that the extremes of the spectrum, the smallest and the largest, are beyond our understanding at present and could possibly forever be?[21] For Nietzsche, science, religion and philosophy are all Apollonian illusions constructed to provide us reasons for existence in our inexplicable world. They explain the world and try and provide us some comprehensible order as to its construction. Yet these too, are mere illusion and fancy, such as our desire for play which we internalize and modify in our shift from childhood to adult.[22] We need them to maintain our mental security, for as Hamlet's brief glimpse into the Abyss stunned him to indecision and suicide, so too will our own minds warp and shatter underneath the weight of true chaos. It is because we thrive upon order and rational, logical progression that we are so horrified by the curious injustice of this antagonistically "arranged" universe.

When we look up to heaven and cry for justice, we are disappointed that none comes. It is then and only then, when the human mind fully realizes it is alone until it dies and ceases to exist, that we can understand the figure of Œdipus and the nature of his suffering. He is the great Primordial Oneness of community forced into the singular existence of a mortal. Suffering from this plight, he is driven to madness and insanity when he realizes his deeds; through pride and the defeat of the Sphynx he has tried to emphasize his importance as a one, which is everything the Dionysian aspect denies. In furthering his opposite, he endures endless torture and eventually takes his own sight. By seeing this imitated upon the stage by human beings, we can truly come to understand how this type of tragedy is the combination of Apollonian and Dionysian elements.

What we may not so readily see however, is how this relates to us here and today. As individuals separated from the Chaotic-All, we suffer. The Greek understanding of the human being born as half of a person searching for his/her other half exemplifies this.[23] We can find our other half, but the breach can never be mended, and we are forever separated from ourselves and the oneness of nature. Thus we too, are tragic figures: we try to explain in a rational and logical manner the creations of the universe; we try to love and find unity in society and other beings as the Bacchic revelries exemplified; we try to find meaning in a mad world where the truth not only blinds, but also kills us. In conclusion, I quote Bertrand Russell:

> The life of Man is a long march through the night, surrounded by invisible foes, tortured by weariness and pain, towards a goal that few can hope to reach, and where none may tarry long. One by one, as they march, our comrades vanish from our sight, seized by the silent orders of omnipotent Death.[24]

NOTES

1 Aristotle, *Poetics* 1449b 24-30.

2 "...Apollo, the god of all plastic energies....is the 'shining one,' the deity of light, is also ruler over the fair appearance of the inner world of fantasy. The higher truth, the perfection of these states in contrast to the incompletely intelligible everyday world, this deep consciousness of nature, healing and helping in sleep and dreams is at the same time the symbolical analogue of the soothsaying faculty and of the arts generally which make life possible and worth living. But we must also include in our picture of Apollo that delicate boundary, which the dream-picture must not over-step..."[Translation by C. Fadiman]{Friedrich Nietzsche, *Werke I Die Geburt der Tragödie aus dem Geiste der Musik*, Frankfurt: {May} 1980. Page 23}

3 "Not only, however, is it merely the pleasant and friendly pictures/experiences that he [the Apollonian] encounters clearly within his very being, it is also the earnest ones, the disconcerted, the melancholy, the sinister and the unsettled affectations [he experiences]..."[My translation]{Nietzsche, *Die Geburt der...* page 22}

4 The Apollonian illusion which covers the horrid reality of the world/nature.[Translated by C. Fadiman]{Nietzsche, *Die Geburt der...*page 55}

5 "the terrible awe which seizes upon man, when he is suddenly unable to account for the cognitive forms of a phenomenon, when the principle of reason, in some one of its manifestations, seems to admit of an exception..."[Translation by C. Fadiman]{Nietzsche, *Die Geburt der...* page 24}

6 For a more recent analysis of this, see W. V. Quine and J. S. Ullian, *The Web of Knowledge*. New York: Random House, 1978.

7 "the most savage instincts were unleashed, including even that horrible mixture of sensuality and cruelty..."—"the phenomenon that pain begets joy, that ecstasy may wring sounds of agony from us..."[Translation by C. Fadiman]{Nietzsche, *Die Begurt der...* page 27}

8 "...to be, is either to be perceived or to perceive..." George Berkeley, *Three Dialogues Between Hylas and Philonous*.

9 This is, of course, assuming that we do away with God's role as a

supreme perceiver.

10 Kuhn, Thomas S. *The Structure of Scientific Revolution* 3rd ed. The University of Chicago Press, 1962.

11 Euripides himself turned from his constant satires wherein gods treated men as objects—and thereby critiqued the religious views of his day—to recognize the power of the *Ur-Einen* and the importance of gods in the human world.

12 Fadiman translates *Ur-Einen* to mean "Primordial Unity." *Einen* means "one-ness" while *Ur* tends to mean a universality or essence in some primitive fashion. As a result, I disagree with his choice in that it seems cumbersome and too vague an idea. I shall use the terms *Ultimate-One, Ultimate Unity, Chaotic-Oneness*, and *Chaotic-Unity* interchangeably here, for they all have the ring of accuracy.

13 Here is a significant side-point of relevance. A quick examination of Nietzsche's work *Jenseits Gute und Böse* (*Beyond Good and Evil*) will reveal how Nietzsche attempted to rise above these two relative and subjective terms. Not only is it an explanation and defense of his best known work *Also Sprach Zarathustra*, it tries to rise above the blind dismissal of anything as inherently good or bad.

14 "Miserable people, Chance's miserable children, why ask you for me to say that which it is best for you never to hear? The best thing of all is for you, impossible—unachievable: not to be born, *not to be, to be nothing*. The second best, however, *is* for you: A quick death."[My translation]{Nietzsche, *Werke I Die Geburt die*...page 29-30}

15 By being, I mean the act of existing.

16 As a further side-note, consider the mythology of human creation as is evident in Plato's *Symposium*. Human beings originally had four arms and four legs. As a punishment for some crime (often the crime is made to be man's acceptance of fire from Prometheus) they were split in half, and it is for the other half—the other person—we seek all our days. Until we find them we are alone, separated and incomplete. Expand this to fit a grander scale, and we have the horror inherent to the Dionysian impulse within us.

17 "...only now can we more clearly behold the ideal of *aesthetic Socrates* [theoretischen Menschen], whose ultimate code says that 'Everything, to be beautiful, must be intelligible,' as the respective

counter-part of the Socratic character: 'Knowledge is virtue.'"[My translation]{Nietzsche, *Werke I Die Geburt die*...page 72}

18 The understanding of the harmony between soul and man, man and community and community and universe is evident in much Greek and modern writing. See Jamie James' *The Music of the Spheres: Music, Science and The Natural Order of the Universe* and Plato's *The Republic*.

19 Plato's *Phaedo*, 118a-b.

20 Cf. Martin Heidegger, *The Question Concerning Technology*.

21 For an interesting examination of polarity in ancient Greek thought, there is an excellent work well: Lloyd, G.E.R. *Polarity and Analogy: Two types of argumentation in early Greek thought*. Cambridge University Press, London; 1966.

22 For further reading, see Winnicott, D. W. *Playing and Reality*. Basic Books Inc. Publishers, New York, New York; 1971.

23 Cf. Aristophanes' speech in *The Symposium*.

24 Bertrand Russell, "A Free Man's Worship," from the collection: *Why I Am Not a Christian*. New York: Simon and Schuster, 1957.

REFERENCES

Berkeley, George. *Three Dialogues Between Hylas and Philonous*. Mineola, New York: Dover Books Publications, 1994.

James, Jamie. *The Music of the Spheres: Music, Science and The Natural Order of the Universe*. New York: Copernicus Press, 1993.

Kuhn, Thomas S. *The Structure of Scientific Revolutions*. 3rd edition. Chicago: The University of Chicago Press, 1962.

Lloyd, G.E.R. *Polarity and Analogy: Two types of argumentation in early Greek thought*. London: Cambridge University Press, 1966.

Nietzsche, Friedrich. *The Birth Of Tragedy in the Spirit of Music*. Translated by C. P. Fadiman. New York: The Modern Library, 1927.

________. *Werke I: Die Geburt der Tragödie aus dem Geiste der Musik*. Frankfurt Press: 1980.

________. *Werke IV: Jenseits Gute und Böse*. Frankfurt Press: 1981.

Winnicott, D. W. *Playing and Reality*. New York: Basic Books, 1971.

ANTI-ESSENTIALISM AND RE-IDENTIFICATION

Michael D. Day
Syracuse University

In this paper I argue for essentialism. I break down anti-essentialism into two camps, namely relativistic anti-essentialism and accidentalism. After giving arguments that neither can be taken independently, I contend that we should be inclined to accept essentialism.

The second portion of the paper is devoted to an exploration of the function of accidental properties in identification and diachronic re-identification. I contend that bundles of perceivable accidental properties are responsible for identification and re-identification. Moreover, I hold that the very thing responsible in identification and re-identification is not individual essential properties separate from this bundle of perceivable properties because such essential properties are often not accessible. I move that since we continue to pick out the same entity, namely a person, over time, even if most or all of the accidental properties have changed, there is an essence underlying the accidental properties. I suggest that this essence is a unique pattern of perceivable accidental properties.

Introduction

In the following paper I shall provide a defense of essentialism with regard to human beings. I begin by dividing anti-essentialism into two camps, namely relativistic anti-essentialism, roughly the doctrine that there are essential and accidental properties only relative to background groupings, and accidentalism, the doctrine that there are only accidental properties[1]. I then argue that we should abandon relativistic anti-essentialism and accidentalism and accept essentialism. That is, we should recognize that human beings have both accidental properties as well as essential properties. And, perhaps more interestingly, I shall go on to argue that accidental properties play a unique role in diachronic re-identification in human beings.

In *Material Beings*[2] Peter van Inwagen argues that lives are internally caused. Just as a living organism gains and loses mereological simples, a club of people gains and loses its members. Over time a living organism may have all new mereological simples, and the club may have all new members. However, we hold that the living organism and the club still exist[3]. In this same spirit, I shall argue that our perceivable accidental properties are very much like bundles of mereological simples or bundles of people. Over time we loose our perceivable accidental properties and gain new ones. For example, I may find that over time my brown hair turns gray. It may be the case that at some future time all of one's perceivable accidental properties will be different, but we very often continue to pick out the same person using a bundle of perceivable accidental properties. And thus, I shall argue that underlying these bundles of properties is an essence that persists diachronically and allows for re-identification.

Relativistic Anti-Essentialism

Relativistic anti-essentialism is the doctrine that there exist essential and accidental properties only relative to background groupings. That is, there are no essential and accidental properties absolutely for any entity. For example, as Quine puts it, it is necessary for any bicyclist to have two legs, but it is not necessary for any bicyclist to be rational.[4]

We consider whether an individual has certain properties essentially and accidentally only in reference to background groupings.

This does seem to be a useful suggestion. We are able to avoid considering whether something is essential or accidental to an individual absolutely. For example, as Descartes thought, thinking may be an essential property of human beings. But what happens when we are sleeping and not dreaming? Since these and other problems arise with absolute essential properties we may be motivated to accept relativistic anti-essentialism.

John Locke and Willard Van Orman Quine are thought to be, for the sake of the texts that I will be examining, paradigmatically relativistic anti-essentialists.

Locke holds,

> ...as it is *essential* to this thing I write on, To contain words, if I will give it the name *Treatise*, and rank it under that *Species*.[5]

Quine holds,

> Mathematicians may conceivably be said to Be necessarily rational and not necessarily Two-legged; and cyclists necessarily two-Legged and not necessarily rational.[6]

Locke begins his anti-essentialist project with a discussion of nominal essences. To demonstrate his relativistic anti-essentialism, Locke holds that essences relate to sortals, or background groupings, and particular beings have essential properties *only* when these properties are grouped under the sortals to which they apply, i.e., to which they are necessary. Locke holds, "'Tis necessary for me to be as I am; God and nature have made me so: But there is nothing I have, is essential to me."[7] However, Locke then urges us to examine our own thoughts, suggesting that when speaking about something being *Essential*, the consideration of a *Species* or even a complex *Idea* will come into play and we will see, "…'tis in reference to that, that this or that Quality is said to be *essential*."[8] It should be noted that the emphasis here is on the reference to background groupings. Thus, in the capacity of reference to a particular background grouping, entities have essential and accidental properties. A background grouping is selected and with it the essential or accidental property changes.

In order to tease out Locke's relativistic anti-essentialism we must examine his doctrine of real essences.

Locke writes,

> But *Essence*, even in this sense, *relates to a Sort*, and supposes a *Species*: For being that Real Constitution, on which the Properties Depend, it necessarily supposes a sort of Things, Properties belonging only to *Species*, and not To Individuals…[9]

Here Locke makes it clear that he is relativizing within his doctrine of Real essences. Correlatively, we see that his doctrine of real essences jibes with his doctrine of nominal essences. Thus, the thing at issue in both doctrines is the relativity of essential and accidental properties.

The above allows us to get clear about why Locke is a relativistic anti-essentialist.[10] Locke is not blindly choosing a relativity of essential and accidental properties. Consider the following. When I grip my coffee mug I may be unusually startled by the heat from the coffee emanating through the ceramic cup, quickly warming my hand. So I pick out the property of heat by having an idea of it. My idea relates to the fact that the cup really is hot. This relates to the fact that the molecules in the ceramic cup are moving more rapidly than the molecules in the ceramic cups in my cold cupboard. In terms of Locke's doctrine of real essences we choose a particular property, e.g., two-leggedness, and by doing so, we will find a sortal, e.g., bicyclist, to which it is essential.

Quine, on the other hand, fleshes out his relativistic anti-essentialism through the paradox of the mathematical bicyclist.

1. It is necessary for every bicyclist to have two legs.
2. It is not necessary for every bicyclist to be rational.
3. It is necessary for every mathematician to be rational.
4. It is not necessary for every mathematician to have two legs.
5. Jones is both a bicyclist and a mathematician.

/∴ Jones is necessarily rational and not necessarily rational.

/∴ Jones is necessarily two-legged and not necessarily two-legged.[11]

The relativistic anti-essentialism of Quine will eliminate the paradoxical conclusions. Let us restate the paradox of the mathematical bicyclist (for just the bicyclist) with the "*qua* solution" given by the relativistic anti-essentialist.

1. It is necessary for every bicyclist to have two legs *qua* bicyclist.
2. It is not necessary for every bicyclist to be rational *qua* bicyclist.
3. Jones is a bicyclist.

/∴ Jones is necessarily two-legged *qua* bicyclist.

/∴ Jones is not necessarily rational *qua* bicyclist.[12]

The "*qua* solution" allow us to resolve the paradox. The focus is put on Jones's capacity to be something, i.e., to fill some role. Once we identify a certain capacity of Jones, then we are able to determine the particular attribute that is essential or accidental to that certain role. Thus, when we speak about Jones as a mathematician we will say, 'Jones is necessarily rational *qua* mathematician,' and 'Jones is not necessarily two-legged *qua* mathematician.' When we choose to speak of Jones in reference to a different background grouping, we must attribute to Jones the essential property of that group.

It must be conceded that this doctrine seems like a useful one. For it does not commit us to holding that there exists absolute essential and accidental properties for a particular entity. Rather, every property can be thought essential and accidental when grouped under a particular sortal, e.g., sortal: bicyclist; property: two-leggedness. [In this case the property of two-leggedness is essential to an entity in the bicyclist sortal.] We take on different roles in our lives, e.g., being a bicyclist or a mathematician, and for each role or for each capacity we have different properties essentially and accidentally.

Accidentalism

In its purist form accidentalism is the doctrine that all properties of particular entities are accidental. That is, there exist no essential properties for any entity.

However, there is another aspect of accidentalism. It may allow us to individuate one thing from another. The best way to see this is to accept essentialism, i.e., the doctrine that there are both essential and accidental properties. Through doing this we will get a feeling of the work being done by accidental properties. Before we begin an explanation of this, let me set the stage holding that (for example) Michael and Bob essentially have the property of being rational. This property allows Michael and Bob to exist as members of the human being group. Despite the fact that they have the same essential property, how can we tell Michael apart from Bob? Michael and Bob both have certain characteristics that, when taken in aggregate, differ. For example Michael may have blond hair, a height of 5'11", two children and so on. Bob, on the other hand, may have brown hair, a height of 6'4", no children and so on. Thus, we can use a certain group of the perceivable accidental qualities of these two individuals as a type of mechanism to identify each within the group of humans.

This does not, of course, rule out each individual having unique essential properties, i.e., individual essential properties, within the human group. However, it may be difficult to have access to these individual essential properties. And thus, sorting by a group of perceivable accidental properties, to which we often have access, will allow us to individuate Michael from Bob. That is, since we all share the same essential property sorting us into the human group, we obviously cannot be individuated on the basis of that property. In such cases we will have to look to accidental properties for inter-sortal individuation, and indeed such properties are readily perceivable, e.g., Michael is 5'11".

Abandonment of Relativistic Anti-Essentialism and Accidentalism

Relativistic anti-essentialism is a useful theory because it does not commit us to holding that there are absolute essential and accidental properties of any entity. Rather, there exists essential and accidental properties only in the capacity of being matched to some background grouping. However, herein exists the problem with relativistic anti-essentialism.

The relativistic anti-essentialist's concern to group things relative to a background grouping commits her to the position that there is some *thing* that can be talked about without reference to background groupings. For example, if the relativistic anti-essentialist sees Jones riding his bicycle in order to get to his office in the mathematics department, then she will concede that not only does Jones the bicyclist and Jones the mathematician exist, but moreover, *Jones* exists, i.e., Jones *qua* Jones. This is speaking purely referentially, i.e., without reference to any background grouping.

The accidentalist will then be concerned to confront the relativistic anti-essentialist. He will ask her to consider Jones purely referentially. The relativistic anti-essentialist considers Jones purely referentially and concedes that Jones exists. Let us now say that Jones loses his right leg in a bicycling accident. The accidentalist asks the relativistic anti-essentialist whether Jones still exists. Speaking purely referentially, she will say that Jones still exists. The important point here is that, originally, the relativistic anti-essentialist was not committed to absolute accidental properties, but she conceded that Jones existed before and after losing his leg without referring to a background grouping. Thus, she was really committed to absolute accidental properties, and this runs counter to relativistic anti-essentialism.

This should be a motivational factor to abandon relativistic anti-essentialism. She claimed not to be committed to essential and accidental properties absolutely. But when we asked her to consider Jones purely referentially, she was forced to accept Jones' right leggedness as an absolute accidental property.

Pure accidentalism, however, has problems of its own, and in the end it seems to be more confused than relativistic anti-essentialism. To say that all properties are accidental is to hold that one can begin stripping an entity of all of its properties, and he must still concede that the entity exists. How many properties can he strip away before the entity no longer exists? This is the problem. A property is accidental to an entity if the entity can exist without that property. And thus, herein lies the difficulty. There is no concrete structure that constitutes a particular entity. There is nothing essential, absolutely or in reference to a background grouping, to an entity.

In the end it seems that we want to speak about a thing in itself. That is, we will not want to always speak about something relative to a background grouping. Thus, it seems that in abandoning relativistic anti-essentialism and accidentalism we will want to accept essentialism. Essentialism will allow us to dissolve the problems associated with both types of anti-essentialism. In doing so, we can accept the existence of both essential and accidental properties. We will then be in a position to use bundles of perceivable accidental properties as re-identification devices.

Accidental Properties and Re-Identification

Many will hold that we do have essential properties. Perhaps the essential property for humans is having a brain. Or Peter van Inwagen may be right in holding that it is having a *life-like* arrangement of mereological simples in living organisms.[13] Or, as Crawford Elder argues, having copied devices may be essential to all things.[14] Although these contemporary views (and there are plenty more) differ in the particular attribute humans have essentially, they do share in the phenomenon that an attribute may be chosen which will allow one to group entities.

Let us say that it is the case that there exist essential properties of particular entities. How shall we deal with distinguishing between the entities? For example, if all humans are essentially rational, then is it the case that Michael and Paula have the same essential property? Yes, for the purpose of grouping them into the human group. (There may be other essential properties unique to just Michael and to just Paula, which I shall discuss in the next paragraph.) However, this is where accidental properties become important, namely for the purpose of numerical distinction. If Michael and Paula share the same essential property, i.e., they are both rational, then we can distinguish them from one another by their accidental properties. Michael has short brown hair and so on, and Paula has long red hair and so on. Thus, it seems that accidental properties allow us to distinguish between two entities that share essential properties. And in doing so, accidental properties operate as a sort of identification mechanism.[15]

I should stress the fact that there may be individual essential properties of Michael and Paula that are not shared. For example, Michael and Paula both share the essential property of rationality, but Michael has the individual essential property X and Paula has the individual essential property Y. So it seems that in addition to a different bundle of accidental properties, Michael and Paula may also have essential properties that differ from one another. However, I would like to note that we may not always have access to these essential properties that differ between two people. On the other hand, we often have access to some group of perceivable accidental properties that allow us to tell Michael from Paula.[16]

I shall want to argue that perceivable accidental properties of an entity, taken in aggregate, i.e., a bundle of perceivable accidental properties, allow us to draw these distinctions over time. For it may have been the case that Paula dyed her brown hair red in 1991. Those who knew her before and after the dying would, after 1991, no longer use her brown hair as a distinguishing property. Rather, they would have a new property, namely "having red hair," as a new accidental property to add to all of the other accidental differentiating properties.

I argue that Paula has the essential property of rationality *qua* human being. However, once Paula finds herself in the group of human beings, we may want to hold that there exists something unique about Paula, something essential to Paula teasing her apart from the group of human beings. She may have one or more individual essential properties to which we may not have access, but I argue that in aggregate Paula has a unique bundle of accidental properties that differ from all other members of the human group. Paula may change her hair color, lose her personality through shock therapy or something of the like. However, all of her accidental properties are not altered at the same time. It is the case that over time they begin to be altered, and over some longer duration of time all of her perceivable accidental properties may be completely altered. But I argue that diachronically there is an essence underlying her accidental properties allowing us to differentiate Michael from Paula over time.

In arguing for his thesis that the only things that exist as medium-sized object are living organisms, van Inwagen holds that *lives* are very much like clubs of people, as stated earlier in this paper. To improve our understanding of my thesis let us substitute van Inwagen's mereological simples with accidental properties. First, let me set the stage. Van Inwagen argues that if there exists a club of people it may be the case that over several years some members will leave and new members will join. And it may happen that over the years all of the members will change. However, we are not willing to hold there exists a different club. Van Inwagen argues that, in the case of *lives*, mereological simples are lost and added, but the life still persists.[17] Compare this to the biological discovery that we loose all of our atoms over a seven year (or so) period, but we are not willing to hold that we no longer exist or that something else exists in place of us. Now compare this to our project. Paula may loose some (or even all) of her perceivable accidental properties and gain new ones, but we are not willing to hold that she no longer exists at some particular point in time, because, after all, these are only accidental properties. (And as we stated above, the existence of an entity is not dependent upon its retention of its accidental properties.) Rather, diachronically speaking, I hold that this unique arrangement of accidental properties is the very thing that allows us to re-identify and individuate Paula from Michael and others over time.

The following issue now arises: if the unique arrangement of perceivable accidental properties allows us to distinguish Paula, and only Paula, from the group of all humans, then it seems that this unique arrangement of perceivable accidental properties is essential to just Paula. And if it is the case that over time we still pick out Paula from other humans, even when Paula has different perceivable accidental properties, then there is an essence underlying her accidental properties. And moreover, this essence does not seem to depend upon any one accidental property, but rather it is dependent upon the persistence of the bundle or the arrangement of the properties. (Compare this to van Inwagen's club of people.)

One may want to hold that the club of people and the bundle of properties are nothing more than sets of people and properties, respectively. If there is a group of 10 doctors, then we can say that those 10 doctors constitute a set of doctors. Let us say that the same 10 doctors are also lawyers. Then we can say that those same 10 people constitute a set of lawyers. So if the members of S_1 are the same as those of S_2, then $S_1=S_2$. This, however, differs from the case of the club of people. Van Inwagen contends that the club's existence is not dependent upon its members, and thus, different members can constitute the same club. And so, we can state a general rule: a set is defined by its members but a club (and a bundle of properties) is not.

If this is the case then we may not want to call the club of people a set of people. Likewise, we may not want to hold that living organisms are a set of mereological simples, or atoms. However, on all of our accounts, it seems that something still exists. Consider the following: Let us call the club of people, 'The Greenwich Country Club,' and in 1902 it got this name and has had it ever since. Let us say that the club began in 1902 and is still in existence today in 1997. I do not wish to discuss whether it should have the same name in 1997 as it had in 1902. Rather, I would like to consider the following: If all of the members are different today in 1997 than they were in 1902, then when we speak about The Greenwich Country Club are we in fact speaking about the same club? If the club is nothing more than a set of people, then we are not because its members define a set. However, I think that most people will hold that the club still exists.

In holding that the club still exists with all new members, we are holding that something other than the members still exists. It can't be the name of the club nor the building in which its members congregate, because these are simply accidental properties of the club. What is essential to the club? I hold that, among other things to which we may not have access, it is the internal causal relation that the members bear on each other.[18] And in our project, if each accidental property can be changed without losing anything essential, and there is something essential underlying the accidental properties, then it must be the case that the essence is found in the causal relations that the properties have on one another.

Consider a further commonsensical fleshing out of the issue. Let us say that the club of people has always had, and still has, just the president as the only executive board position. When the club began the first few presidents were very lenient, and the members began to lose respect for each president. However, years later, the presidents became more strict and accomplished great tasks bettering the club. With increased morale from the members, more people began joining and the club began prospering like it never had before.

I wish to highlight the fact that something in the club has remained the same. Indeed it is the case that the club's existence is not dependent upon its number of members, and perhaps even the executive positions could change through amendments to the club's constitution. Moreover, it seems that a pattern persists. The actual rules that the club follows may change through amendments, but there must be an order concerning the way in which these changes are made. This order seems to be reflected through a unique pattern.[19]

Over a duration of many years my brown hair may become progressively gray. As well, the tight skin on my face may become rather loose and drawn downward. (Having a particular shape to my face and having a particular hair color are accidental properties.) However, after many years I meet a high school friend. She recognizes me. She tells me that she recognized me because of the way my hair stands up on the top of my head and because of the rosiness of my cheeks. However, "standing up" is a property attributed to different hair than I had earlier in my life. And moreover, my hair is now gray and less plentiful. As well, the property of rosiness attributed to my cheeks is a different property of rosiness than I had when I was younger. My cheeks are now no longer red in color, but rather, there is only a faint pink. But just like the case of the club, the pattern of properties persisted diachronically, and this allowed for re-identification.

This is obviously a hypothetical case since I have yet to age as described above. And so, in terms of bettering my account, I would only urge the reader to compare one of his or her child-photographs to one of his or her most recent photographs, and pay special attention to the resemblance or pattern underlying his or her perceivable accidental properties.

Conclusion

I have discussed reasons for holding that there are essential and accidental properties of humans. I then devoted some time to explaining the claim that perceivable accidental properties allow us to numerically distinguish between different entities. As well, I spoke about bundles of perceivable accidental properties being responsible for diachronic re-identification. And if this is the case, i.e., accidental properties are responsible for individual diachronic re-identification, then it must be the case that there is something essential underlying these bundles of properties, perhaps a unique pattern or a pattern-instance, i.e., that which can be viewed on par with quality-instances but which is a pattern of qualities, rather than an individual quality. And if it is a pattern-instance that is essential, perhaps such an essence would count as an individual essential property that is accessible to the senses.

If people are less sympathetic to holding that a completely different group of accidental properties can make up the same bundle, then I will hold that these unique bundles are still responsible for identification (if not also re-identification). That is, the haecceity of the bundle or the patter-instance is what allows us to numerically distinguish one thing from another. For even in the case where a complete stranger stumbles upon twin siblings, who may both have individual essential properties that are not accessible to the senses, she can use one or more perceivable accidental properties to individuate one from the other. It may be as subtle as one throwing a temper-tantrum in the middle of a restaurant and one sitting complacent eating his meal that allows the onlooker to diachronically track the twins throughout dinner.

Notes

1 I thank Professor José A. Benardete for making me aware of this distinction.

2 Van Inwagen, Peter. *Material Beings*. Ithaca: Cornell University Press, 1990. p. 84.

3 *Ibid.* p. 84.

4 Quine, Willard Van Orman. *Word & Object*. Cambridge: The MIT Press, 1960. p.199.

5 Locke, John. *An Essay Concerning Human Understanding*. (ed. By Peter H. Nidditch) Oxford: Oxford University Press, 1975. p.441.

6 Quine, p.199.

7 Locke, p.440.

8 Locke, p.441.

9 Locke, p.442.

10 I would like to note that there are some who hold that there are hints of accidentalism in Locke. I will not take up this issue in this paper. My desire with presenting Locke and Quine as relativistic anti-essentialists is to show two different facets to this doctrine.

11 Quine, p.199.

12 Quine, p.199.

13 Van Inwagen, p.82.

14 Elder, Crawford L. "On The Reality of Medium-Sized Objects." *Philosophical Studies* 83 (1996): 191-211.

15 A potential worry may arise. If we follow this train of thought it might seem that we end up with two things which are different but have all their properties, i.e., their essential and accidental properties, in common. And thus, it may seem that we are committed to a violation Leibniz's identity of indiscernibles. However, this is not the case. Indeed any two humans share the same essential property sorting them into the human group. If we are able to individuate one from the other, then there seems to be either accidental or essential properties, namely individual essential properties, that the two do not share. I argue in the next paragraph that we may not

have access to the latter, and thus the former are usually more readily available for individuation. But even in the case of identical twins, who share most of their accidental properties, there is nothing to say that they don't have unique individual essential properties. In the end, my view does not commit us to accepting the above worry.

16 However, we may want to investigate a case when individuation will occur through the use of individual essential properties rather than through accidental properties. Again, let us consider the case of identical twins. Even if two twins have different accidental properties, it may be the case that it is quite difficult to use these to individuate one from the other. In such cases we can turn to unique individual essential properties. However, it must be noted that these cases might be difficult in terms of individuation because we may often have difficulty determining individual essential properties for any human being, twin or non-twin.

17 Van Inwagen, p.87.

18 This is roughly van Inwagen's argument on p.84 of *Material Beings*.

19 Someone may want to hold that it is impossible to tell two clubs apart with the same constitution. However, if two clubs have the same constitution and choose to make different decisions within it, then we can diachronically track two different clubs. If, however, they make all of the same decisions, then it may be more difficult to tell them apart. In such a case, we may need to look to the two clubs' individual essential properties, to which we may not even have access.

REFERENCES

Elder, Crawford L. "On The Reality of Medium-Sized Objects." *Philosophical Studies* 83 (1996): 191-211.

Locke, John. *An Essay Concerning Human Understanding.* (ed. By Peter H. Nidditch). Oxford: Oxford University Press, 1975.

Quine, Willard Van Orman. *Word & Object.* Cambridge: The MIT Press, 1960.

Van Inwagen, Peter. *Material Beings.* Ithaca: Cornell University Press, 1990.

Keynote Addresses

THEMES IN CONTEMPORARY ANALYTIC PHILOSOPHY AS REFLECTED IN THE WORK OF MONTY PYTHON

Gary L. Hardcastle
Virginia Tech

This talk is perhaps best described as a semi-silly, semi-serious illustration of various themes in analytic philosophy (e.g. verificationism, semantic holism, the role of human reasoning) by way of skits presented by the British comedy troupe Monty Python. It was written in response to a request from the Philosophy Club at Virginia Tech, and has been delivered there several times in the last few years.

My aim in this talk is to present a comprehensive overview of each and every one of the main themes endured by analytic philosophy in the last sixty years or so, and to argue the bold historical claim that the whole lot is well represented—indeed, often best represented—in the work of Graham Chapman, John Cleese, Terry Gilliam, Eric Idle, Terry Jones, and Michael Palin, collectively and henceforth referred to as "Monty Python." Since I have all of fifty minutes to make my case, I expect we'll have time for a song at the end. So let's get to it.

Analytic philosophy has spent the last seventy years engaged in two successive revolts. If you didn't know this, don't feel bad—philosophers engaged in revolt look pretty much exactly like philosophers not engaged in revolt. They go to the office, teach introduction to philosophy, make a few phone calls, have office hours, work on a rough draft, and head home. There's no storming of the parliament building, ripping up of city streets, or lobbing of Molotov cocktails for your revolting philosopher, or, I should say, the philosopher in revolt.

To see philosophical revolt you have to go to the philosophical journals, and indeed that's where you find the first revolt, the famous revolt against metaphysics. This occurred in the 1920s and 30s and was carried out by the logical positivists, who are now regarded in analytic circles as something like folk heroes. If you have been conditioned by college life to feel guilty if you have not yet written something down, then write down the names of the leading logical positivists: 'Moritz Schlick', 'Rudolf Carnap', 'Hans Hahn', 'Otto Neurath', 'Herbert Feigl', 'Philipp Frank', and 'A. J. Ayer'.

The positivists' revolt against metaphysics was really successful. Really, really, successful. It was so successful that even now, when everyone agrees that (a) logical positivism is dead, and that (2) even if it isn't dead, its arguments against metaphysics, to use the technical phrase, suck pond water, upper-level courses in metaphysics taught in universities throughout the analytic world—indeed, in this very university—typically begin with self-conscious multi-week probing reflections on whether or not it's really okay to now do metaphysics.

There's a wonderful irony behind this revolt against metaphysics. It's that the logical positivists, whose basic complaint against metaphysics was that it was all irretrievably confused and fuzzy, themselves had a notion of metaphysics that was, you guessed it, somewhat confused and fuzzy. The fuzziness was manifested in a couple of now-famous technical glitches in the positivist program. Whenever anyone came up with a means of sorting out the good philosophy from the metaphysical, some young upstart logic whiz always pointed out that the proposed means either ruled out some clearly good philosophy or ruled in some ghastly bit of metaphysics. Even worse, nobody could ever find an acceptable way to defend the main sail on the positivist's ship, the verifiability criterion. The verifiability criterion said that the meaning of a meaningful statement was conveyed completely by the means by which it is verified. The criterion was enormously useful in accomplishing sort of an end-run around metaphysics; since metaphysical statements couldn't be verified, the criterion told you they were meaningless. The positivists were pretty happy about all this until it sank in that the verifiability criterion itself couldn't be verified. Think about it—to verify the verifiability criterion, you'd have to sort out all the meaningful statements beforehand, and that you couldn't do without first assuming the verifiability criterion! So the verifiability criterion is not verifiable. If it's not verifiable, then, according to itself, it's meaningless. So the verifiability criterion might as well be a bit of metaphysics. In the possible world in which Homer Simpson is not only a real person but a logical positivist living in Vienna in the 1930s, Homer just said "D'oh!"

Now, I'm sure you're wondering when I'm going to stop rambling on about logical positivism and show something from Monty Python. Hang on, I've got one more thing to say. It's now pretty clear that the positivists weren't revolting against metaphysics per se, but against philosophy itself. Really, they were quite upset that philosophy had not made much progress. Other sciences had of course; consider, for example, physics, chemistry, astronomy, biology, metallurgy, geology, geography, archeology, agriculture, mathematics, genetics, political science, poultry science, economics, anthropology, horticulture, nutrition, medicine, psychology, sociology, forestry... well, you get the idea. It seemed like philosophy had even had a head start over all the other intellectual enterprises, but had somehow forgotten to keep in touch with the real world. Instead it spiraled off into bizarro metaphysics, where you could say anything at all and get away with it because there was no way to determine the truth of what you said or indeed if you even really said anything at all in the first place. This is really the first, and the biggest theme, of contemporary analytic philosophy—the contempt for innumerable philosophers of yore, who managed to get nothing done while everyone else was off figuring out neat things like natural selection and the heliocentricity of the solar system. Now let's look at our first clip.

Clip #1: International Football
(From Live at the Hollywood Bowl)

Notice a few things. First, not one of the players is a logical positivist. That's because all the logical positivists are in s the stands (if they've come to the game at all), screaming omething like "Kick the ball already, you silly nits!" Okay, there is Wittgenstein, playing for Deutschland, but you can tell by the tweed that it's the *later* Wittgenstein, the Wittgenstein who wrote *Philosophical Investigations*, and who was reviled by Russell, for example, for having abandoned good (i.e., analytic) philosophy. Notice also that it's not even a philosopher who starts the ball rolling, so to speak, but Archimedes, an engineer. You saw all the others wondering around, isn't it annoying? Well, the positivists were annoyed too, and that's why they revolted.

The positivists' version of the Molotov Cocktail, you'll recall, was the verifiability criterion. I have a good clip for that, too, but I have a thing or two to say first. Despite its troubling aspects, the verifiability criterion became the cornerstone of verificationism, which is roughly the position that the only way to say something meaningful about the world is to say something that can, in principle, be determined to be either true or false in light of experience. Central to verificationism is the notion that for each statement about the world there is a definite set of experiences that by itself determines whether the statement in question is true or false. This is sometimes called "semantic reductionism" at the level of statements, as in: any meaningful statement can be reduced to a set of experiences (more correctly, statements about experience, if you favor the brand of philosophy I call "annoying particularism"). If you're out to verify the statement 'The cat is on the mat', for example, then presumably you're in search of certain experiences—like seeing the cat on the mat. Having the experience guaranteed the truth of the statement, or at least that is what verificationism told you. A really important spear that fell the mastodon of positivism—more important, perhaps, than the embarrassing bit about the verifiability criterion not itself being verifiable—was the discovery that reductionism simply wasn't true. It couldn't be true! To determine the truth or falsity of a statement you not only need a set of special experiences, but you need to know the truth or falsity of a host of other different statements as well. That is, verifying that the cat is on the mat is not a matter of experience alone, but of accepting all sorts of other different statements, all the way from 'Light rays travel in straight lines' to 'I am not having another one of those darn flashbacks.'

Now, in response to this you might be inclined to say, as is my wife on occasion, something along the lines of "So what? Big deal." Well, hang on. We've just shown that if you admit that language gets its meaning by being hooked up with the world, so to speak, then you have to deny that, strictly speaking, sentences have meanings all by themselves. Instead, they have meanings only when they hang out with other sentences. Willard van Orman Quine, a philosopher whom I admire so much that I am hoping to convince my wife to name our third child either Willard, van, or Orman (her choice), put it best in 1951. He said, "statements about the external world face the tribunal of experience not individually but only as a corporate body" (Quine 1951, p.41). Quine's remark is an expression of that view which opposes semantic reductionism, semantic holism. The key idea of semantic holism is that meaning is had by the whole language, but not by any of its parts alone.

Semantic holism has some absolutely marvelous consequences. One is that you can't really assert a meaningful statement without sort of implicitly asserting a bunch of other statements—indeed, perhaps the entire language—at the same time. Another is that it seems possible to hold any arbitrarily chosen statement as true no matter what empirical evidence is presented against it, and to do so rationally, by rejecting and accepting the right related statements. So if you want to maintain that the cat is on the mat when everybody else denies it, you can do so by deciding that certain atmospheric phenomena are making it look like there's no cat, or that the cat on the mat is a special kind of transparent cat, and so on. And you can maintain these claims by making still further adjustments in other claims. This sounds like silliness, but the point is that it is just the kind of silliness that verificationism had hoped to do away with.

I know, it's been a long time since a clip. So let's have two. First, watch how Monty Python conveys this conflict between verificationism and semantic holism, by means of parrot.

Clip #2: Dead Parrot
(Monty Python's Flying Circus, Full Frontal Nudity)
http://www.stone-dead.asn.au/sketches/petshop1.htm

Mr. Praline, the man attempting to return the parrot, is our verificationist, as is evidenced by his attempt to verify the death of the parrot by reference to experience, such as seeing that it's dead, its falling to the ground when sent aloft, its being nailed to its perch, and so on. The shopkeeper is our philosophically more sophisticated holist. He knows that maintaining the truth of other statements, concerning for example the bird's strength and its affection for the fjords, will allow him to maintain that the parrot is alive. Notice who wins: the shopkeeper is never brought to accept that the parrot is dead. Indeed, the sketch could go on indefinitely without that ever happening.

Here's a rather more graphic depiction of holism.

Clip #3: Arthur Meets the Black Knight (MPHG)
http://www.stone-dead.asn.au /sketches/others/blckkngt.htm

Despite the successive loss of limb, it is the Black Knight who is our holist. That's because he maintains as true that he shall prevent the bridge from being crossed, and he knows how to maintain it come what may. If King Arthur ultimately triumphs over the Black Knight to cross the bridge, it is for contingent and empirical reasons, I would argue, and not for any weakness in the Knight's arguments. And you realize that I could even argue that Arthur didn't cross the bridge at all; now that's semantic holism.

I bet you've guessed by now what the second of the two revolts in contemporary analytic philosophy is. It's the revolt against logical positivism, of course! If you're starting to feel guilty again for not having written anything down, then write down the names 'Carl Hempel', 'Thomas Kuhn', 'Norwood Russell Hanson,' 'Nelson Goodman,' 'Hilary Putnam', and, of course, 'W. v. O. Quine'. These are just a few of the prominent post-positivists. There are lots more. Indeed, it's much easier to list all the living positivists, and barring a change in the philosophical winds it's going to get easier and easier with the passing of every year.

At any rate, unlike most revolts, the revolt against positivism was either sufficiently sensitive or sufficiently indiscriminate—it's hard to tell which—to retain the essentially correct aspects of what it was revolting against. Specifically, it retained positivism's love affair with language. Post-positivists, like the positivists, believed that understanding anything really important, like how we know, what there is, or what's right and wrong, meant first understanding our language, which after all is pretty much the best and only means by which we express what we know, what there is, and what's right and wrong (There are a few exceptions—philosophers who have given up the linguistic orientation of logical positivism. Bas van Fraassen, Ian Hacking, and Richard Rorty come to mind). Throw in semantic holism, and it should come as no surprise that the story of analytic philosophy since the downfall of logical positivism is essentially the story of successive, multi-pronged and somewhat uncoordinated attempts to sort out the consequences of the fact that the unit of meaning in a language is not the sentence but the language itself.

One consequence of semantic holism, believe it or not, comes in the form of a threat to the very foundation of society. Let me explain. Holism seems to warrant bad reasoning, for it allows one to rationally maintain any statement come what may. That's bad enough. But it took about a half second for analytic philosophers to realize that things were, potentially, much worse. You see, philosophers from way, way, back in the analytic tradition believed deeply that, one way or another, reason was the proper foundation for society; it was both the mechanism that runs society and the grease on which the mechanism turned. Ever interested to be of use, philosophers have worked hard at coming up with a theory of argument to describe how reason ought to work in daily life. This is why undergraduates are subjected to classes like Introduction to Logic; philosophy departments sincerely believe that this class will make better citizens. But, as some of you might have noticed, the theory of argument asks that you grant certain crucial statements beforehand, without argument. Statements like, for example, that something can't both be true and false at the same time. Well, if holism is true, then we can't count on our fellow citizens accepting such statements. Nor can we count on being able to convince them that they ought to accept such statements, if they don't! We shouldn't even call them crazy if they don't accept such statements, though we do it anyway! In short, if holism is true then the whole notion of argument, and of reason, is up for grabs. Would you like to see what that looks like?

Clip #4: The Argument Clinic
(Monty Python's Flying Circus, The Money Programme)
http://www.stone-dead.asn.au/sketches/argument.htm

Ah, you laugh, you laugh. But be aware, on some philosophical accounts, you've just witnessed a small piece of the end of civilization.

Of course, not all the post-positivists were so imbued with the apocalyptic vision. Indeed, some were decidedly unimpressed by the news that rationality could not be the foundation of society, they having already decided that rationality was over-rated. After all, we'd been managing marginally well as a species so far without much of it, so there was no reason now to worry about everything falling apart. What grabbed these folk about semantic holism was that it suggested that it took only a very small difference in the linguistic behavior of two individuals to warrant the conclusion that they were speaking altogether different languages. For example, if you and I mean very different things when we make the noise: "My brain hurts", and if this difference reverberates throughout the rest of our linguistic utterances, then maybe it makes sense to say that we are speaking different languages, despite the fact that each sounds like English and even despite the fact that we think we understand each other perfectly well. Now, if you also suspect that a speaker's language plays a big role in determining the nature of the world in which the speaker lives, then you can put these two together and conclude that each of us has our own world, perhaps wildly different than our neighbors'. This line of reasoning has been tossed around in the philosophical literature quite a bit in the last thirty years; you could run off and read all about it in the library, or you could get the basic idea from Monty Python.

Clip #5: Nudge Nudge
(MPFC, How to recognise different types of trees...)
http://www.stone-dead.asn.au/sketches/nudge.htm

Different worlds, indeed, and perhaps different languages too. They eventually do "connect," of course, though not quite in the manner desired by Norman, the man on our left.

I spoke about the project of founding society on reason, and about the blow that that project was dealt by semantic holism. Very recently, things have gotten even worse for that particular project. Imagine that holism could somehow be circumvented, so that we could all be assured that we shared the same language and the same world. It now looks, in light of empirical evidence about human reasoning, like even these rosy conditions shouldn't make for optimism about rationality in society. What the empirical evidence has suggested—and, to be fair, this is the topic of heated debate—is that, from the point of view of logic, human reasoning is very bad indeed, and that there's little hope of improving it. We're wired up, psychologically speaking, to reason badly. How badly, exactly? About as badly as the individuals in the following clip.

Clip #6: the witch trial (Holy Grail)
http://www.stone-dead.asn.au/sketches/others/witch.htm

The folks who fail to see what's so funny about this, by the way, are exactly the folks who at one time or another have taught Introduction to Logic; they don't need psychologists or their empirical studies to tell them about the reasoning abilities of the average citizen. To the rest of the analytic world, however, it's been something of a shock, although, as I said, there's quite a bit of debate over the whole matter.

I know what some of you are thinking. It's something like, "Okay, I'm convinced. The best expositor of *contemporary analytic* philosophy is Monty Python. But let's not get carried away. There's a lot more to philosophy than analytic philosophy, and what do these Monty Python people have to say about all of that? Not much, I imagine!" Those of you saying this have in mind continental philosophy, named I believe after both Continental Airlines and the continental breakfast, in each case in honor of the failure to satisfy. I could go on at length in thorough refutation of this complaint, but as my area of specialty, not to mention my topic today, is analytic philosophy, I'll refute it with a single counterexample. Here it is.

Clip #7: The Cheese Shop (MPFC, Salad Days)
http://www.stone-dead.asn.au/sketches/cheese.htm

Now I hope you see that Mr. Mousebender's attempt to get a little cheese resembles various other life experiences, most obviously, perhaps, a typical attempt to register for classes. But I'd like to suggest something more grand. I'd like to suggest that the cheese shop is life itself, as described to us by existentialism. Mr. Mousebender is our existentialist hero, creating himself through choices of cheese in an uncooperative, nay, unfeeling world. Mr. Wensleydale, the keeper of the cheese shop, is the burden of life incarnate, who, in the fashion of Sisyphus' rock, unfailingly returns a negative answer only to be queried again by our hero. Did Nietzsche, Sartre, or Camus, those all-stars of Continental philosophy, ever put it any better, in any of their often abstruse and sometimes impenetrable scribblings? Say no more, say no more.

I know there are some folks out there who are still unconvinced of the philosophical stature of Monty Python. This is not because they worry that Monty Python has ignored continental philosophy, but because they think Monty Python is insensitive to THE HISTORY OF PHILOSOPHY. Philosophy is a conversation going back to Thales, they will say, and if you don't know what's been said then you're simply not doing philosophy, let alone good philosophy. This is a criticism leveled not infrequently at contemporary analytic philosophy, and though I agree with the sentiment, I do not agree that it works against Monty Python. As before, I rest my response on a single counterexample, prefaced with a comment or two. Good history of philosophy doesn't just tell you what past philosophers said. It reveals connections between what they said, and connections between the philosophers themselves. And even better history discovers connections which are novel, surprising, and provocative. And the absolute best history of philosophy ties all this together and presents it in a manner so striking and harmonious that it just must be true. And since song is that thing which is striking and harmonious, the absolute most spectacularly best history of philosophy must be done in song. With this in mind, I present Monty Python's Bruces' Philosophers Song. It speaks for itself, and so, out of respect for Monty Python, whose brilliant explications of the central themes of contemporary analytic philosophy have gone unnoticed until today, and out of respect for the glorious history of philosophy, let us rise and sing the Bruces' Philosophers Song with the members of Monty Python. You'll see the lyrics on the screen.

Themes In Contemporary Analytic Philosophy As Reflected in the Work of Monty Python

Clip #8: Bruces' Philosophers Song
(LHB); armed thugs force all to rise and sing.
http://www.stone-dead.asn.au/lyrics/bruces-philosophers-song.htm

Thank you.

References

Quine, W. v. O. "Two Dogmas of Empiricism," in *From a Logical Point of View.* Cambridge, MA: Harvard University Press, 1951.

"WHEN ARTISTS READ PHILOSPHERS…": A STUDY IN THE ORIGINS OF THE 'POSTMODERN'

Jere Paul O'Neal Surber
University of Denver/Johannes Gutenberg Universität-Mainz

A note to the reader: This essay was specifically written and delivered as an oral presentation to a general academic audience; I have decided to retain most of the style in which it was originally formulated. Also, the "live" presentation utilized numerous illustrative visual images; in the printed format, I refer only to those essential to main argument of the essay.

Introduction: The Traditional Relation between "Philosophers" and "Artists"

To start my presentation, I'll have to ask you to make, with me, one big assumption: it is that we can, at least up until relatively recent times, make a fairly unproblematic distinction between philosophers and artists. Let's be very simplistic to begin with and just assume that "philosophers," historically speaking, are those persons who have written texts which today are typically taught and studied in most academic departments of philosophy (folks like Plato, Aristotle, Thomas Aquinas, Descartes, Hume, Kant, Hegel, Heidegger, Wittgenstein, and so forth), and that "artists" (in the most common meaning of this term) are those persons who have produced the sort of visual artifacts that are today studied in most academic programs in art history (folks like Praxiteles, Michaelangelo, Dürer, Rubens, David, Delacroix, Manet, Van Gogh, and Picasso). Now, we know that some of the folks we call philosophers in fact, at one point or another, viewed some of the works produced by folks we call artists, and that some of the folks we call artists occasionally read texts written by philosophers. But until quite recent times, it would be difficult to claim, on the basis of the available evidence, that such experiences on the part of either significantly affected their own creative activity in their respective fields of endeavor.

There was a good reason for this. Philosophy, as first developed in our tradition by Plato, was principally concerned with those purely intellectual "truths" which only the mind, not the senses, could apprehend, and works of visual art, however "real" they might appear, were, at best, "images of images," copies of sensually perceived "objects," which were themselves only "copies" or "images" of the "real realities" which Plato regarded as the "eternal forms." For most of our philosophical tradition, the philosopher had his or her hands full trying to relate the vagaries and mutability of the directly perceived world to clear and immutable ideas, and any sort of copies or mirror reflections of these fell below the threshold of philosophical interest. Producers of visual art, for their part, were primarily concerned with a diverse range of issues including materials, technique, patronage, popular iconology, and so forth, to none of which the abstract speculations of the philosophers had much to contribute. (I realize that this is a broad generalization, to which there are likely a few notable exceptions—some of the artists and Classicists of the Italian Renaissance and Albrecht Dürer come to mind—but I think it is by and large true of the vast majority of canonical artists and philosophers.) This situation began to change gradually during the Enlightenment, especially in the 18th century. Several historical developments played into this. On the side of the artists, mention should be made of the increasing demand, on the part of the burgeoning academies, that the training of artists include some general cultural literacy; the development of more public occasions, and eventually museums, in which artworks could be exhibited, discussed, and critiqued; and, perhaps, the general permeation of pre-revolutionary society by discussions of liberal philosophical ideas, promoted especially by the salons and the gradual relaxation of censorship. For their part, philosophers during this period gradually came to recognize "aesthetics" as a distinctive branch of their own enterprise. In fact, it was the German philosopher Alexander Baumgarten who, in the 1735, first employed the term "aesthetics" in something of the sense in which it is still used today. Thanks to such figures of the German *Aufklärung* as Lessing, Mendelssohn, and, most of all, Kant, "aesthetics" became well established, by the end of the 18th century, as a basic and important field of philosophy.

However, it was not until the advent of the Romantic movement in the last years of the 18th century that these developments would bear significant fruit. Understandably, the first serious encounters between artistic practice and philosophical theory occurred in the area of literature: it is well-known, for example, that such figures as Goethe, Schiller, Coleridge, Wordsworth, Novalis, and Hölderlin made serious efforts to read philosophy (especially the works of Kant, Fichte, and Schelling) with care, and that such philosophers as the Schlegel brothers, Schelling, Schleiermacher, Hegel, Schopenhauer, and Nietzsche returned the favor. The situation among visual artists has been a bit more difficult to determine (and scholarly work in this direction is still very much underway). However, it is already well established that the philosophical concept of the sublime, especially as developed by Kant and Burke, was familiar and utilized by many visual artists; that Friedrich and Runge, leaders of the German Romantic movement in painting, were at least familiar with the general outlines of Kantian philosophy and its developments; and that there was at least a general interest in philosophical aesthetics on the part of such major figures as Turner, Constable, Delacroix, and Ingres. Nonetheless, despite the beginnings of a flirtation between philosophers and visual artists during the Romantic period, it would be difficult to claim on the basis of presently available evidence either that any specific philosophical work or position was *directly* influenced by a serious encounter with the visual arts, or that any visual artist produced artworks based upon a direct engagement with an identifiable philosophical position.

I. Hegel's *Philosophy of the Fine Arts*: A New Rapprochement between Art and Philosophy

I want now to propose that we can fairly precisely trace the beginning of one important characteristic of "modern" and "postmodern" developments in the visual arts to those writings of G. W. F. Hegel, mostly dating from the 1820s, which comprise his "Philosophy of the Fine Arts." While Hegel's "aesthetics" is admittedly embedded in the final division of a much more comprehensive "system" which included Logic, the Philosophy of Nature, and the Philosophy of Spirit, his treatment of art is important and original for several reasons.

First, Hegel, speaking as a technical academic philosopher, nonetheless came to assume the role traditionally reserved for the "critic" or "connoisseur" in explicitly discussing and, in some cases, passing critical judgment upon specific works of visual art. Second, he accords to art in general, along with religion and philosophy, full membership in the realm of "Absolute Spirit," the sphere of the highest and most profound productions of human culture. Gone is the "third remove from the truth" theory of art prevalent from Plato to, arguably, even Kant. Finally, and most importantly for our purposes, Hegel goes so far as to claim that all three of these realms—art, religion, and philosophy—express the same "true content" and differ only in the various "forms" in which this is expressed.

While Hegel himself sees these three realms as ordered in relation to their adequacy to express the ultimate "Truth" of human spirit and culture, giving precedence to philosophy over art and religion, and to religion ("revealed Christianity" is what he has in mind) over art, he nonetheless opens the door to the dual possibilities that art can express philosophical "truth" in its own distinctive media and that philosophy can (perhaps even must) be, in some important ways, instructed by aesthetic forms of expression.

Now my purpose in making this historical point is the following: I want to propose that one suggestive way of approaching later developments in the visual arts (and, to some degree, philosophy as well) in the 20th century—so-called "modernism" and "postmodernism" in particular—is to regard them as interpreting and exploring, in various ways, the possibilities first opened by Hegel's aesthetics. In particular, I want to suggest, with respect to the visual arts of the 20th century, that we can identify an ongoing engagement and, within limits, a sort of "dialectical development" of the cross-appropriation and interpenetration of philosophical ideas and artistic practice. Let's begin with the so-called "modernist movement" (which admittedly deserves a good deal more attention than I can give it here).

II. A Brief Characterization of Modernism's Philosophical Engagement

Very roughly put, what occurred between Hegel's aesthetics and the advent of Modernism in the visual arts in the first decades of the 20th century was the fading of religion as a crucial element of the cultural landscape. Where Hegel had seen the relation between art and philosophy as mediated by a Christianity still robust in his day, its fading from the cultural scene became increasingly registered, most famously by Nietzsche and his thesis of the "Death of God," as the 19th century drew to a close. The decline of religion as a significant cultural force left art and philosophy free to confront one another directly, another point made with great force by Nietzsche. More accurately, perhaps, at least for some of the early founders of Modernism such as Joyce, Pound, Eliot, Kandinsky, Malevitch, Mondrian, and Schoenberg, religion became assimilated to art under the rubric of art's alleged "spiritual function." For its part, philosophy, which had been disentangling itself from religious concerns for the last century since Kant's critique of theology, was, at least for a while, satisfied to concede such "spiritual remnants" of religion to the side of art with little fuss, and to focus upon such issues as logic and methodology, the foundations of science, and the formal structure of consciousness bound up with these.

The result of the cultural repartitioning signaled by Modernism was something quite novel and something which even Hegel probably could not have anticipated. It did not, right away, result in a new rapprochement between the *discipline* of philosophy and the visual arts, but rather marked an opening where the artwork became "visual philosophy" and the artist himself or herself came to assume the earlier role of the philosopher concerned with the sort of "ultimate questions" concerning human beings, nature, and society which "academic philosophy" seemed to have left aside.

Modernism's most famous and self-appointed "official" theorist, Clement Greenberg (not an "academic philosopher" be it noted), was probably right in holding that one basic impulse of Modernism was the sort of universal critique begun by Kant and that this was to be accomplished by purging from the visual arts all historical detritus, including any "representational content," that did not directly concern the artwork's own distinctive medium and its formal possibilities. His further view that the "modernist artwork" thus represented the maximum degree of self-reflexivity, that it was simply and solely "about itself," at once and seamlessly signifier and signified, was also highly suggestive as well as widely influential.

However, Greenberg's account overlooked (or perhaps deliberately ignored) three equally important features of Modernism as it existed in fact, if not in theory, characteristics which would eventually be foregrounded—sometimes, as we will see, with a vengeance—in what will come to be called "Postmodernism." The first was precisely that allegedly "spiritual" dimension of art claimed, in one form or another, by virtually every modernist artist. The second was the fact that the alleged "self-reflexivity" of the modernist artwork, even if granted, remained "mediated" (to use a Hegelian term) by a great deal of theoretical and social discourse on the part of artists themselves, issuing in a massive archive of manifestos, position papers, essays, exhibition notes, interviews, and unrecorded discussions. This, by the way, clearly violated Greenberg's own emphatic separating of the roles of artist and critic on the grounds that any conflation of these roles would threaten the seamless character of the modernist artwork. Finally, while Greenberg admittedly shared some of the more "formalist" ideas of such Frankfurt School theorists as Theodor Adorno, he tended to discount the other indispensable element of their philosophical orientation shared with most practicing artists: that, in general, "art," whatever else it may be, is a social institution and, in particular, that even a maximally "self-reflexive" artwork can be seen to be such only against a historical background and within specific conditions which themselves fall short of such seamless "self-reflexivity." (To be fair, Greenberg himself eventually came to recognize some of these points, but by that time they had already been made more forcefully and decisively by others, including artists themselves, leaving his name associated mostly with his earlier views.) To spell out my general suggestion on this point, it is that modernist artists functioned within a framework of contradictions between an "official" modernist theory and aesthetic, and a set of actual artistic concerns and practices opposed to it in important ways, and that it was precisely these contradictions which became thematized in postmodernist critiques of modernism.

III. From Modernism to Postmodernism

To return to the philosophers, in the meantime and certainly by the 40s and 50s, they had begun to awake from their methodologist and positivist slumbers of the early part of the century. Most importantly, from whatever direction, whether Anglo-American analytic philosophy, Continental phenomenology and existentialism, French structuralism and semiotics, or new developments in psychoanalysis, philosophers had begun to converge upon a single overarching theme: the problem of language and, more broadly, of human signification and meaning itself. This new focus upon the act and structure of human signification called into radical question any possibility of achieving some sort of context-, history-, politics- or system-independent self-reflexivity that could function as the aim, if not the actual accomplishment, of the modernist artwork. At the same time, however, it suggested a new ground of rapprochement between philosophy and the visual arts. If modernist theory had abandoned disciplinary philosophy in search of its own forms of "spiritual discipline," "truth," and "absolute reflexivity," it could now look to these newly emergent philosophical trends as suggestive of novel directions for overcoming its own growing social isolation, commercial co-optation, and aesthetic elitism.

Most revolutionary in the dynamics of this development of postmodern ideas and artforms was a new division of labor between philosophy and the visual arts. Since Kant and up through existentialism, the hallmark of much mainstream philosophy had precisely been its claims to radical self-critique and self-reflexivity, an aim which modernist art had attempted to take over on its own independent terms. In the period after the Second World War, however, philosophy came first to doubt and then to reject self-reflexivity entirely as a "metaphysical prejudice" inherited from a now-discredited tradition. (I have in mind here such critiques of the "Western tradition" as those of Heidegger, Derrida, Foucault, and Lyotard.) But to many philosophers as well as artists, this did not mean that all forms of reflexivity could or had to be abandoned, only that, after all was said and done, philosophy as a specific mode of *linguistic* discourse might not, at least drawing exclusively on its own resources, be equipped to explore or elucidate this very effectively. Rather, it fell to the "postmodern artwork" both to assay the variety of types of incomplete reflexivity of which finite and historically embedded human beings are actually capable and, at the same time, to reveal their limits, to register concretely, as it were, the unavoidable gaps and spaces between signifiers and signifieds.

In a sense, then, I am suggesting that, within the intellectual economy of postmodernism, the traditional roles of artist and philosopher have, in a certain sense, become reversed. To employ a Hegelian formulation, art has increasingly become the "content" of philosophy, and philosophy has assumed the "form" of art. Or, put in different terms, it has fallen to artists forcefully to confront the problematic history of philosophy, ideology, and art and its lingering effects upon us, while philosophy can, at least in certain of its most currently notorious varieties, only propose necessarily limited discursive accounts and interpretations of the "logic of culture" which is principally carried forward by art. (If you detect in my description of the current situation a tacit criticism of much contemporary philosophy, you would be right; however, this is another story and my purpose here is only to help locate where we may be at the present cultural moment. As Hegel said, "the Owl of Minerva spreads her wings only at dusk," and perhaps the sun is now low on the horizon. Still, I believe that this recent, almost incestuous, liaison between art and philosophy may yet prove salutary for both as we move into the next millennium.)

After more than a decade of contentious and often just plain confused, but always inconclusive, theoretical debate over the terms "modernism" and "postmodernism"—whether they mean anything at all and if so what—it may now be more helpful to consider specific cases. After all, no artist or philosopher ever went to sleep one night thinking he or she was a "modernist" and awoke the next morning with a "postmodern agenda." Rather, the journey from a "modernist" to a "postmodernist" outlook, like any other such change of cultural orientation, occurred within the work (and lives) of specific artists and philosophers as their own creative paths unfolded, oblivious to the labels that second-order and after-the-fact accounts might later give them. In what follows, I want to chart the path from a modernist to a postmodernist orientation of an artist whose development is, I think, particularly illustrative and illuminating for the question of the relation between art and philosophy with which we began. The artist whom I have chosen as a "case study" for my presentation is the still productive Joseph Kosuth, once described in the *New York Times*, at a relatively early stage of his career, as "the *eminence grise* of conceptual art while remaining its *enfant terrible*."

Kosuth's work is instructive for our dual questions of the relation between modernism and postmodernism and between art and philosophy in a number of respects. First, because Kosuth refuses to draw a line between his artistic production and his own philosophical theorizing about it, between his activities as an "art maker" and an essayist, his own engagements with specific philosophical views are explicit and relatively easy to chart. Second, his work has unfolded in a specifically American context where the assimilation of the often jargon-ridden discourses of deconstruction and postmodernism has been gradual and sometimes guarded. Although I will suggest that Kosuth eventually arrives at some key insights announced in these predominantly Continental movements, he does so mostly through his own creative practice, not as some more dogmatic attempt to instantiate or illustrate ideas derived from elsewhere. Third, his creative activity began precisely at the time that "modernism" was being questioned, but before "postmodernism" had yet solidified into any specific form of theory or practice. We can therefore trace, in the development of his work, a gradual process of transition from a "critical modernist" to a more postmodernist stance, without having to say, at any given point, that this is where he "becomes a postmodernist." Finally, I think that Kosuth himself has consistently aimed for a sort of intellectual clarity about his artistic practice that many other artists (and philosophers) who have traveled similar paths have either neglected or avoided.

IV. Joseph Kosuth's Path from "Critical Modernism" to "Postmodernism"

In most histories of recent developments in the visual arts, Kosuth is usually presented as a paradigmatic representative of the Conceptualist movement, and this latter is, in turn, generally treated as a sort of "transitional phase" in the development from Modernism to Postmodernism. (Although both claims might require some qualification, I won't quibble with them here.)

The work of Kosuth, an American born in 1945, first came to public attention in the mid-60s in a New York art world still dominated by the "in house" modernist struggle between the Abstract Expressionist painters and the more sculpturally-inclined Minimalists. At the same time, Pop art, at least implicitly critical of both and of the modernist program in general, was beginning to make serious inroads into the discussion. Originally, Kosuth felt himself closest to the minimalist views of Ad Reinhardt and Donald Judd, and in a broader sense, to the ultra-critical avant-gardism of Marcel Duchamp. In fact, he frequently cites Duchamp's infamous "ready-mades" as the real beginning of what Kosuth himself calls "Conceptualist Art." However, his essay "Art after Philosophy," published in 1969, announced conspicuously and unmistakably that his reading of a number of philosophers, but most importantly Ludwig Wittgenstein, had led him to begin charting a new path beyond the lingering modernism of his early influences.

IV.1. *Kosuth's First Engagement with Wittgenstein: The Artwork as "Analytic Proposition"*

In this essay, the precocious (now 24-year-old!) Kosuth presented one of the first major manifestos of "Conceptualist Art." A very tightly argued piece, as such documents go, the essay made the following points in clear and forceful prose:

(1) Beginning (as we did above, in fact) with Hegel, Kosuth observes that the sort of grand metaphysical project launched by German Idealism and, in a way, incorporated into the "modernist artwork" is now at an end. Specifically, it was conceptually laid to rest, once and for all, by, more than anything else, the radical linguistic and logical critique set forth in Ludwig Wittgenstein's *Tractatus Logico-Philosophicus* (1921). This founding document of Logical Positivism had demonstrated, or so Kosuth thought, that the realm of "meaningful propositions" was exhausted by two mutually exclusive classes: on the one hand, logical "tautologies" (also called "analytic propositions"), that is, pure statements of logical equivalence or identity like definitions or mathematical equations; and, on the other, factual empirical statements. This directly implied that since most traditional philosophical or aesthetic statements were neither one nor the other, they must, one and all, be regarded as logically "meaningless" or, literally, "nonsense." For Wittgenstein and Kosuth, this signaled nothing less than the "end of philosophy."

(2) For Kosuth, this "end of philosophy" represented, at the same time, "the beginning of art." Here, Kosuth immediately departed from Wittgenstein, who, in the *Tractatus*, seemed to suggest that art was not "propositional" at all but should be regarded, rather, as a sort of "expression of emotions." Kosuth, however, took a radically different course by claiming that the artwork must now be regarded as itself a sort of analytic proposition or tautology. Specifically, according to Kosuth, every work of art is, first and foremost, a *definition* of the nature of art, an answer to the purely conceptual question, "What is art?," and it is significant solely because of the sort of definition which it provides.

(3) A corollary of this is that the "physical experience," "aesthetical qualities," "style," "look"—all these summarized by what Kosuth calls the "morphology" of an artwork—are entirely irrelevant to what makes it an artwork, which is purely conceptual. Put in other terms, the nature of an artwork is to be sought not in any of its material, perceptual, or "formal" features but solely in the concept or idea which it *proposes* (remember here that it is a "*proposition*"). In this sense, modernist theory was misguided in thinking that "every artwork is about itself" or is some "purely self-referential object." Rather, for Kosuth, both of these formulations are suggestive but incorrect: just as every mathematical statement instantiates the whole language and conception of mathematics but is, in no way, "about itself," so every artwork proposes a definition of the whole of art but tells us nothing about itself, since there is nothing further to tell. Likewise, and even more radically, no *artwork* is a mere object in any event: rather, it is a concept which is only contingently or accidentally embod-

ied by a given but dispensable object or series of objects. (Upon this rests Kosuth's rejection of Modernism: the entire Modernist movement is boring and tedious precisely because it amounts merely to the endless reiteration of the self-same and identical "definition" of art: if you've seen one modernist work, you've conceived them all!)

(4) Kosuth's rejection of "realism" in art also follows directly from this. If the artwork is essentially an "analytic proposition," a definition of "art" itself, then it tells us nothing about "the way the world is" but "pictures" for us a concept of the nature of art. Representational art, viewed as art and not as something else (for example, a record of a beautiful mountain vista), is interesting only in that it *proposes* "reference to the world" as part of the definition of art: again, for Kosuth, if you've seen one representational painting, you've conceived them all.

(5) The real task of art, viewed in this way, is to continually question and critique the nature of art itself. Thus, as Kosuth suggests, the artist assumes from philosophy (now dead) the mantle of unremitting and continual self-critique. Going even further, Kosuth suggests that, "In this period of man, after philosophy and religion, art may possibly be one endeavor that fulfills what another age might have called 'man's spiritual needs.' Or, another way of putting it might be that art deals analogously with the state of things 'beyond physics' where philosophy [formerly] had to make assertions."

(6) There follows from all this the sort of "repartitioning of the division of labor" of art and discourses about it which I mentioned above. It is worth spelling out here.

First, for Kosuth, the distinction between the artist and the art critic, one of the pillars of modernism, disappears: because the role of the critic is strictly dependent upon "objects" produced "elsewhere" upon which to comment, and because these are irrelevant to art in any event, the critic who is not himself or herself an artist has nothing relevant to say about art. Rather, the only relevant "art criticism" is the course of the artist's own work as it continues to critique its own concepts and definitions of art. Consistent with this, Kosuth maintains that, inasmuch as art is purely conceptual, no line can be drawn between the "objects" which the artist makes and the linguistic "texts" which he or she writes: rather, Kosuth presents his own essays as themselves artworks and, in several exhibitions, offers them very literally as such. Further, since "concepts" (as Kosuth uses the term) can be indifferently presented verbally or visually, many of his "exhibitions" involve linguistic texts shown as "objects" (or we could just as well say, "objects" which are, in fact, linguistic texts). Finally, like that of the art critic, any autonomous role for the discourse of philosophy vanishes. For Kosuth, the last relevant philosopher was Wittgenstein, and it was Wittgenstein's distinctive role in the history of philosophy to lay philosophy to rest, turn out the lights, lock the door, throw away the keys—and finally leave artists free to do the conceptual work, formerly usurped by philosophers, that they should rightfully have been doing all along.

IV.2. *Kosuth's "works"*

Let's now consider some "works" (if we can still call them that) by Kosuth which may serve to illustrate some of these ideas.

- IV.2.1. The "Conceptualist Artwork" as "Analytic Proposition." *(One and Five Clocks*, 1965, the Tate Gallery)

This "work" consists of (1) a photocopied image of a clock, (2) the actual clock which was photocopied, set at some arbitrary time, which may or may not be the "present" time, and photocopied enlargements of dictionary entries for (3) "time," (4) "machination," and (5) "object."

- It was Kosuth's intention, as with many of his other works, that this "artwork" would have no "unique" status of its own, but could be easily reproduced at any other time or place, i.e. that its actual "temporal existence" was indefinitely repeatable. (In fact, he merely gave instructions for the photocopying and had someone else do it.) In other words, it was the "concept" underlying the assembling and juxtaposing of the "objects" and "texts" that was the "artwork" itself, not something that the artist himself physically produced.
- Similarly, because of this simple reproducibility, the "artwork" itself would have no commercial value, since, of course, only "objects," not "concepts," can be bought and sold.
- The juxtaposing of a copy of an object, the object itself, and three definitions of words implied in the meaning of the word "clock" invites us, with the title, to view these "objects" as simultaneously "one" and "five." In other exhibitions, Kosuth simply presented single pho-

tocopied definitions, which are, in logical terms, themselves "tautologies." Here, just as Wittgenstein argues in the *Tractatus*, the logical conjunction or juxtaposition of tautologies remains itself a (compound) tautology. Thus, viewed separately, each "object" is itself a tautology and all five become a single (compound) tautology by logical conjunction. None of them, taken singly or together, give us any additional information about the "world beyond"—rather, taken together, they merely serve to stake out a "logical space" within which our concept of "clock" functions. One could even say that the most important element of this "exhibit" is not the "objects" but their logical and completely immaterial, because conceptual, relations.

➢ In sum, then, this work proposes neither to clarify for us any meaning of "clock" which we didn't already know, to engage us in any deep philosophical meditation about the nature of "time itself," or, indeed, to tell us anything about "the world beyond the work" at all: rather, as Kosuth suggests, it is an "analytic proposition" about the nature of art, inviting our reflection, perhaps, on the conditions under which we are willing to call something "art," the status of "art objects," the logical space within which meaning arises, and the "relations among objects and their relations," or, as Kosuth sometimes expresses it enigmatically, "art as idea as idea."

IV.2.2. The "Conceptualist Artwork" as Interplay between "Text and Context": Kosuth's "*Investigation* series." (Specific reference is to *The Seventh Investigation (Art as Idea as Idea), Context B: Public-General, Chinatown, New York*, 1969.)

Shortly after the appearance of "Art after Philosophy," Kosuth commenced a series of "conceptual works" which he called "*Investigations*" (the title possibly derived from Wittgenstein's own later *Philosophical Investigations*, published in 1953 although documenting the results of a path of reflection commenced soon after the appearance of the *Tractatus*). Wittgenstein had soon become aware of the conceptual limitations of his earlier logical positivism for understanding the manifold and concrete ways in which human language and signification actually functioned in concrete contexts. Likewise, Kosuth soon realized the limitations which the "artwork-as-tautology concept" imposed upon his own need to thematize the broader linguistic, social, and historical conditions under which a given "object" could be regarded as "art." Even more, he realized that his own earlier view of the artwork as a closed, analytic definition still came dangerously close to the modernist "self-reflexive" concept of the artwork. Kosuth, in pursuing his own *Investigations*, which formed the center of his work for most of the decade between the mid-60s and the mid-70s, continued to maintain his earlier theses that art was essentially conceptual, that the specific "art-object" existed purely in the service of the concept and had no value in its own right, and that "Conceptualist Art" had replaced philosophy as the most adequate vehicle for undertaking such "conceptual inquiries." The new elements which appeared in his work, however, closely paralleled Wittgenstein's own development.

- Just as Wittgenstein, after the *Tractatus*, had come around to rejecting a theory of meaning based upon the logical analysis of the structure of propositions in favor of a view of "meaning as usage" within given contexts, so Kosuth's work began to thematize the interplay between the putative "art-object," the contexts within which it was placed by the artist, and, though at this time to a somewhat lesser degree, the role of the viewer in interpreting its "meaning-in-context."

- Also in agreement with Wittgenstein, Kosuth continued to maintain that language was the paradigmatic case of human signification, so that written texts continued to dominate his works, but the emphasis had now shifted. Rather than the mechanically reproduced "definitions" of the earlier works and the "logical space" which they specified, Kosuth now experimented, in an extremely methodical and systematic manner, and still accompanied by a great deal of theoretical discussion, with a variety of reproduced texts, often mutilated, incomplete, or problematically juxtaposed with one another, and set in a variety of diverse spaces and contexts.
- Finally, just as the later Wittgenstein had come to the view that various types of language-use formed a family of "games" which were rooted in "forms of life," so Kosuth's *Investigations* increasingly tended to move out of the museum and into a variety of public and other non-museum spaces.
- The result of all this was that "meaning" could no longer be viewed as some "logically stable," immediately intuitable entity directly presented by definition-like "analytic propositions," but that it now became a complex "play" among problematic texts, contexts, and interpretations. While "art" remained "idea," the "idea" had become fluctuating, multivalent, intertextual, and polysemic.

As a sort of an almost symmetrical countermove to his taking the "conceptual art-object" into various contexts of public space, thus transforming the meaning of the "object," his gallery and museum shows during this period typically involved "installations" of various "information archives" (as he called them) within the galleries or museums, e.g. bookshelves, file cabinets, and so forth—often containing within them his own written texts. Just as its presence in public space transformed the concept of "art" from its significance when shown in galleries and museums, so his "art" in museums and galleries sought to transform their own meaning from places for display of objects to "archives" of various concepts of art.

IV.3. *From Languages to "Cultural Practices": 'The Artist as Anthropologist.'*

Kosuth's second major theoretical "manifesto," "The Artist as Anthropologist," was published in 1975 and can be read as an outline of a concept of art which Kosuth himself now explicitly called "post-modern." In this essay, while he does not abandon the basic notion he had already developed of art as essentially conceptual under the earlier slogan "art as idea as idea," he considerably expands the scope of what factors must be considered in "proposing" new conceptions of art. In particular, like the Continental structuralists who followed in the path first charted by the renowned French anthropologist Claude Lévi-Strauss, he comes to reject the priority of spoken or written language as the fundamental source of meaning, seeing it, rather, as only one element functioning in a much broader and richer set of structures called, perhaps for lack of a better word, "culture." While much of this essay documents, through direct and often lengthy quotations, his own engagement with such diverse views as the Frankfurt School and contemporary critical anthropology, he eventually comes around to stating his own position succinctly and clearly.

- He now describes the artist as practicing a type of "*engaged anthropology*." He cites, as the background of this phrase, the debates in disciplinary anthropology between proponents of the more traditional view which see it as, like other "sciences," "objectively detached" and "descriptive," and the more radical critics who view it as intimately involved with the cultures which it studies and capable of intervening in them at certain points. Siding with the latter, he sees the contemporary artist as likewise immersed in cultural practices and called upon to critique and intervene in them by enhancing the viewer's self-awareness about them.
- As such, he concludes that "Conceptualist Art" has a far higher calling than merely to "propose" new definitions for art. Rather, because artistic praxis is itself fully immersed in and engaged with a given ideological conception of society, its "proposal" of new conceptions of art must necessarily serve to uncover the limits of this "ideological complex" in which it is embedded and open spaces for its possible reconfiguration.
- With this, he entirely and explicitly parts ways with any remnant of "Modernism." Specifically, he claims that "Modernism" pursued two paths, both of which were based on the artistic counterpart of "scientism" and its claims to "objectivity." On the one hand, which he calls the "high road," Modernism subscribed to a view of the artwork as a "pure objectivity," standing apart from the dynamics of culture in its own pristine realm of "pure aesthetic experience." On the other, the "low road," Modernism lionized individual subjective styles in pursuing its "objectivist aim" and saw no problem in submitting their products to the "ultimate objectifying matrix" of the "art-historical marketplace."

- In perhaps his most radical formulation, Kosuth goes so far as to suggest that, just as earlier Conceptualist Art had taken over what was once the province of philosophy, the newer Conceptualist Art (which he is now elaborating) will come to displace disciplinary anthropology as well. Whereas the tradition of "detachment" and "objectivity" continues to haunt contemporary anthropology, even in its critical varieties, the "Conceptual Artist," as embedded in his or her own culture and deliberately employing its own materials, has no such baggage to shed. Indeed, he or she should be able to transcend even Marxism in its critical capacities: "In the face of the conspicuous absence of any sophisticated (that is, real in terms of its complexity) alternative Marxist model, we must use as a given the model of art as it has come to us in this Post-Modern period."

Again, the artworks which date from the years following this essay instantiate and illustrate this development in orientation. Such projects as the "*Text/Context*" series abandon the confines of gallery/museum space entirely and literally take to the streets. Now, although written texts continue to figure prominently, they are typically juxtaposed with visual images drawn from contemporary politics or advertising and aim to provoke a sort of critical dialogue among Kosuth's own intervention as an artist, the signs by which contemporary capitalist culture and politics are represented, and the "viewer on the street" who encounters them. Precisely as he suggests in his essay, they function as forms of "engaged anthropological praxis" literally embedded in the midst of contemporary cultural activities and designed to intervene in them by forcing their participants to question their "naturalness" or "taken-for-grantedness" in favor of a new, art-induced "self-reflexivity."

IV.4. *From "Engaged Anthropology" to "Deconstruction": Kosuth's work from the 80s.*

In a general way, since his essay of 1975, Kosuth seems to have remained true to his conception of "artist-as-anthropologist" and has never explicitly repudiated this notion (at least so far as I am aware). However, one can discern a subtle and gradual change in his approach. I would put it in this way. Whereas his earlier engagement with the writings of the Frankfurt School and critical anthropology offered a model whereby prevalent cultural meaning-formations or ideologies were relatively stable but in need of critique and intervention, he gradually came to confront the problem, especially associated with such "deconstructionist" thinkers as Derrida, Foucault, and Lyotard, that "meaning" itself may not be something stable enough to support any frontal critical assault. Perhaps, that is, the problem of the "postmodern era" is not so much one of opposing some monolithic and oppressive ideology, but of pursuing *any* effective artistic or political praxis in a world where meaning refuses to arrest or coalesce into any determinate and opposable form at all—a world in which everything, including art and philosophy, is indifferently "information" without form or accent, constantly transforming itself into yet other "information."

Kosuth's numerous attempts to "conceptualize" this new "postmodern condition" and redefine art in relation to it is well illustrated by a remarkable and powerful series of installations which he produced during the second half of the 80s. They are all titled "*Zero @ Not*" and are based upon an admittedly complex "concept." Each involves a specific architectural ordering of "space" divided by various arrangements of walls and openings in them. Upon the walls are repeated a long excerpt from the German text of

Freud's *Psychopathology of Everyday Life*, which is systematically obscured by lines crossing it out, thus making it sometimes only barely legible and other times entirely illegible. (It is perhaps also significant that the site of one of the installations was the Freud Museum at Freud's former residence in Vienna.) All of this invites lengthy and complex commentary, which I will spare you. However, a couple of more straightforward points are worth making about its broad features.

- Kosuth is clearly employing a notorious device first used by Heidegger and borrowed by Derrida whereby one "writes under erasure." To summarize a complicated discussion, it is the nature of any occurrence of language both to "reveal and conceal," to convey one meaning at the same time as covering over, concealing, or suppressing others. And it is precisely this "revealing/concealing" effect of language that constitutes the inherent instability of all meaning. (By the way, it was Freud who, in his theory of dream-interpretation, first introduced the idea, learned from his patients under analysis, that what one doesn't say may be far more important than what one does.)
- Kosuth's installations serve, among other things, to problematize the relation between language and space. While this had long been an interest of his as far back as the billboard "investigations" and "information installations," language and space now seem to implode: it is impossible to say whether the architecture is dictated by the linguistic texts or the texts ordered architecturally. In a sense, in these installations, language literally extends into the architectural space of the viewer; or, perhaps, architectural space "warps" the language of the viewer. And in any event, both the lin-

guistic and architectural aspects of his installations are constantly both revealing and concealing new perspectives.

- Whether intended by the artist or not, the overwhelming effect of these installations is the feeling of being trapped within a barbed-wire compound, a hostile labyrinth of obscured words and constricted spaces simultaneously inducing physical claustrophobia and conceptual overload.

In Conclusion.......

To be honest, I don't know quite what to say after this chilling image, except that I, for one, would like to get out as quickly as possible. But go where? Back to a precious and naïve view of philosophy which tries to forget or deny its recent liaison with radical art? Back to a more pristine, "modernist" view of art as a vehicle of transcendence to another realm undisturbed by the uncertainties and instabilities of contemporary social existence or the complexities of philosophical reflection? Maybe just to another part of the gallery, maybe one with comfortable representational paintings of historical events, horses, or bowls of fruit? Out to the street, lined with yet other self-erasing and ambiguous images? Or maybe we should just pull up some chairs in the labyrinth, break out a few beers, order a pizza, and share with each other what we make of it all, and not worry too much about whether we are artists, philosophers, or whatever at the moment. That will have to do for now, until someone tries to sell us one of the beer cans as "art" or presents us a shopping list and calls it philosophy, and then we will be at it again.

State University of New York
College at Oneonta

Undergraduate Philosophy Conference

April 3 - 4, 1998

Sponsored by the Philosophy Club, the Student Association, Oneonta Philosophy Studies, the Ninash Foundation, OAS, the Religious Studies Program, the English Club, and the President's Office.

Oneonta Philosophy Club

The Philosophy Club allows students, as well as faculty, to engage one another in intellectual discussion. Meetings are held Thursday evenings at 8:00 p.m. in Morris Hall. Students are encouraged to express their interests in a comfortable environment created by close student/faculty relationships. As indicated by our activity list below, we like to combine cognitive stimulation with physical activity.

Through our boundless interest, we have formed a club that meets the intellectual and creative needs of students and allows then to engage in extracurricular activity. All meetings and activities are open to all members of the college community. For more information, please visit our web page, stop by the department office, or contact us at the email address provided below.

Sample activities:

- Monty Python's **Search for the Holy Grail**
- Free Tibet Activities
- Discussion: Sexual repression in America
- Halloween Mask-A-Raid
- Trip to Michigan to meet with Daniel Quinn
- Images and Forms: A lesson in Play Doh

Outdoor activities and excursions include:

- The Cloisters - "Philosophy and the Middle Ages"
- Skiing at Deer Run - "Testing out Aristotle on the Slopes"
- Great Barrington, MA - "Mountain Climbing with Nietzsche"
- Camping in Paradox, NY - "Back to Nature with Rousseau"
- Phonecia - "Tubing down the Esopus river with Heraclitus"
- Buddhism in America - Touring the Karma Triyana Dharmachakra Buddhist Monastery in Woodstock

Officers:	President	- Lily Stolzberg	(607) 432-1631
	Vice President	- Emily Martines	(607) 431-2364
	Treasurer	- Kevin Goetz	(607) 436-9135
	Advisors	- Achim Köddermann	(607) 436-3037
		- Douglas Shrader	(607) 436-2456

Email: philosc@oneonta.edu

HTTP://WWW.ONEONTA.EDU/~SHRADEDW/PHILCLUB.HTML

Undergraduate Philosophy Conference
Oneonta, New York
April 3-4, 1998

FRIDAY

Registration and Reception (1:30 - 2:00 p.m.) {Craven Lounge}

Concurrent Session (2:00 - 4:00 p.m.)
Science, Religion, and Human Values {Craven Lounge}
It's About Time {Morris Activity Lounge}

Concurrent Session (4:00 - 6:00 p.m.)
Poetry and Metaphor {Craven Lounge}
Moral Knowledge {Morris Activity Lounge}

Dinner (6:00 - 7:30 p.m.) {Otsego Grill}

Featured Presentation (8:00 - 9:00 p.m.) {Craven Lounge}
Contemporary Analytic Philosophy
as Reflected in the Work of Monty Python
Gary Hardcastle (Virginia Tech)

Friday Evening Social (9:00 - 11:00 p.m.) {Cafe Union Square}

SATURDAY

Continental Breakfast (9:00 - 9:45 a.m.) {Multicultural Center}

Concurrent Session (9:45 - 11:45 a.m.)
Of God and Love {Craven Lounge}
Philosophy and Politics {Morris 103}

Lunch (11:45 a.m. - 1:00 p.m.) {Multicultural Center}

Concurrent Session (1:00 - 3:00 p.m.)
Textual Analysis {Craven Lounge}
Foundations of Knowledge {Morris 103}

Concurrent Session (3:00 - 5:00 p.m.)
Kant, Foucault, and Tibetan Buddhism {Craven Lounge}
Human Nature {Morris 103}

Keynote Address (5:00 - 6:30 p.m.) {Craven Lounge}
When Artists Read Philosophers:
From Modernism To Postmodernism
Jere Paul Surber (University of Denver)

Dinner and Awards Ceremony (6:30 - 8:00 p.m.) {Otsego Grill}

Saturday Evening Social (8:00 - 11:00 p.m.) {Cafe Union Square}

Friday Afternoon: Concurrent Sessions

Science, Religion, and Human Values

(2:00 - 4:00 p.m.) {Craven Lounge}

Chair: Amanda Joy Schwarz

Science vs. The Cosmological and Teleological Arguments for the Existence of God
Fritz Allhoff – William and Mary
Discussant: Lauren M. Bleser

More Human Than Human: A Critique of Life at the Margins
Neal D. Carlson – United States Military Academy
Discussant: Jessi Gottlieb

Physician-Assisted Suicide: The Moral-Legal Tensions
Yelena Paranyuk – Adelphi University
Discussant: Denise Nicoletti

It's About Time

(2:00 - 4:00 p.m.) {Morris Activity Lounge}

Chair: Alexander Slater

Temporal Incongruity in Zeno of Elea and its Philosophical Consequences
Jeffery M.J. Murphy – Xavier University
Discussant: Meghan Callahan

The Representative Theory of Memory: A Basic Exegesis of Hobbes, Locke and Hume
Gary Jay Schwenk – Nazareth College
Discussant: James Ryan

An Explanation and Commentary of W. H. Walsh's Analytical Theory of Historical Knowledge
Albert Castelo – Hunter College (CUNY)
Discussant: Michael J. Brisendine

Friday Evening

CONFERENCE DINNER

(6:00 - 7:30 p.m.) {Otsego Grill}
reservations required

WORDS OF WELCOME

(7:45 p.m.) {Craven Lounge}
Alan B. Donovan
President of SUNY-Oneonta

FEATURED PRESENTATION

(8:00 - 9:00 p.m.) {Craven Lounge}

Contemporary Analytic Philosophy
as Reflected in the Work of Monty Python
Gary Hardcastle
(Virginia Tech)

Gary Hardcastle earned a B.S. from the University of Pittsburgh. His M.A. and Ph.D. are from the University of California, San Diego. Professor Hardcastle's research encompasses Epistemology, Philosophy of Science, History of Twentieth Century American Psychology, and Philosophical Issues Related to Communications Technologies. Publications include "Accomplishing Translation: The Notion of Evidence in the Discipline of the History of Science," in *Science and Hermeneutics* (Boston Studies in the Philosophy of Science, 1997).

Professor Hardcastle describes his presentation, which is punctuated by videoclips, as "a semi-silly, semi-serious illustration of various themes in analytic philosophy in the century (e.g. verificationism, semantic holism, the role of human reasoning) by way of skits presented by the British comedy troupe Monty Python."

FRIDAY EVENING SOCIAL

(9:00 - 11:00 p.m.) {Union Square Cafe}

Refreshments, entertainment, and good conversation.

Saturday Morning: Concurrent Sessions

Continental Breakfast
(9:00 - 9:45 a.m.) {Lee Hall – Multicultural Center}

Of God and Love
(9:45 - 11:45 a.m.) {Craven Lounge}

Chair: Shuba Fikru

Does the Ontological Argument Need Salvaging?
An Analysis of St. Anselm's and Plantinga's Theistic Proofs
Erin Kathleen Carter – Taylor University
Discussant: Gary Jay Schwenk

Divine and Human Love
Michael D. Day – Syracuse University
Discussant: Justin Mandel

A Woman's Place: French Neoplatonic Feminism vs. Platonic Love
Amy Katrin Ferrara – SUNY-Oneonta
Discussant: Jennifer Campoli

Philosophy and Politics
(9:45 - 11:45 a.m.) {Morris 103}

Chair: Jim Gilbert

The Republic and Totalitarianism:
Did Plato Have A Political Philosophy?
Phil Jenkins – Hunter College (CUNY)
Discussant: Michael Frazer

Whiteness: Being and Seeing White
Joanne Molina – American University
Discussant: Alexander Slater

The Bed of Power
John Costa – SUNY-Oneonta
Discussant: Lily Stolzberg

Saturday Afternoon: Concurrent Sessions

Buffet Luncheon

(11:45 - 1:00 p.m.) {Lee Hall – Multicultural Center}

Textual Analysis

(1:00 - 3:00 p.m.) {Craven Lounge}

Chair: George Savvas

Wittgensteinian Hermeneutics? Sketch of a Reading of Wittgenstein's **On Certainty** *in Comparison to Ricoeur's* **From Text to Action**
Kevin Goetz – SUNY-Oneonta
Discussant: Nikolai C. Schulman

"Hear Say Yes in Joyce": Otherness, Gender, and Derridian Repetition
Litia Perta – Vassar College
Discussant: Alissa T. Kokkins

A Critical Re-Evaluation of the Esoteric Character of Maimonides' **Guide of the Perplexed**
Michael Frazer – Yale University
Discussant: Daniel J. Bristol

Foundations of Knowledge

(1:00 - 3:00 p.m.) {Morris 103}

Chair: Lily Stolzberg

Descartes' Recurring Problems with Circles
Harjeet S. Parmar – Clark University
Discussant: Howard Fitzpatrick

Putnam, Realism and Perception
Clinton Tolley – Wheaton College
Discussant: Darin Somma

The Hard Problems in Dennett's Evolutionary Account
John Hartmann – Alfred University
Discussant: Michael J. Brisendine

Late Saturday Afternoon: Concurrent Sessions

KANT, FOUCAULT, AND TIBETAN BUDDHISM

(3:00 - 5:00 p.m.) {Craven Lounge}

Chair: Alissa T. Kokkins

The Transcendental Ideality of Space and Its Fundamental Assumption
Julie Kirsch – SUNY-Buffalo
Discussant: Thomas Rome

Alarm Security, Cyborgs, and Foucault
Anton Soderman – Vassar College
Discussant: John Hartmann

Great Perfection: The Practical Phenomenology of Tibetan Buddhism
Daniel J. Bristol – SUNY-Oneonta
Discussant: Jonah Ladner

HUMAN NATURE

(3:00 - 5:00 p.m.) {Morris 103}

Chair: Kerri Lynn Nicholas

Apollonian, Dionysian and Socratic Views: A Nietzschian Exegesis
Gary Jay Schwenk – Nazareth College
Discussant: David Schaaf

Rousseau Roulette
Amanda Joy Schwarz – SUNY-Oneonta
Discussant: Keith Reischmann

Anti-Essentialism and Re-Identification
Michael D. Day – Syracuse University
Discussant: Eitan Zachodin

Saturday Evening

Keynote Address

(5:00 - 6:30 p.m.) {Craven Lounge}

When Artists Read Philosophers: From Modernism To Postmodernism

Jere Paul Surber

(University of Denver)

Jere Surber, author of *Culture and Critique* (Westview Press, 1997), is a Professor of Philosophy at the University of Denver. Professor Surber earned his B.A. and M.A. from Texas Christian University. He holds a Ph.D. from Pennsylvania State University and the University of Bonn. Professor Surber's areas of research include Nineteenth and Twentieth Century Continental Thought, Social and Political Philosophy, Philosophy of Law, and Aesthetics.

In "A Framework For Thinking About Philosophy and Its History" (1997), Professor Surber argued that postmodernism lead to a destabilization of

> the prevalent faith in a "philosophical canon," opening it out to other historical meanings of "philosophy" and associated texts and orientations which it should never have jettisoned in the first place, and ... made it aware that "philosophy" itself had a history–indeed a very contorted and contested one–which, perhaps for the first time, can make "philosophers" aware of the intrinsic advantages as well as limitations of the distinctive type of discourse in which they have chosen to speak. Perhaps, now, "philosophers" may both begin to find a larger audience and be less like to alienate it once they have it.

Dinner and Awards Ceremony

(6:30 - 8:00 p.m.) {Otsego Grill}

reservations required

Saturday Evening Social

(8:00 - 11:00 p.m.) {Union Square Cafe}

Refreshments, entertainment, and good conversation.

SUNY INTERSESSION IN INDIA

Learn and Serve for Three Weeks

Earn Three Credits

Tentative Dates

December 28, 1998

to

January 16, 1998

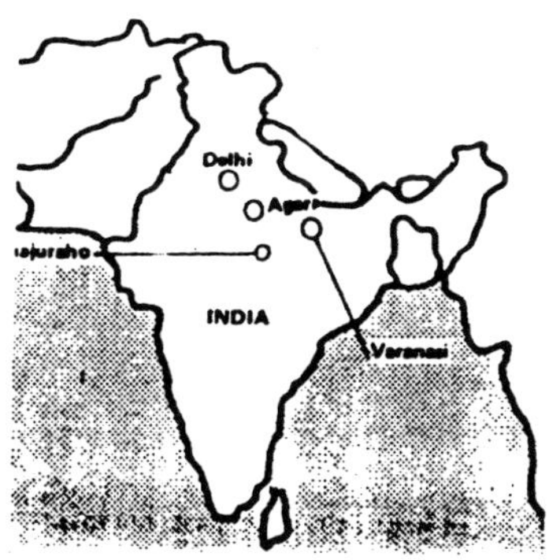

General information and slides of previous trips will be presented in Morris 104 throughout the day on Saturday, April 4.

For additional details, contact:

Mr. Robert Brzozowski

Director of International Education

Telephone: (607) 436-3369

or

Dr. Ashok Malhotra

Department of Philosophy

Telephone: (607) 436-3220

Abstracts

Fritz Allhoff
Science vs. The Cosmological and Teleological Arguments for the Existence of God
William and Mary (Williamsburg, VA)

The philosophical tradition abounds with attempts to prove the existence of God through both empirical and metaphysical arguments. Theologians and philosophers present five different arguments for the proof of God: the argument from contingency, the argument from design (teleological argument), the ontological argument, the argument for God as a presupposition of value and morals, and the argument for proof by religious experience. The arguments from contingency and design both center on the state of the world and shall be the focus of this paper.

An argument based on empirical evidence must be consistent with that evidence. The physical reality presupposed in the cosmological and teleological arguments defies modern physics' conception of the laws of nature which include quantum mechanics and relativity. These breakthroughs shattered the principal concepts of the Newtonian world view: "the notion of absolute space and time, the elementary solid particles, the strictly causal nature of physical phenomena, and the ideal of an objective description of nature" (Capra, *The Tao of Physics*, 61).

Kathryn Blum
Can a Utopia for the Masses Ever Exit?
Fordham University (New York, NY)

The paper imagines an exchange between Thomas More and Robert Nozick. Ultimately, it is argued, Nozick's position is the stronger one. A single utopia could never exist in the actual world. The only possible way that one utopia could exist, successfully, is in your mind. Otherwise you would run into too many conflicts with people who wanted the world their way – that would only cause animosity between neighbors, war, and unhappiness leading ultimately to more of a hell than a utopia.

Daniel J. Bristol

Great Perfection: The Practical Phenomenology of Tibetan Buddhism

SUNY-Oneonta (Oneonta, NY)

Perhaps the most intriguing of the teachings of Tibetan Buddhism ar the Dzogchen ("Great Perfection"). According to the Great Perfectio teachings, the whole of phenomenal experience, including the basi nature of human awareness, is equal to the realization of the Buddh: Usually considered esoteric in nature, the Dzogchen teachings are highly incisive form of phenomenology that combines theory an practice as inseparable elements. We will be examining three text: Longchengpa's *Great Perfection: The Nature of Mind, The Easer* (*Weariness*, Namkhai Norbu Rinpoche's *The Cycle of Day and Night*, an the contemplative instructions of Padmasambhava as found in collection entitled *Advice From the Lotus Born.*

Neal D. Carlson

More Human Than Human: A Critique of Life at the Margins

United States Military Academy (West Point, NY)

The paper advances an argument concerning the Quality (Personhood. At the center is the fundamental equation of personhoo as a function of genetic fabric and moral community. Subsequer sections concern implications for abortion, euthanasia, and anim: rights. Specific authors whose views are critiqued include Aldoı Huxley, John Noonon, Carl Sagan, Mary Anne Warren.

Erin Kathleen Carter

Does the Ontological Argument Need Salvaging?
An Analysis of St. Anselm's and Plantinga's Theistic Proofs

Taylor University (Upland, IN)

Since St. Anselm formulated the first ontological argument in tł eleventh century, philosophers and theologians have debated whethe such an argument is sound and thus succeeds in proving the existen of God. In the course of this paper, I examine whether St. Anselm original formulation of the ontological argument succeeds as a theist proof, and if not, whether Alvin Plantinga's modal version circumven the problems in the Anselmian argument.

Ian Cashman

On the Impossibility of Deriving Moral Import Solely From Reason

Marymount University (Arlington, VA)

I will argue in this essay that a rationalist foundation of ethics, as developed by Alan Gewirth and Immanuel Kant, depends upon a particular conception of the moral agent, i.e. a rational agent. Given this conception, I will further argue that Gewirth's and Kant's theories of ethics do not necessarily follow from their notions of agency; in order to accomplish this task, an evaluation of the "is-ought" debate is developed. Additionally, I will argue that the notion of agency, as presented by Kant and Gewirth, is too simplistic to sufficiently account for moral experience.

Albert Castelo

An Explanation and Commentary of W. H. Walsh's Analytical Theory of Historical Knowledge

Hunter College (New York, NY)

In his *Introduction to Philosophy of History*, W. H. Walsh presents an analytical theory of historical knowledge largely consisting of a synthesis incorporating elements from competing general theories of knowledge, including Idealism and Correspondence on one hand, and Positivism and Coherence on the other. Walsh arrives at his views by comparing the respective objectives and methods employed by science and history, noting that although both disciplines bear significant differences, history is, nevertheless, an autonomous enterprise with a distinctive subject matter and methodology, or "a kind of science in its own right." What ultimately separates historical from scientific knowledge, Walsh argues, is the fact that while scientists are concerned with the objective formulation of universal laws, historians seek to explain past human events by reliance on an a priori or subjective understanding of human nature. A fuller explanation of Walsh's theory of historical knowledge is the subject of the first half of this paper, followed by a demonstration of the inappropriateness of his comparison between historical and scientific knowledge, with the conclusion that historical knowledge is harder to achieve on account of the complexity of its subject matter, and thus subject to entirely different standards of objectivity.

John Costa

The Bed of Power

SUNY-Oneonta (Oneonta, NY)

Where does power come from, where does it lie, slumb Conventional opinion seems to be that power is a dormant enti Power traditionally lies in the hands of the "heavy weights"; power l weight. When somebody comes into a room with what society c: power, we might hear somebody say, "Here come the heavies." A of things change when Power is in the room: ideologies change, tru change, privacy or lack-thereof changes, and education changes. W is it that power changes these things? Where does the perception power as weight come from?

Michael D. Day

Anti-Essentialism and Re-Identification

Syracuse University (Syracuse, NY)

In this paper I argue for essentialism. I break down anti-essentiali: into two camps, namely relativistic anti-essentialism and accidentalis: After giving arguments that neither can be taken independently contend that we should be inclined to accept essentialism.

The second portion of the paper is devoted to an exploration of t function of accidental properties in identification and diachro re-identification. I contend that bundles of perceivable acciden properties are responsible for identification and re-identificatic Moreover, I hold that the very thing responsible in identification a re-identification is not individual essential properties separate from tl bundle of perceivable properties because such essential properties : often not accessible. I move that since we continue to pick out t same entity, namely a person, over time, even if most or all of t accidental properties have changed, there is an essence underlying t accidental properties. I suggest that this essence is a unique pattern perceivable accidental properties.

Michael D. Day
Divine and Human Love
Syracuse University (Syracuse, NY)

In the following paper I argue that human parental love is a paradigmatic case of a human behavior mirroring a divine behavior, namely divine love. I discuss the traditional Judeo-Christian conception of divine love, and I explain two aspects of divine love from Aquinas: (1) God loves all things equally, and (2) God has greater love for "better" things. I argue that although both of these are aspects of divine love, human behaviors that come close to mirroring divine behaviors, even for a short amount of time, are more like the former rather than the latter. Although God can encompass both of these aspects, humans seem more divine when they exercise behaviors similar to aspect (1), i.e., those behaviors that are all-encompassing, stable and unchanging. For when human beings show variability or mutability in their behaviors toward others, they seem less like God, even though such behavior may be advantageous.

Robb E. Eason
The Thinker as Poet
University of New Hampshire (Durham, NH)

Martin Heidegger proposed in *Being and Time* that we, in the Western Philosophical tradition, must again "raise anew the question of the meaning of being" (p. xix). This question, since the ancients, has been forgotten, subtly put aside and has "ceased to be heard as a thematic question of actual investigation" (p. 1). This "forgotten question" has permeated all of Western Metaphysics, leaving it ultimately unsatisfying in portraying an accurate account of how it is that we and other beings are in the world. According to Heidegger, Plato plays a constitutive role in leading metaphysics into an ultimately problematic position. This paper attempts to show that Heidegger's interpretation of Plato is, in fact, incomplete and thus inaccurate. A new interpretation of Plato's *Symposium* might reveal an understanding of Plato which reaches beyond the "theory of the Forms", beyond "metaphysical language", and beyond Heidegger's interpretation.

Amy Katrin Ferrara
A Woman's Place: French Neoplatonic Feminism vs. Platonic Love
SUNY-Oneonta (Oneonta, NY)

What is love? So simple a question and yet so difficult to answer, i to each of us the mere idea of love encompasses so many possibilit and emotions making it a concept both relative and, at the same tin universal. I will begin by examining the viewpoints presented in Plat *Symposium* and *Phaedrus*. Following this, I will explore parallels a differences in the French Neoplatonic concept of love through t exploration and careful dissection of the poetry of Louise Labe a Pernette de Guillet. Many of the poems used in this paper have nev before been translated from their original middle French.

Michael Frazer
A Critical Re-Evaluation of the Esoteric Character of Maimonides' **Guide of the Perplexed**
Yale University (New Haven, CT)

It is impossible for the modern student of the *Guide of the Perplexed* escape the esotericist school of Leo Strauss. Maimonides' philosophic opus is now widely agreed to be a work meant for a learned elite th can only be understood if one, to use a dead metaphor, is willing read between the lines. This view has in the past few decades led to full re-appraisal of almost all of Maimonides' treatise. Strangel however, one essential section of the Guide has not been criticall re-evaluated, those very passages dealing with the esoteric nature of tl work itself. After discussing the nature of an esoteric text ar examining a number of rival esoteric interpretive techniques, this pap will apply these techniques to passages in the Guide which discuss tl treatise's "secrets." When interpretive techniques based on tl assumption that the Guide is an esoteric work are applied Maimonides' description of his work as esoteric, then one mu confront the possibility that the work may not be esoteric at all. It wi become evident that to solve this scholarly liar's paradox will requi an examination of the subtle conflict between religious law an philosophy in the Middle Eastern Jewish communities of Maimonide day.

Kevin Goetz

Wittgensteinian Hermeneutics? Preliminary Sketch of a Reading of Wittgenstein's On Certainty *in Comparison to Ricoeur's* From Text to Action

SUNY-Oneonta (Oneonta, NY)

On Certainty is a compilation of a number of the personal notes of Ludwig Wittgenstein. The notes were written towards the end of his life, and center on the difference between the common use and the proper use of the word "Knowledge". To say, as some do, that the work is addressed only to the positivists of the day is to leave out many incidentals. An assumption of this paper is that many of these "incidentals," the ideas and arguments which are passed through on the way, form a philosophy which takes its place in a larger area than only that of the logical empiricist community, which positivism was a part of; that there are also other traditions addressed in *On Certainty* in specific, and Wittgenstein's philosophy in general. The thesis of this paper is that one of the traditions which may also be addressed in Wittgenstein's notes, though it remains fairly undeveloped, is the Hermeneutic tradition. As a result of this possibility, there is a place for a non-positivist reading of Wittgenstein's work. The arguments for the thesis will be drawn from the similarity which Wittgenstein's writings and method shared with the thought of some of the ideas which are important in the history of the hermeneutic tradition.

John Hartmann

Nietzsche's Use of Metaphor

Alfred University (Alfred, NY)

This paper is an examination of Nietzsche's metaphoric style and thought, and the structure of the genealogy that maintains it. Perhaps the most interesting result of this line of thinking is the idea that post-metaphysical philosophy is indeed possible, insofar as post-metaphysical thought can generate interpretations that derive concepts from active metaphorizing. Epistemology is replaced with an economy of forces, with an aesthetic. In this light, our understanding of ideas like the Will to Power and the Eternal Return must be reinterpreted as metaphoric, and this reinterpretation has certain implications both for the scholarship surrounding Nietzsche's works, as well as our reading of the works themselves.

John Hartmann

The Hard Problems in Dennett's Evolutionary Account

Alfred University (Alfred, NY)

In this paper, I will attempt to show that Dennett's evolutiona account of consciousness is lacking in two key areas, both of whi might best be described as the "hard" problems in Dennett's work, aft the term popularized by David Chalmers. First, I will consider wh Polger and Flanagan call "the other hard problem" – that of explaini consciousness through evolutionary means. My argument here is th any evolutionary account of consciousness runs into the problem explaining *qualia* – what could the selective advantage of *qualia* b This leads directly into my second criticism of Dennett's account. H despite his own beliefs, falls prey to the problem of the explanatory g between *qualia* and the (perhaps futile) search for neural correlates.

Phil Jenkins

The Republic and Totalitarianism: Did Plato Have A Political Philosophy?

Hunter College (New York, NY)

Plato's description of a good city in the *Republic* appears to be extreme form of conservatism at best, totalitarianism at worst, upon literal reading. Some scholars have criticized Plato by focusing on the political ideas as presented by Socrates and attributing them directly doctrines held by Plato. But the setting up of the city in the *Repub* is done for the aim of giving a comparison with the soul in the cour of defining justice in the person. I argue that Socrates' description what makes a good state is primarily a literary device Plato uses f examining his theories on what makes a good person and the deta were never meant to be taken literally as an example of Plato's ideas what would make a good state. Examining examples from differe parts of the *Republic* as well as from other dialogues, it is shown th inconsistencies between Socrates' city cannot be explained if Plato held doctrinally responsible for every detail of Socrates' politic explications. I suggest that if one reads the founding of the city in t *Republic* with more attention to Plato's general vision and less attenti to an analysis of literal political details one will more likely encount Plato's intended thought.

Julie Kirsch

The Transcendental Ideality of Space and Its Fundamental Assumption

SUNY-Buffalo (Buffalo, NY)

In the *Critique of Pure Reason* Kant attempts to transform metaphysics into a science. Fundamental to this investigation are the pure forms of the intuition: time and space. Kant contends that both time and space exist as transcendental idealities and resemble no qualities whatsoever in the *Ding-an-Sich*. In particular, Kant argues that the most rudimentary attributes of our spatial reality are aspects of our subjective experience which are independent of all sensation. Kant, however, offers no substantial proof of this claim. Thus, in my paper, I shall propose several possible rationales for Kant's position. The first view considers the presence of beings who might have modes of perceiving different from our own; the second examines problems with contemporaneous views of Newtonian space; and the third position deals with the inability humans have to sense space, and the problems which this condition entails. Still, not one of these arguments is strong enough to verify Kant's assertion.

Joanne Molina

Whiteness: Being and Seeing White

American University (Washington, DC)

Lewis Gordon's account of the Sartrean model allows us to understand the existential foundations that shape our relationship with race. Using this model, we can turn to a discussion of how race is addressed in the classroom. As we examine multicultural education, I hope to anticipate claims of conservative agendas by exploring how whiteness is created through the discussions and activities in these classrooms, and how the classroom atmosphere can be used to create a format for discussion that focuses on how race is part of everyone's identity. This will include an examination of the structural constraints that define whiteness and also the way the forms of discourse allow for the shaping of racial identities. George Lipsitz will provide the structural analysis that is necessary to see how racial categories are formed and maintained through social policies. Ruth Frankenberg and Phyllis Palmer will provide reconstructive narratives of racial identity that defy the category of bad faith and promote an important segue for the emergence of a society where everyone has the tools to combat racism.

Jeffrey M.J. Murphy

Temporal Incongruity in Zeno of Elea and its Philosophical Consequences

Xavier University (Cincinnati, OH)

When the antinomies and paradoxes of Zeno of Elea are analyzed, o can observe a dual description of temporality. In the antinomies agai plurality, Zeno treats time conceptually as if it were *continuo* non-discrete, *infinitely divisible*, and not composed of individı "nows," whereas in the paradoxes against motion, time is treated *discontinuous* and *finitely divisible into indivisible units* of no tempoı magnitude, beyond which no further division is possible. What drawn from Zeno's treatment of time are that: (1) time is treat conceptually in two different ways – as infinitely divisible in proc against plurality and as finitely divisible in proofs against motion, aı (2) in order to disprove motion, Zeno was forced to concede to a less species of theoretical plurality and in order to disprove plurality, was forced to concede to a lesser species of theoretical motion.

Yelena Paranyuk

Physician-Assisted Suicide: The Moral-Legal Tensions

Adelphi University (Garden City, NY)

Can a civilized society morally absolve an action that ultimately resul in a death of a human being? While some argue that physician-assist suicide (PAS) cannot be morally justified, the majority of opinio today seems to reflect the opposite. However, helping someone d continues to be prohibited by law and legal actions are frequently tak against physicians who do assist their patients in dying. It seems though the law fails to reflect the moral convictions of the societ Moreover, the hesitation to legalize assisted suicide seems to stem fro the fear of the possible abuse of the legal system. In attempt to resol the issue I would like to propose a set of guidelines designed to prote such a law and minimize its abuse. Among some of the requiremen outlined in the policy are: patient's own initiative in the request assisted suicide, a careful investigation of each individual case, tl presence of a physically unbearable suffering and the provision of a kinds of palliative care available. I believe that a similar policy wou make legalization of physician-assisted suicide possible, helping relea the tension created between the moral and the legal sides of the issu

Harjeet S. Parmar
Descartes' Recurring Problems with Circles
Clark University (Worcester, MA)

The traditional dispute over Descartes' philosophy stems from his view that clear and distinct propositions are required to justify the existence of a non-deceiving God, while God's veracity is utilized to guarantee our clear and distinct propositions. The new charge of circularity involves Descartes' philosophical beliefs on remembering. He insists that clear and distinct propositions currently under the focus of the mind's eye do not require God's guarantee, because they are not susceptible to methodological doubt. If the clear and distinct propositions utilized to justify divine veracity do not themselves require reliance on recollecting the demonstration of or belief in divine veracity, then Descartes has been exonerated from the charge of circularity. Under my interpretations of the text, this involves him in another kind of circle. Furthermore, this contradicts Descartes' assertions that all clear and distinct propositions, including divine veracity, require the use of divine veracity. On the other hand, if the clear and distinct propositions utilized to demonstrate divine veracity do require reliance on recollecting divine veracity, then Descartes' argument is obviously circular. In either case, I will show that Descartes' philosophy entails a circularity of some kind.

Litia Perta
"Hear Say Yes in Joyce": Otherness, Gender, and Derridian Repetition
Vassar College (Poughkeepsie, NY)

The paper, written as a response to a piece by Jacques Derrida entitled "Ulysses Gramophone: Hear Say Yes in Joyce", focuses primarily on the role of affirmation in communication, and on the role of communication within human reality. The question of self-hood is raised, and whether or not this self is compromised by the necessary externality surrounding linguistic communication. The mechanization of communication in the age of technological convenience is also explored, with particular focus on the absentminded repetition of the affirming Yes.

Litia Perta
Poetry, Time, and the In Between
Vassar College (Poughkeepsie, NY)

The essay is primarily concerned with the similarities of Poetry, Tim and Mankind, as existents which lie always in between. The notion a temporal instant, and its relation to an uttered poetic phrase, explored. The status of man as an in between is drawn largely fro "...Poetically, Man Dwells...", in which Martin Heidegger discusses tl wonder of man's cognition, which will allow him to see all that he ca without allowing him to always have it.

Amanda Joy Schwarz
Rousseau Roulette
SUNY-Oneonta (Oneonta, NY)

Using Rousseau's *Émile* as a primary text, this paper examines a seri of interconnected issues concerning human nature, gender identity, ai education. Specific attention is given to the relationship betwe children and parents, the lessons of the tutor, the supposed separatic between nature and society, the differential treatment of boys and gi (Émile and Sophie), and the unique role which teachers play in the liv of their students.

Gary Jay Schwenk
Apollonian, Dionysian and Socratic Views: A Nietzschian Exegesis
Nazareth College (Rochester, NY)

In *Birth of Tragedy Through the Spirit of Music*, Nietzsche describes tv basic impulses of human psychological behavior in relation to t world, and art's role in that dichotomy. This monumental work gi us revolutionary insight into Greek Attic Tragedy (470-410 B.C.). F the Apollonian, life is an illusion; for the Dionysian, Reality is ward off by an intoxicated state of revelry and Bacchic ritual. But, this wo does not merely explain the audience's viewpoint of sixty years Greek theatre; it gives us a glimpse into the mind of the ancient Gree as well as ourselves. What do we learn about the Greek gods from tl theory? What psychological significance does this have for us? Who the theoretical man and what connections can we find between tl aspect and our own scientifically-oriented 20th-21st century world?

Meghan Tadel

Counter-Intuitive Ethics

George Washington University (Washington, DC)

This paper investigates the plausibility of conscience and intuitiv thought as an epistemic foundation for ethics as proposed by Josep Butler (1692-1752) and Wang Yang-Ming (1472-1529). It is found th although both philosophers offer significant contributions to the stud of ethics, neither one succeeds in successfully and absolutely assertin conscience or intuition as the basis for ethical systems. Instead, both fa to clearly delineate intuition from other internal faculties and therefor allow for other internal ethical foundations such as sentiment or reason Moreover, due to a lack of anchoring ethics in intuition and conscienc both philosophers leave open the possibility for an external source c ethical systems, in fact, their suppositions almost require such a sourc Although this point is not argued as a more plausible solution, it used to demonstrate the difficulty in locating a precise fundament ethical principle.

Clinton Tolley

Putnam, Realism and Perception

Wheaton College (Wheaton, IL)

Hilary Putnam has spent much of his time trying to navigate a vi media between the Scylla of Relativism and the Charybdis of Metaphysical Realism with a capital "R." En route, Putnam has com to espouse an epistemology of "direct realism" in his defense again charges of relativism: the mind perceives the real world directly, nc through some intermediary such as the modern "way of ideas" or th positivist's "sense data." The mind just perceives the world. Th Realists (such as John Haldane) appear delighted at such a move, for the mind is to apprehend the real world directly, and one gives an kind of weight to the notion of intentionality, it would seem that th world must already be divided into "objects" in itself prior t perception for the mind to then have something to intend. Ca Putnam maintain this insistence on a direct encounter with the worl which endures independently of the mind, and still escape the Realist' other (unwanted) metaphysical baggage?

Participants

Fritz Allhoff
Brett Bisgrove
Lauren M. Bleser
Kathryn Blum
Michael J. Brisendine

Daniel J. Bristol
Meghan Callahan
Jennifer Campoli
Neal D. Carlson
Erin Kathleen Carter

Ian Cashman
Albert Castelo
Diana Chiappinelli
John Costa
Kevin Curran

Michael D. Day
Robb E. Eason
Amy Katrin Ferrara
Shuba Fikru
Howard Fitzpatrick

Michael Frazer
Jim Gilbert
Kevin Goetz
Jessi Gottlieb
Gary Hardcastle

John Hartmann
Phil Jenkins
Julie Kirsch
Alissa T. Kokkins

Jonah Ladner
Justin Mandel
Emily Martines
Joanne Molina
Jeffery M.J. Murphy

Kerri Lynn Nicholas
Denise Nicoletti
Yelena Paranyuk
Harjeet S. Parmar
Litia Perta

Amanda Rasnick
Thomas Rome
Keith Reischmann
James Ryan
George Savvas

Gary Jay Schwenk
David Schaaf
Nikolai C. Schulman
Amanda Joy Schwarz
Gary Jay Schwenk

Alexander Slater
Anton Soderman
Darin Somma
Lily Stolzberg
Jere Paul Surber

Meghan Tadel
Clinton Tolley
Eitan Zachodin

Acknowledgements

Many thanks to the following organizations and local merchants fc their generous support -

The Student Association
The Ninash Foundation
The Philosophy Club
The English Club
The Religious Studies Program
The Philosophy Department
Organization for Ancillary Services
Oneonta Philosophy Studies
Campus Grocery
Center Street Deli
Drury Lane Bakery and Cafe
Elena's Sweet Indulgence
Hannaford Foods
J & B Subs
Oneonta Bagel Company
P & C Food Market
Subway
Wal-Mart
Woody's Market
Gary's Flowers and Gifts
Stoeger Florist
Wyckoff's Florist

Faculty, Staff, and Students at all Institutions who helped post fliers and disseminate conference information.

We would also like to recognize the following individuals -

Gary Hardcastle, Ph.D.
Jere Paul Surber, Ph.D.
Alan Donovan, Ph.D.
Achim Köddermann, Ph.D.
Marjorie Holling
Eric Sloan - O.A.S. Catering

And finally a heartfelt **Thank You** to all the Presenters, Chairs, and Discussants – for without them there would be no Conference.

Thanks Again,
The Philosophy Conference Planning Committee

Daniel J. Bristol
Kevin S. Goetz
Alissa T. Kokkins
Kerri L. Nicholas
David K. Schaaf
Lily E. Stolzberg

Amanda Joy Schwarz
Committee Chair

Douglas W. Shrader
Faculty Advisor

ONEONTA PHILOSOPHY STUDIES

HISTORICAL AND CULTURAL PERSPECTIVES

Oneonta Philosophy Studies is a scholarly series that promotes exchange concerning traditional and contemporary issues in philosophy. Because comparative study often fosters appreciation and tolerance as well as understanding, special consideration is given to manuscripts that illuminate relationships between diverse or seemingly discrete views. Historical and cultural studies are especially welcome.

Submission is open to all—without regard to institutional affiliation, political preference, religious belief, gender, or national origin. Manuscripts are subject to external review. Published material does not necessarily reflect the views of the Editorial Board, the Philosophy Department, or the State University of New York.

A series such as this depends on the vision, good will, and labor of many. Special appreciation is extended to the *Institute of Global Cultural Studies* (IGCS), *Society for Ancient Greek Philosophy* (SAGP), *Society for the Study of Islamic Philosophy and Science* (SSIPS), and the State University of New York at Oneonta—especially Michael Merilan (Dean of Science and Social Science), Anne Cairns Federlein (Provost and Vice President for Academic Affairs) and Alan B. Donovan (President).

DOUGLAS W. SHRADER
EDITOR IN CHIEF

Books

Virtue, Order, Mind:
Ancient, Modern, and Post-Modern Perspectives
Peter Vincent Amato, editor

On Choosing a Teacher: Plato's *Protagoras* (MARIE I. GEORGE); Words of Love: Rhetoric and Eros in Plato's *Phaedrus* (DOUGLAS W. SHRADER); Tragic *Katharsis* (MARTHA HUSAIN); *Metaphysics* Z and H: Spurious V. Genuine Genera (WALTER E. WEHRLE); Aquinas, Aristotle, and the Convertibility of Being and Truth (JAMES T. H. MARTIN); Toxic Shame and the Lonerganian Concept of Conversion (DENNIS D. KLEIN); Jonas on the Crisis for Modern Man (OSCAR MOHL AND ANGELO JUFFRAS); A Roadmap for Ethics in the Twenty-First Century (EDDY SOUFFRANT); Communicative Rationality, Communicative Ethics and the Political Space of the Public Sphere (EVANGELOS KOBOLAKIS); A Pragmatic Reading of Gadamer's Philosophical Hermeneutics (VINCENT MARK VACCARO); Reconceiving Power and the Social Through Baudrillard (MARC HANES); A Feminist Analysis of Value-Neutral Observation (MAUREEN LINKER); Modernity, Kolakowski and Myth (PETER VINCENT AMATO).
1994 –203 pages – ISBN 1-883058-16-3

Essays in Islamic Philosophy, Theology, and Mysticism
Parviz Morewedge

Basic Dimensions of Islamic Theology; Basic Concepts of Neoplatonism; Greek Sources of Some Islamic Philosophies of Being and Existence; Substance and Process Theories of the Self in Islamic Mysticism; Mystical Icons in Rumi's Metaphysical Poetry: Light, the Mediator and the Way; Sufism, Neoplatonism and Zaehner's Theistic Theory of Mysticism.
1995 – 265 + xxviii pages – ISBN 0-9633277-7-1

❧ Jean Paul Sartre's Existentialism in Literature and Philosophy
Ashok Kumar Malhotra

This book offers innovative approaches to the reading of the novel *Nausea*, considering it as a philosophical and a psychological novel, and as a work of art. After depicting the existential themes in *Nausea*, the author compares the existential philosophy of *Nausea* to that of *Being and Nothingness*, and then deals with the ethical and social dimensions of Sartre's philosophy before exploring the interconnection between philosophy, art, and literature.
1995 – 154 + x pages – ISBN 1-883058-14-7

❧ Seeds of Wisdom
Douglas W. Shrader, editor

Biological Research and Feminist Obligation (JENNIFER BURKE); Subjective versus Objective Reality: An Examination Through Physics and Philosophy (MICHAEL JOSEPH); Exploring the Universe: From Plato to Einstein and Beyond (ALEX SLATER); Observing, Observability, and the Importance of a Smiler: A Partial Defense of Strawsonian Events (DAVID MIGUEL GRAY); Follow Your Bliss: The Philosophy of Joseph Campbell (ANGELA CASE); Concepts of Self: East and West (GABRIELLE LEVIN); Quality, Love, and Madness: Pirsig versus Plato (KERRI NICHOLAS); Nietzsche's Appropriative Representation *or* Is the Overman a Hermaphrodite? (JOHN DEVINE); The Impossibilities, Irrationality, and Contradictions of Immanuel Kant's Ethical Theories (DAVID SCHAAF); Descartes and Nietzsche (TATIANA ZELIKINA)
1997 – 167 + xii pages – ISBN 1-883058-08-2

Language, Ethics, and Ontology
Douglas W. Shrader, editor

Between Eastern and Western Thought: Individuation in a Western Setting (JOHN R. HARTMANN); The Paradigm of Emptiness: A Commentary on the *Diamond Sutra* (DANIEL J. BRISTOL); Rational Systematic Thought: Aristotle and Ancient Cultures (JOHN F. VELONA); Evolution of the One During the Early Medieval Period: Plotinus to Proclus (DAVID SCHAAF); Inversion of Fate: Boethius' Philosophy From Within (DAVID JUSTIN HODGE); The Nature of Rhetoric in Plato's *Gorgias* (ANNA CHRISTINA S. RIBEIRO); Discussing an Education, as Found in the *Phaedrus* (KEVIN GOETZ); Existence Communication and the Arbitrary Nature of Language (JEFFREY F. DUECK); On the Priority of Epistemic Issues to the Metaphysical Issues of Realism (DARIN SOMMA); Surface Spectral Reflectance and Color Objectivism (CHRISTOPHER O'CALLAGHAN); Events, Objects, Tropes, and Explanation (DAVID MIGUEL GRAY); Nietzsche and the Eternal Recurrence (DAVID MORGAN SVOLBA); The Possibility of Permissible Suicide Within Kant's Ethical Theory (PAUL NGUYEN); Emotions, Gender, and Kantian Morality (EMILY D. PORTER); Woman Philosopher: An Oxymoron? (HAZEL E. BARNES)
1998 – 352 + xvi pages – ISBN 1-883058-74-0

Children of Athena
Douglas W. Shrader, editor

Temporal Incongruity in Zeno of Elea and its Philosophical Consequences (JEFFERY M.J. MURPHY); Does the Ontological Argument Need Salvaging? (ERIN KATHLEEN CARTER); Putnam, Realism and PERCEPTION (CLINTON TOLLEY); Great Perfection: The Practical Phenomenology of Tibetan Buddhism (DANIEL J. BRISTOL); Counter-Intuitive Ethics (MEGHAN TADEL); The Thinker as Poet (ROBB E. EASON); Nietzsche's Use of Metaphor (JOHN HARTMANN); Wittgensteinian Hermeneutics? (KEVIN GOETZ); "Hear Say Yes in Joyce": Otherness, Gender, and Derridian Repetition (LITIA PERTA); A Critical Re-Evaluation of the Esoteric Character of Maimonides' Guide of the Perplexed (MICHAEL FRAZER); Apollonian, Dionysian and Socratic Views: A Nietzschian Exegesis (G. J. SCHWENK); Anti-Essentialism and Re-Identification (MICHAEL D. DAY); Contemporary Analytic Philosophy as Reflected in the Work of Monty Python (GARY HARDCASTLE); When Artists Read Philosophers: From Modernism to Postmodernism (JERE PAUL SURBER)
1999 – 334 + xxii pages – ISBN 1-883058-67-8

Research Papers

✣ **The Logic Beneath the Caution: An Analysis of the Buddha's Responses to Questions About the Self**
Douglas W. Shrader
1992 – 22 pages – ISBN 0-9633277-3-9

✣ **On Hindu Philosophies of Experience: Cults, Mysticism, and Meditations**
Ashok K. Malhotra
1993 – 75 pages – ISBN 1-883058-03-1

✣ **Near-Death Experiences: Scientific, Philosophical, and Religious Perspectives**
Douglas W. Shrader
1995 –56 pages – ISBN 0-9633277-9-8

Department of Philosophy
SUNY-ONEONTA
Oneonta, NY 13820-4015

HTTP://WWW.ONEONTA.EDU/~SHRADEDW/OPS.HTML